Introduction to Media Laws and Ethics

Introduction to Media Laws and Ethics

Juhi P. Pathak

SHIPRA

(PoD 2023)

Rs. 1295; US$ 43

ISBN: 978-81-7541-751-9

2017 Impression
First Published in India in 2014

Introduction to Media Laws and Ethics

Published by:
SHIPRA PUBLICATIONS
LG 18-19, Pankaj Central Market,
I.P. Ext., Patparganj, Delhi 110092
Ph. 91 11 22235152/ 6152; 9650028065
info@shiprapublication.com
www.shiprapublication.com

Preface

Media Laws and Ethics is a subject that students of Journalism and Mass Communication have to deal with, not only at their Graduation and Post-Graduation levels, but also when they enter the media industry as professionals.

Now-a-days, so many Media related programmes are coming up under different names that provide short and long term courses to students with a view to equip them with the knowledge needed to be a part of the Media industry; and it has been noted that all these programmes have included the subject of 'Media Laws and Ethics.'

Today's students will be entering the profession tomorrow. And in this era of sensationalism and yellow journalism, it is important that we teach these students the importance of professional ethics, which in our case, would be Media Ethics.

It is important that these future Media professionals are made aware of the laws related to their profession, so that, whenever the need arises, they can have instant solution to the problems. In fact, the knowledge of these laws is required to avoid falling into any trap. They should know the practices to avoid so that cases of defamation, contempt etc. are never clamped on them.

But, being a student of Journalism myself since graduation, I have felt that most students just mug up all the laws without understanding their importance and relevance. They find it difficult to relate it with other topics or draw distinctions between them.

This book does not just state the laws verbatim, but tries to study it keeping in view their historical implications, critically analyses them, understands their salient features, draws similarities and differences among various related aspects, looks at their limitations and throws further light on them through relevant case studies.

Sincere effort has been made to analyse and explain each topic thoroughly and in an all-encompassing way. I believe that the students of Mass

Communication need not remember all the Acts and laws by heart, but they should know their practical applications in their field. They should know their salient features, history, applicability, comparisons with related laws, limitations and everything else to gather a comprehensive knowledge of the subject. So, this book has been written with the desire to provide them with everything that I believe a student of media is supposed to know. This book discusses comprehensively major aspects of Media related laws and ethics applicable to the profession.

While writing this book, best possible care has been taken to use the authentic sources of knowledge available. Various leading scholars and authors on the subject and related fields have been referred to; and their ideas, thoughts and writings have been incorporated to enrich the content of the book for the users. I wish to acknowledge sincere gratitude to all the writers and the publishers mentioned in the Bibliography and also to those whose names have been inadvertently omitted.

The desire behind writing this book is to provide to the students a better understanding of Media Laws by going beyond merely stating various sections and provisions of those laws. As we all know that laws, with the complexity of its construction along with legal jargons further intertwined with clauses and sub-clauses, makes it very tough for students of non-legal disciplines to decipher and understand them. This problem is also faced by students of Journalism, who find it a little difficult to decipher the various provisions of laws, which are wrapped up in legal vocabulary. The book is written in a way that the students understand and grasp the meaning of the laws and not just memorize them to pass the examinations.

The book, designed as a textbook, caters to the needs of the students, both Undergraduate and Post-Graduate students of Journalism and Mass Communication and other such related media courses. It is also important that I state the fact that the content of this book is nothing but a compilation of the notes that I have collected over my scholastic years; and so if ever at any place I have unintentionally or inadvertently skipped necessary acknowledgements and credits, I whole-heartedly seek forgiveness for the same. What use would my notes be if I hold it close to my heart? I think it would be wise to give it out to all those who would need it more in the future.

I welcome suggestions from all sections of readership for improvement of the book. However, I take all the responsibility for any deficiency in the book.

Juhi P. Pathak

Acknowledgements

I wish to express my gratitude to my parents and beautiful sister Hridisthita Pathak, after Almighty God, for being my constant support throughout my life. I specially thank my father, who let me freely use his personal library, which is a treasury of law related books and my mother, who spent sleepless nights giving me company, while I was working on the manuscript of the book.

This book would not have been complete without the contributions of the renowned Journalist Mr. Prabhu Chawla of the Indian Express, sting operation specialist Mr. Shripal Shaktawat and one of the first newsreaders of Doordarshan Mr. Ved Prakash; their individual contribution to the field of journalism being immense.

I also take this opportunity to thank my teachers for providing me with the best of knowledge and making me capable enough now to give it back to the society. I specially thank Mrs. Padmaja Arvind, Mr. Mithun Pillai and Mr. Rajiv Dogra of SIES, Nerul, Mr. Mahendra Maharishi from Delhi and Mr. Chandan Goswami from Gauhati University for their constant motivation and encouragement that helps me keep my focus fixed on my goals.

I thank my friends, especially Mr. Pranesh Kumar Roy, and well wishers, who have always inspired me to write on the subject. I also sincerely thank Mr. D. Kumar, the Publisher, for keeping faith in me and happily agreeing to publish my work.

Juhi P. Pathak

Contents

Unit 1: Constitutional Provisions, Press Freedom and Law

1

History of Press Laws in the Pre and Post-Independence India

In India, the history of laws directed against the Press dates from the days of the East India Company almost simultaneously with the growth of newspapers, which, from their inception, took up the criticism of the administration and officials responsible for it.

Historically, however, the history of Indian press was the history of increasing diminution of its liberty, in spite of minor vicissitudes. The history of Indian nationalism proves that, in the proportion that it grew, the freedom of press in India suffered a proportional curtailment.

Raja Ram Mohan Roy was the pioneer of Indian Nationalist Press. He was also the first fighter for the freedom of press in India.

Pre-Independence Period

Mass Media laws in India have a long history and are deeply rooted in the country's colonial experience under the British rule. The earliest regulatory measures can be traced back to 1799 when Lord Wellesley promulgated the Press Regulations, which had the effect of imposing pre-censorship on an infant newspaper publishing industry.

Press censorship was imposed for the first time in 1795. The 'Madras Gazette' was asked to submit all the materials to the Military Secretary before printing. Pre-censorship, restriction on mailing facilities and extradition were three major restrictions that were imposed on the editors/newspapers that were not following the government orders. In 1799, Wellesley also made it mandatory to publish the names of printer, publisher and editor in the newspaper. He had appointed an official censor entrusted with the duty of passing all matter for publication and framed drastic rules to punish those, who infringed them.

Lord Warren Hastings abolished the press censorship and removed most of the restrictions in 1818. The atmosphere of relative freedom of press, which the measures of Hastings created, stimulated the emergence of Indian newspapers, like the '*Bombay Samachar*' published in 1822.

The first ever press law, popularly known as Adams Regulations, was imposed by the then Governor General Adams Smith on 18 December, 1823. The Court of Directors duly approved this. Under this law, a license was necessary from Governor-General-in-Council to publish anything except intellectual articles, advertisements, exchange rates, commodity prices and other commercial information. The license was signed by the Chief Secretary of the government. The applicant had to furnish, in his application, the name of the printer, publisher, name of owner(s); their addresses, address of the press and the name of the journal. In case of change in any of the above, the applicant had to file a fresh application for license. The Governor may reject or cancel any application on his sole discretion. The law provided Rs. 400 fine for publishing journals without license and maximum four months imprisonment in case the person was unable to pay the fine. The licensed presses had to publish the name and address of the printer on the first and last page of every printed material. Besides, the printed materials were to be submitted to local Magistrate on payment basis. Such types of regulations were imposed in Mumbai in 1825 and in Madras in 1827.

The Adams Act provoked the protest of Raja Ram Mohan Roy and his nationalist compeers. Roy, along with his enlightened nationalist Indians, such as Chandra Kumar Tagore, Harchandra Ghose, Dwarkanath Tagore, Gauri Charan Banerji and Prasanna Kumar Tagore, drafted a petition to be submitted to the Supreme Court of Calcutta.

The petition condemned the attack on the freedom of the press as undemocratic, inexpedient and reactionary. The signatories of this petition were the pioneers of the freedom of press in India.

Miss Sophia Collet extolled this petition as the 'The Areopagitica of Indian History'. R.C. Dutt described it as the beginning of 'that system of constitutional agitation for political rights, which their countrymen have learnt to value so much in the present day'.

Their petition was, however, rejected by the Supreme Court and the press remained subjected to new restrictions till 1835.

The onset of 1835 saw the promulgation of the Metcalfe Act, which undid most of the repressive features of earlier legislations on the subject.

Metcalfe, assisted by liberal Macaulay, through the Act of 1835 repealed the restrictions on the press in Bengal and Bombay. The license required for printing books and newspapers was abolished by the Act. Now press was free to express views on any social issue within the moral framework.

Till 1857, there was considerable freedom of the press in the country.

The outbreak of the Sepoy Mutiny prompted Lord Canning to pass the Press Act of 1857 known as the 'Gagging Act' due to its drastic nature. He re-imposed licensing system through this Act.

It was on 18 June 1857 that the 'Gagging Act' was introduced, which among various other things, introduced compulsory licensing for owning or running printing presses; empowered the government to prohibit the publication or circulation of any newspaper, book or other printed material and banned the publication or dissemination of statements or news stories, which had a tendency to cause a furore against the government, thereby weakening its authority.

In other words, under the Act, the government could control the establishment of printing presses and prevent, if it wished, the circulation of printed books and papers.

1860 was a landmark year in as much as it saw the passing of the Indian Penal Code, which, though not directed specifically towards the Press, laid down offences, which any writer, editor or publisher must avoid, for example, the offences of defamation, obscenity, etc. Later amendments introduced the offences of sedition (Section 124A inserted in 1870); promoting enmity between classes (Section 153A inserted in 1898); imputations or assertions prejudicial to national integration (Section 153B inserted in 1972); outraging religious feelings (Section 295A inserted in 1927).

Then followed the 'Press and Registration of Books Act' in 1867, which continues to remain in force till date. This is the earliest surviving enactment specifically directed against the Press. The object was, however, not to establish government control over the freedom of the Press. It was a regulatory law, which enabled the government to regulate printing presses and newspapers by a system of registration and to preserve copies of books and other matter printed in India.

Lord Lytton became the Viceroy of India in 1876. The Vernacular Press Bill aimed at better control over language press was submitted to the Governor General's Council, which was passed as Act IX of 1878. The law provides means 'to punish and repress seditious writing calculated to produce dissatisfaction towards the government in the minds of the ignorant population.' It was also aimed to 'prevent unscrupulous writers from using their papers as a means of intimidating and extortion.' This Act imposed serious restrictions on the vernacular press that was rapidly growing at that time and was becoming the organ of nationalist views and platform for criticism of the British government.

The Vernacular Press Act was comprehensive and rigorous. The District Magistrate and Commissioner were empowered to call a printer or publisher and to ask them to furnish a bond or undertaking not to publish certain kind of material, to demand security and forfeit the money and printing presses whenever they think it fit. They were also empowered to confiscate the published material that they thought were objectionable.

Lord Rippon, who had liberal views, repealed the Vernacular Press Act in 1882.

1898 saw the passing of two legislative measures relating to the general law of crimes, some provisions of which particularly concerned the Press; one was the amendment of the Indian Penal Code, 1860; and the other was the enactment of the Code of Criminal Procedure, 1898, to consolidate and amend the law relating to criminal procedure and to replace the Criminal Procedure Code of 1882.

Till 1908, the Indian press enjoyed considerable freedom. However, due to phenomenal growth of the nationalist movement in the previous decade, the government decided to curtail the freedom of press.

The Official Secrets Act first came into existence in 1884 during the tenure of Lord Dufferin as Viceroy. It was aimed at punishing those newspapers that were publishing secret papers of the Government. It was later replaced by Official Secrets Act, 1923, which is effective even till date.

In 1908, Lord Minto promulgated the 'Newspapers (Incitement to Offences) Act, 1908, which authorized local authorities to take action against the editor of any newspaper that published matter deemed to constitute an incitement to rebellion. The Act gave the magistrate the power to seize the newspaper and forfeit the press that published any material that incited provocation to murder, violence or other crime.

Later to make the 'Newspapers (Incitement to Offences) Act of 1908 more rigorous, the Indian Press Act, 1910 was brought forth.

The Press Act of 1910 was the most severe measure adopted by the British government in India against the Indian press. It considerably extended the power of the executive over the press and its free functioning by empowering it to demand heavy securities, which could be forfeited at will and to confiscate printing plants of offending papers. Though the right of appeal to the courts was provided, this right was not of much value.

There was a country wide nationalist agitation against the Act as well as the previous repressive Acts. As a result, the Press Law Repeal and Amendment Act of 1922 was passed whereby the Newspaper Act of 1908 and the Press Act of 1910 were repealed and the Press and Registration of Books Act and the Post Office Act were relaxed.

The Indian press enjoyed relative freedom till 1930. The nationalist movement, in its mass form, had declined and subsided between 1922 and 1929. But, again, with the rise of new wave of movement in 1929, the government decided to arm itself with powers to curb the press.

The Indian Press Emergency Powers Act was passed in 1931. It imposed on the Press an obligation to furnish security at the call of the Executive. The

Act (as amended by the Criminal Law Amendment Act, 1932), empowered a Provincial Government to direct a printing press to deposit a security, which was liable to be forfeited if the Press published any matter by which any of the mischievous acts enumerated in Section 4 of the Act, like bringing the Government into hatred or contempt or inciting disaffection towards the Government; inciting feelings of hatred and enmity between different classes of people, etc. The very Preamble of the Act, which stated: 'for the better control of the Press', was offensive.

While the Draft Constitution was under consideration in the Constituent Assembly, the Government of India appointed a Press Laws Enquiry Committee to 'review the Press Laws of India with a view to examine if they were in accordance with the fundamental rights formulated by the Constituent Assembly of India.'

This Committee recommended, *inter alia*, a repeal of the Press (Emergency) Powers Act, 1931 and the incorporation of some of its provisions in the general statutes laying down the law of crimes.

Post-Independence Period

However, the most significant day in the history of Media Regulations was 26 January 1950 – the day on which the Constitution was brought into force. The colonial experience of the Indians made them realise the crucial significance of the 'Freedom of Press'. Such freedom was, therefore, incorporated in the Constitution; to empower the Press to disseminate knowledge to the masses and the Constituent Assembly, thus, decided to safeguard this 'Freedom of Press' as a fundamental right. Although, the Indian Constitution does not expressly mention the liberty of the press, it is evident that the liberty of the press is included in the freedom of speech and expression under Article 19(1)(a). It is, however, pertinent to mention that, such freedom is not absolute, but is qualified by certain clearly defined reasonable restrictions under Article 19(2) in the interests of the public.

Thus, although the freedom of the press is guaranteed as a fundamental right, it is necessary for us to deal with various laws governing different areas of media so as to appreciate the vast expanse of media laws.

After independence, a revision committee was appointed to examine the existing press laws. The Revised Press (objectionable material) Act came into existence in 1951 on the recommendations of the committee, which was abolished in 1957.

The Cinematograph Act, 1952: The Cinematograph Act of 1952 was passed to make provisions for a certification of cinematographed films for exhibitions by means of Cinematograph. Under this Act, a Board of Film Censors (now renamed Central Board of Film Certification) with advisory panels at regional centres was empowered to examine every film and sanction it whether for unrestricted exhibition or for exhibition restricted to adults. The Board was also empowered to refuse to sanction a film for public exhibition.

The First Press Commission constituted in 1952 gave its report in 1954. In 1955, the Working Journalists and other Newspaper Employees (Conditions of Service and Miscellaneous Provisions) Act, came into existence. It laid down the minimum standards of service conditions for newspaper employees and journalists.

Delivery of Books and Newspapers (Public Libraries) Act, 1954: According to this Act, the publishers of books and newspapers were required to deliver, free of cost, a copy of every published book to the National Library at Calcutta and one copy each to three other public libraries specified by the Central Government.

Newspaper (Price and Page) Act, 1956: Though it was an ameliorating measure, but the Supreme Court of India interpreted that it had an indirect restrictive effect. The Act was annulled by the Supreme Court in 1962. This Act was made with the apparently laudable object of preventing unfair competition among newspapers through price-cutting. According to this Act, the right of a newspaper to publish any number of pages was made to depend upon the price charged to the readers, so that the newspapers could not increase the volume of its publication without raising its price to that extent. The justification offered by the Government was that such a regulation of volume according to price was necessary to protect the smaller newspapers from unfair competition of the bigger newspapers having larger financial resources. Another justification was that the Act was to prevent concentration of ownership in the hands of the few commercial groups, which conducted the bigger newspapers.

Both these contentions were turned down by the Supreme Court with the observation, *inter alia*, that:

(a) The fixing of a minimum price for the number of pages, which a newspaper is entitled to publish, would deter a class or section of its readers from purchasing such newspaper (because of the higher price) and, thus, curtail its circulation;
(b) Limiting the number of subscribers of a newspaper is an infringement of the Freedom of the Press, guaranteed by Article 19(1)(a), even though it is effected through a schedule of rates;
(c) The volume of circulation of a newspaper cannot be curtailed for the purpose of protecting or promoting smaller newspapers or for suppressing unfair practices by other newspapers or for prevention of monopolies.

The Copyright Act, 1957 – According to this Act, 'copyright' meant the exclusive right to commercially exploit the original literary, dramatic, artistic, musical work, sound recordings or cinematographic films as per the wishes of the owner of copyright, subject to the restrictions imposed in the Act.

Defence of India Act, 1962 – This Act came into force during the Emergency proclaimed in 1962. This Act aimed at restricting the Freedom of the Press to a large extent keeping in mind the unrest prevailing in India in lieu of the war against China. The Act empowered the Central Government to issue rules with regard to prohibition of publication or communication prejudicial to the civil defence/military operations, prevention of prejudicial reports and prohibition of printing or publishing any matter in any newspaper.

Civil Defence Act, 1968 – It allowed the Government to make rules for the prohibition of printing and publication of any book, newspaper or other document prejudicial to the Civil Defence.

Press Council Act, 1978 – Under this Act, the Press Council was reconstituted (after 1976) to maintain and improve the standards of newspaper and news agencies in India.

Cine Workers and Cinema Theatre Workers (Regulation of Employment) Act, 1981 – This legislation afforded a measure of protection to those employed in the industry by imposing certain obligations on motion picture producers and theatre owners concerning the former's condition of service.

Cine Workers Welfare Cess Act, 1981 and the Cine Workers Welfare Fund Act 1981 – These Acts sought to create means of financial support to cine employees, the seasonal and unpredictable nature of whose employment often left them impoverished and helpless.

Cable Television Networks (Regulation) Act, 1995 basically regulates the operation of Cable Television in the territory of India and regulates the subscription rates and the total number of total subscribers receiving programmes transmitted in the basic tier. In pursuance of the Cable Television Network (Regulation) (Amendment) Bill, 2002, the Central Government may make it obligatory for every cable operator to transmit or retransmit programme of any pay channel through an addressable system as and when the Central Government so notifies. Such notification may also specify the number of free to air channels to be included in the package of channels forming the basic service tier.

Media Laws of the UK and USA

Tim Crook, in his book, 'Comparative Media Law and Ethics', gives a detailed account of the Media laws of the United Kingdom and United States of America.

He writes that the focus on the United Kingdom and United States of America is justified by the fact that the former is the source of Common law and the latter is the most powerful cultural, political, economic and military power in the world.

There is a difference in the evolution of the media laws in both the nations.

The key difference between the United Kingdom and the United States of America is the First Amendment of the US Constitution, which asserts the right to freedom of the press.

Tim Crook writes, "In history and present day reality, the First Amendment does not have an absolute remit, but it does ensure that freedom of expression and media freedom could be said to be more of a trump card in balancing other rights as compared to the situation in the United Kingdom. The United Kingdom Parliament in the Westminster incorporated the European Convention on Human Rights into legislation in 1998 (enacted October 2000), and Article 10 on freedom of expression is substantially qualified."

Article 10(1) of the Human Rights Act is qualified by Article 10(2), which states;

> 'The exercise of these freedoms, since it carries with it duties and responsibilities, may be subject to such formalities, conditions, restrictions or penalties as are prescribed by law and are necessary in a democratic society, in the interest of national security, territorial integrity, or public safety, for the prevention of disorder or crime, for the protection of health or morals, for the protection of the reputation or the rights of others, for preventing the disclosure of information received in confidence, or for maintaining the authority and impartiality of the judiciary.'

But the First Amendment of the US Constitution is not qualified in this way. Supreme Court Justices Black and Douglas, in the *Sullivan vs New York Time* (1964), speculated that the statement 'Congress shall make no law' abridging speech and press freedoms' meant Congress could make no law.

Thus, we know that in the United States of America, freedom of expression/press is guaranteed by the Constitution. But, it is a legislative principle that guarantees freedom of expression in the United Kingdom. The Article 10(1) of the European Convention on Human Rights (Freedom of Expression) states: 'Everyone has the right to freedom of expression. This right shall include freedom to hold opinions and to receive and impart information and ideas without interference by public authority and regardless of frontiers. This Article shall not prevent States from requiring the licensing of broadcasting, television or cinema enterprises.' This Article appears to subsume the idea of 'freedom of press' within the broader area of 'freedom of expression.'

In the United Kingdom, the Office of Communications established by the 2003 Communications Act and the Federal Communications Commission (FCC) in the USA established by 1934 Federal Communications Act, both have the legal power to fine broadcasters as well as to suspend and cancel licenses. Their codes, guidelines and decisions generate what is known as administrative law.

The broadcasters in the United Kingdom and United States face huge financial penalties and their right to broadcast is also withdrawn at times as a penalty.

The Press Complaints Commission, which is a voluntary body, regulates the print, magazine and online media in the United Kingdom. The print or online bodies that do not adhere to the codes or norms face the embarrassment of a critical adjudication by the Press Complaints Commission getting published in the website www.pcc.org.uk. No such organization exists in the United States of America, but professional journalists do follow the codes set by the Society of Professional Journalists, National Photographers Association, American Society of Newspaper Editors and others. United States have had a long standing tradition of training and education in media ethics and it can be said that the media in the United States has been much more proactive and progressive in applied ethics.

Conclusion

India has a rich treasure of laws that gives considerable freedom to the press. We are always coming up with new bills and laws to secure and guarantee the freedom of press. Very recently, the Right to Information Act also came into existence in 2005. Our journalists and social activists are taking full advantage of this Act to come out with new stories, most of which are of scams, misappropriation of money and mismanagement of funds and arbitrary decision making.

But as India is on its way to progress and all round development with more emphasis on science and technology, we are in need of more laws to cater to the needs of the present times.

Our Convergence Bill is yet to become a law. It would be a very important step, as this present stage is the age of convergence where the distinctions between different forms of media, like print, broadcast, online are gradually blurring and everything is merging into one another.

India is yet to develop its umbrella Intellectual Property law, which is presently scattered and divided into various other laws relating to copyright, patent, trademarks, merchandise symbols, etc.

We are also required to take an in depth look into our cyber laws, which are still in their embryonic state.

Thus, we can say that we need to implement new laws that will overcome the slight lacuna that we have in the field of media related laws.

2

Fundamental Rights and Duties

Part III of Constitution of India deals with the Fundamental Rights. Its contains an exhaustive list of fundamental Rights. The inclusion of these rights in the Constitution prevents the government from becoming despotic. The rights are above all other laws of the land. Fundamental rights have been rightly regarded as the soul of the constitution. P.B. Gajendra Gadker says: "A fundamental right is a legally enforceable right governing the relations between the state and the individual. It has both a negative and positive aspect. It must, as the world indicates, be fundamental. It does not only mean a right of liberty permissible under the law; it also means a right of liberty in a positive sense which enables an individual to develop his personality and his faculties and to live his life in his own interest and in the interest of the community as a whole"

Dr. Kripesh Chandra Paul and *Durga Kanta Sarmah* in their individual books written on the subject of Political Science give an elaborated description on the concept of Fundamental Rights. Their ideas have been adapted in this book for the better understanding of the readers.

The Americans were the first to incorporate the fundamental rights in the constitution and gave these a constitutional status. In America, the Philadelphia conference in its 'declaration of Independence' recognized some basic rights of the individual. The Universal Declaration of Human Rights has also recognized the value of human rights. Today, right has become a condition of civilized life. Democracy cannot work if the people do not have rights. In India, the demand for 'fundamental rights' was frequently made during the British Rule. The Congress passed many resolutions demanding civil rights and equality of status with Englishmen. The Motilal Nehru Committee Report of 1928 recommended that the people of India should be given certain fundamental rights. Simon Commission of 1930 rejected this demand of the Congress. There was no provision for fundamental rights in the Government of India Act, 1935. The Karachi session of the Congress also strongly demanded fundamental rights. This time the draft of fundamental rights was framed by Pandit Nehru. But these proposals had no effect upon the then British Government of India. The Karachi Resolution laid emphasis on political as well as economic rights.

The leaders of India convinced about the provision of fundamental rights in the Constitution because of the communal situation in the country. It was necessary to assure the rights of the minorities. Even the cabinet mission plan suggested the appointment of an advisory committee by the Constituent Assembly on fundamental and minority rights. The Constituent Assembly appointed a committee on fundamental and minority rights. It was headed by Sardar Vallabhbai Patel. This committee appointed a sub-committee headed by Acharya. J.B. Kripalani to prepare the scheme of fundamental rights. So, the fundamental and minority rights were incorporated in the constitution according to the recommendations of these committees.

Meaning: A 'fundamental right' is one which finds its sanction in the constitutional provisions of a country. It is protected by the higher law of the land. The fundamental rights have a secured place in the basic law of the land. It puts restriction on the unreasonable powers of the state. D.D. Basu says: "While an ordinary legal is right is protected and enforced by the ordinary law of the of the land, a fundamental right is one which is protected and guaranteed by the written constitution of the state." The Constitution of India subscribes to the liberal democratic order and hence it has fundamental rights relating to equality, liberty, non-exploitation, religion, education and culture and their constitutional remedies. It does not guarantee economic rights.

Necessity of Fundamental Rights

Fundamental rights constitute the backbone of the nation. These rights are very essential to safeguard the interest of the people. The party in the power cannot misuse its powers because of the guarantee of fundamental rights by the constitution. The inclusion of fundamental rights in the constitution will also enable the people to participate in the political affairs of the state. Fundamental rights are also essential for the development of personality of the individual and for social good. The fundamental rights are necessary to lay down the political foundation of democracy. Justice Sapru said, "The object of Fundamental Rights as far as I can gather from a reading of the constitution was to provide certain standard of conduct, citizenship and fair play."

Characteristics of Fundamental Rights

- Fundamental rights are not absolute. They are subject to reasonable restrictions. They strike a balance between individual liberty and social security. But reasonable restrictions are subject to judicial review.

- All fundamental rights can be suspended except the fundamental rights guaranteed under Articles 20 and 21. Right to freedom under Article 19 is automatically suspended during emergency. Other fundamental rights can be suspended by the President under Article 359 in the country as a whole or any part thereof. The fundamental rights remain suspended only during national emergency under Article 352.
- Some of the fundamental rights are meant for citizens only. Other rights can be enjoyed by both citizens and aliens.
- The fundamental rights can be amended but they cannot be abrogated. The abrogation of fundamental rights will violate the basic structure of the constitution.
- The fundamental rights are both positive and negative. The negative rights prevent the state from doing certain things. Articles 15 prevents the state from making discrimination. Fundamental rights are positive as they permit the citizens to enjoy certain rights example, Article 19(1)(a) confers the freedom of speech and expression.
- Some fundamental rights are available against the state. Some rights are available against individuals.
- The fundamental rights are justifiable. A citizen may approach the court of law when his fundamental right is violated.
- Some fundamental rights may not be available to personnel serving in the defence forces. They cannot enjoy all the fundamental rights. The Parliament decides under Articles 33 which rights will not be available to them. The nature of their job requires such restrictions.
- The fundamental rights are social and political in character. No economic rights have been guaranteed to the citizens of India although without them the other rights are of little or of no significance.

Classification

Part lll of the Constitution has 24 Articles which deal with the fundamental rights. The fundamental rights of the Indian citizens have been guaranteed by these articles (Art. 12-35). The fundamental rights are classified into six categories.

1. Right to Equality (Art. 14-18)
2. Right to Freedom and Personal Liberty (Art. 19-22)
3. Right against Exploitation (Art. 23-24)
4. Right to Freedom of Religion (Art. 25-28)
5. Cultural and Educational Rights (Art.29-30)
6. Right to Constitutional Remedies (Art.—32).

Right to Property: Originally, a citizen of India had seven fundamental rights. Part lll of the constitution contained another important right. It is the right to property. But it is no longer a fundamental right. The 44th Amendment Act of the constitution has excluded it from the categories of fundamental rights. It is now an ordinary legal right.

Right to property has been abolished as a fundamental right to make way for socialism in India. Because of the existence of right to property as fundamental right, the state faced difficulties in making socio-economic legislation for the good of the people. Hence, the need arose to take away the fundamental character of right to property. The right to property as fundamental right stood in the way of the state to move in the direction of democratic socialism.

Thus, the 44th Amendment Act of 1978 deletes right to property from Part lll of the constitution. So, it has been converted from a 'fundamental' to a 'legal' right Art. 300A is added in chapter IV of part XII. It says that no person shall be deprived of his property save by the authority of law. The present position of right to property is that it still remains a constitutional right from part lll of the constitution to another part. But it is no longer a fundamental right. It is an ordinary right which can be protected by ordinary law. The states can now legislate for the socio-economic welfare of the people.

The fundamental rights of the citizens of India many qualifying provisions. The six types of fundamental rights are discussed below:

Right to Equality: Right to equality has been given first place in the constitution. It is discussed below:

(a) The state cannot deny to any individual equality before law or its equal protection. Article 14 of the Constitution guarantees the right to equality to all persons including those who are not citizens of India.

(b) Article 15 lays down that no discrimination shall be made on the grounds of religion, race, caste, sex or place of birth.

(c) There can be no discrimination in respect of recruitment to public offices on the ground of religion, caste, place, etc. (Art. 16)

(d) Article 17 has abolished untouchability and its practice in any from is forbidden.

(e) Articles 18 of the constitution provide that the state can confer titles pertaining to military or academic distinctions. Titles have been abolished because they created social distinction. The citizens cannot accept any title from any foreign state without prior approval of the government of India. The titles conferred by the erstwhile British Government stand forfeited.

Right to Equality does not mean absolute equality. Equality before law permits: They are:

(a) Classification of person into different groups for the purpose of legislation;
(b) Establishment of special for certain specific offences for a speedy trial;
(c) The passing of special laws for some areas;
(d) Grant of immunities to certain persons in certain situation and
(e) Discrimination by the state in its larger interests.

The constitution also permits special protective measures for backward classes, scheduled castes and scheduled tribes. In the case of public employment also, a certain percentage of jobs can be reserved for the weaker sections of the society.

It is noticed that the right to equality is subject to qualifying provision. But discrimination cannot be made on artificial grounds as laid down in the constitution. The state has been empowered to take special steps for the welfare of the women, children, or for the advancement of socially and educationally backward section of the society. Establishment of absolute equality is no possible. But the constitution has provided equal opportunities for all the citizens. In the larger interest of the society and the state, there must be provision for special-care for the weaker sections of the people.

Right to Freedom and Personal Liberty: Right to freedom has been given second place in constitution. The various freedoms and rights are discussed below:

(a) *Right to Freedom*: Article 19 of the constitution of India guarantees certain right to the Indian citizens which includes: (1) right to freedom of speech and expression; (2) freedom of assembly; (3) right to form association; (4) freedom of movement; (5) right to reside and settle, at any place of the state; and (6) freedom of profession, occupation, trade or business.
(b) Article 20 provided protection against arbitrary and excessive conviction for the offences committed by the citizens. No person shall be convicted of any offence except for the violation of law. No person shall be punished for the same offence more than once. Penalty shall be imposed as per law in force at the time of commission of the crime.
(c) Article. 21 lays down that no person shall be deprived of his life and personal liberty except according to the procedure established by law.
(d) Art. 22 of the constitution provides protection against arrest and detention. An arrested person shall be informed as soon as possible of the grounds for such arrest. He shall be given the right to consult

a legal practitioner. A person arrested by the police must by produced before the nearest magistrate within a period of 24 hours on whose orders the detention may by revoked forthwith or extended.

Like Right to Equality, Right to Freedom can also be enjoyed under reasonable restrictions. Right to freedom may be restricted in the interest of the sovereignty and territorial integrity of the country. "Right to acquire hold and dispose of property" has been taken away from Right to Freedom under the 44th Amendment Act of the Constitution in 1978. It is no longer a fundamental right. Though Articles 22 ensures freedom against arbitrary arrest, it sanctions preventive detention. Under preventive detention a person may be detained for a period of two months. The term may be extended on the recommendation of an advisory broad.

The various freedoms granted under this right remain suspended when the President of India declares emergency under Article 352 of the constitution of India. Right to freedom cannot be absolute and unlimited. The constitution strikes a balance between individual liberty and social control. Hence, they are put under reasonable restrictions. The restrictions which are excessive or arbitrary are not valid. The restrictions imposed on some of the fundamental rights for the implementation of the Directive principles of state policy regarded as reasonable.

Right against Exploitation: The constitution guarantees the right against exploitation. This right is necessary to supplement the right to freedom. Articles 23 lays down that traffic in human beings and 'begaar' and similar other forms of forced labour are illegal. It is prohibited by the constitution. Any violation of this provision shall be offence punishable in accordance with law. Article 24 prohibits the employment of children below the age of 14 years in any hazardous employment.

Traffic in human beings implies selling and buying of men and women for immoral purposes. It was very common in pre-independence days. It is also present today in some parts of the country. The term 'begaar' means work without payment. To prevent this type of exploitation this provision has been made in the constitution.

Article 21 is also accompanied by some qualifying provisions. It says that nothing shall prevent the state from imposing some compulsory service for a public purpose. While imposing such service, the state shall not make any discrimination on grounds of religion, race, caste, class etc. conscription for army and police is not begaar. Moreover, those persons who have been convicted of offences, can be forced to do work in prison and it will not be 'begaar'.

The right of Indian citizens against exploitation is very important. Now, children and women cannot be exploited. But exploitation in same places in going on as usual. Laws have been passed to stop this evil practice. But without public co-operation and government firmness this cannot be prevented. Poor people are not strong enough to fight against exploitation. They need the help of social organizations in this regard.

Right to Freedom of Religion: Right to Freedom of Religion is called the anchor of India's secularism. The following fundamental rights are very important for the citizens of India.

1. Article 25 gives the citizens freedom of conscience and the right to the practice or propagation of any religion by peaceful means.
2. Article 26 gives freedom to any religious denomination or to any section thereof to establish and maintain institutions for religious and charitable purposes. It can manage its own affairs in matters of religions. It has the right to acquire and own movable and immovable property in accordance with law.
3. No person shall be compelled to pay tax under Article 27, the proceeds of which are specifically appropriated in payment of expenses for the maintenance or promotions any particular religious denomination.
4. Religious instructions cannot be imparted in an institution wholly or partly maintained by the state. Article 28 puts this restriction upon religious intuitions.

Right to Religion is also subject to certain restrictions like other Fundament rights. The right to religion is subject to the norms of public order, morality and public health. The state can regulate or restrict the economic, financial, political or other secular activities associated with religious practices. It can throw open the Hindu religious intuitions of public character to all classes and sections of Hindus to bring about social welfare and reforms.

Forcible conversion have been prohibited by the constitution. Everyone has the rights to propagate his religion. But, he has no right to convert anyone forcibly to his religion. Various states have passed laws prohibiting forcible conversion. The government can charge fee from religious trusts for rendering specific services. Religious instructions can be imparted in institutions established under any endowment or trust. The above mentioned rights to the citizens give India a secular character.

Cultural and Educational Rights: India has religious, racial and cultural diversities. To maintain the unity of the country in the midst of diversity, the framers of the constitution felt that the cultural and educational rights of all citizens of the country should be guaranteed in the constitution. Hence, they have incorporated the cultural and educational rights of the people in the constitution. These rights will ensure the development of culture and language of the minority communities in India.

(a) Article 29 lays down that any section of citizens of India having a distinct language, script and culture has right to conserve the same. This right applicable to all sections of the citizens. It covers both majority and minority communities. This right is not subject to restriction. It is absolute. Because of the existence of this right in the constitution, the majority cannot thrust its language, script and culture upon the minority. No citizen shall be denied admission to any educational institution maintained by the state or receiving financial assistance from the government on the grounds of religion, race, caste, language etc.

(b) Article 30 of the Constitution provides that all minorities based on religion or language have the right to establish and administer educational institutions of their choice. The religious and linguistic minorities can administer only those educational institutions which are established by them. The state cannot discriminate against any educational institution on the ground that it is under the management of a minority, whether based on religion or language, while granting aid to educational institutions. The religious and linguistic minorities have a right to choose their own governing body to administer them and other employees. The linguistic minorities have a right to determine the medium of instruction in the institutions established by them. Without this right they cannot maintain their own distinct culture and language. But the government may make regulations for proper functioning of these institutions.

The aims of the cultural and educational rights are to give cultural protection to the minorities, whether linguistic or religious. Protection of these rights of the minorities is very essential to win their whole–hearted support and co-operation in the task of nation-building. When every citizen will feel assured of his culture and language, he can take part in the political system with a sense of equality. The state must try to protect the rights of the people, particularly of the minorities by all means. Along with right to religion, the right to education and culture is also most important for the minorities.

Right to Constitutional Remedies: Article 32 of the constitutional of India is very important. It provides an effective machinery for the protection and enforcement of fundamentals right. As regards the importance of article 32, Dr. B.R. Ambedkar remarked: "If I were asked which particular article of the constitution is the most important an article without which this constitution would be a nullity I would not refer to any other article except this one. It is the very soul of the constitution and the very heart of it." To make the fundamental rights meaningful, the famers of the constitution provided certain means for their protection and enforcement. All other rights would have been meaningless without this specific right.

Article 32 of the constitution empowers the Supreme Court to issue orders, directions and prerogative writs for the enforcement of the fundamental rights. Besides the supreme court, a person may also approach the High courts for the enforcement of fundamental rights. The High courts, under Article 226 of the constitution, can also issue various writs for the enforcement of the fundamentals rights. The persons concerned will decide whether to approach the High court of his state or the Supreme Court in the first instance. The various kinds of writs which the courts can issue are: habeas corpus, mandamus, Prohibition, quo warranto and certiorari.

The right to move the Supreme Court or the High courts for the protection or enforcement of the fundamental rights can suspended duringy the emergency except for the enforcement of fundamental rights mentioned in article 20 and 21. Article 20 is relating to protection in respect of conviction for offences and 21 is concerning protection of life and personal liberty.

The writs which the Supreme Court or the High courts can issue for the enforcement of fundamental rights are five in number. The Supreme Court can issue these writs under article 32(2). The high courts derive the power to issue writs under Article 226.

Habeas corpus: It is a remedy against wrongful detention of a person. The court may direct the detaining authority to present the detained person before the court. The detaining authority must justify the detention of the person in the court. By this writ illegal detention of a person can be prevented by the court.

Mandamus: it is an order given by the court to some subordinate Authority to perform an act which falls within its jurisdiction. The word 'mandamus' means 'we command'. By issuing this writ court commands a public body or an official to perform a public duty.

Prohibition: this is a writ issued by a superior court to a subordinate court. The superior court prevents the subordinate court to deal with a matter over which it has no jurisdiction.

Quo-warranto: By issuing this writ the court may prevent a person from acting in a office to which he is not entitled. It is in the nature of an injunction. It is issued to a person who acts in a capacity to which he is not entitled.

Certiorari: the literal meaning of word is "to be more fully informed of'. This is issued by a superior court to a court subordinate to it. The latter is directed to submit the records of a case pending before it for its proper consideration.

The power of the courts to issue writs is very wide. But it has certain limitations. When right to freedom is suspended during emergency, the courts cannot issue writs for the enforcement of these freedoms. Moreover, the saving Articles 31(a), 31 (c) may impose limits upon the enjoyment of fundamental rights. In this case, the power of the courts to issue writs is also limited. Again, when Article 359 is enforced during emergency, the courts cannot issue writs.

Article 33 empowers the parliament to modify the rights, conferred by part lll of the constitution in their application to armed forces. Thus there are limits on the enjoyment of fundamental rights by the forces employed for the defence of the country and maintenance of law and order. The fundamental are restricted for them so as to ensure the proper discharge of their duties and the maintenance of discipline among them.

Article 34 imposes restriction on the enjoyment of fundamental rights. When material law is in operation in any area, the parliament may be law indemnify any person in the service of the union or of a state or any other person in the respect of any action done by him in connection with the maintenance or restoration of under in that area. Article 35 concerning legislation to give effect to provision of this part of the constitution.

Right to the Constitutional Remedies is very important for the citizens of India. Without this basic right, there other right will be meaningless. A person may approach the supreme court or the high court's to protect his fundamental rights if violated. The right guaranteed under article 32 cannot be suspended except as otherwise provided for by the constitution of India. The parliament may empower any other court to exercise the power of issuing right within the local limits. We have discussed earlier that too many conditions have been laid down for the enjoyment of this right. This rights becomes inoperative when emergency is in force and Article 359 enforced by the president of India.

Limitations of the Fundamental Rights

Although the fundamental rights incorporated in the constitution of India are praised by all, those rights have certain serious limitation. The limitation of the fundamental rights are discussed below:

1. Part III of the constitution of India does not contain a single economic right. This is the most serious defect of our fundamental rights. In a poor country like India, economic rights are of great necessity. Without economic rights, the other rights are almost useless for the common people. Our rights are not meant for establishing 'economic democracy'. They lay the foundation of political democracy.
2. Rights are supposed to be the fruits of duties. Till the other day the constitution of India was silent about the duties of the citizens. Now, they have certain duties. But, they are not binding upon the people. Legally binding duties would have made the right meaningful.
3. Too many restrictions have been imposed on the fundamental rights. The restrictions and exceptions have made the fundamental rights meaningless.
4. Unnecessary details of the fundamental rights mentioned in the constitution have made them complicated. According to Ivor

Jennnings, "writing of so many duties of the fundamental rights in the constitution was not necessary."

5. The power of the president to suspend the fundamental rights during emergency can lead the country to dictatorship.
6. The power of the parliament to amend the fundamental rights is also subject to criticism. The citizens have no guarantee of their fundamental rights. They may be created by the parliament at any moment by amending the constitution.

Our fundamental rights have been criticized for being offered by one hand and taken away by other due to several qualifying provisions. They highly circumscribe the scope of their exercise and enjoyment. The machinery for the protection of the fundamental rights is also very expensive. The judiciary is beyond the reach of the common people.

Importance of Fundamental Rights

The fundamental rights guaranteed by the constitution of India have been lauded as: "The bed rock of Indian democracy." The framers of our constitution have enshrined in the constitution certain fundamental rights to safeguard individual liberty, Graville Austin says: "In India it appears that the fundamental rights have both created a new equality and have helped to preserve individual liberty."

Some limitations have been imposed upon the fundamental rights, but they do not minimize their importance for the citizens of India. Absolute right is impossible rights can only be exercised under reasonable restrictions.

Many criticisms have been levelled against the fundamental rights, but some of them are not at all sound. If the people remain vigilant, the government cannot misuse its powers and encroach upon the rights of the people.

The fundamental rights have laid down the foundation of political democracy in India. The citizens of India now live in an atmosphere of freedom. Without these rights, democracy in India would have been meaningless.

Although our fundamental rights are not economic in character and the makers of the constitution have failed to give us economic security, necessary direction have been given to the state to look after economic interest of the people.

The secular character of the fundamental rights is another important factor. They have made the foundation of secularism in India strong.

The courts of law are also serving useful purpose in safeguarding and enforcing the fundamental rights of the people. These rights have put a check on the arbitrary exercise of power by the state.

Adequate steps have been taken to safeguard the interest of the minorities and improve the condition of the socially deprived sections of the society, the fundamental rights have weakness for a minorities and the backward sections of people.

It has been said earlier that the provisions of fundamental rights have laid down the foundations of a democratic order in our country. Now if the people of India remain vigilant and see that elected representatives are of character and integrity, these fundamental rights are of immense value.

Ambedkar observed: "in politics we have equality and in social economic rights we will have inequality. In politics we will be recognizing the principle of one man one vote. In our social and economic rights we shall, by reason of our social and economic structure, continue to deny one man, one value." Although Ambedkar holds this view about the fundamental rights, it should be remembered that the Constitution of India is a dynamic document. It is subject to changes and it can be changed as per the needs of the people. Hence the provision in Part III should change in response to the changing social and economic aspirations of the people and the conditions of the country.

People should also guard against the misuse of fundamental rights. Very often, it is the people who are responsible for violating the fundamental rights of their fellow citizens. So, we should develop a habit of honouring the rights of others. It must be noticed that the fundamental rights guaranteed by the Constitution must be made available to the common man of our society.

Amendment of the Fundamental Rights

Fundamental Rights were amendable by the Parliament from 1950 till the verdict of the Supreme Court in the famous Golaknath's case in 1967. Before the Golaknath case ruling Fundamental Rights were amended to implement the Directive Principles of State Policy.

The Fundamental Rights were made un-amendable since 1967 by the Golaknath verdict of the Supreme Court which came as a shock to the Parliament. 24th Constitutional amendment of 1972 made the Fundamental rights amendable again. It nullified the decision of the famous Golaknath case which declared the Fundamental Rights as un-amendable.

In Keshavananda Bharti's case of 1973, the Supreme Court held that the Fundamental Rights can be amended but the basic structure of the Constitution cannot be destroyed.

The judgment in the Keshavananda Bharti's case provided a basis for stability and progress. It maintained a balance between the powers of the Parliament and the rights of the people.

Under the 42nd Constitution Amendment Act, the Parliament again possessed unlimited powers to amend the Fundamental rights. But the Minerva Mills case judgement of the Supreme Court in 1980 has again restored the status of the Keshavananda Bharti's case verdict. From then onwards, all constitutional amendments are subject to judicial review. Thus, Fundamental rights can be amended but the basic structure of our Constitution cannot be destroyed.

3

Freedom of Speech and Expression and the Freedom of Press

The Freedom of speech and expression implies two important pillars of democracy.

The Freedom of speech and expression is guaranteed to all citizens under Article 19(1)(a) of the Indian Constitution. This freedom is considered as the bulwark of democracy and is essential for its proper functioning.

Article 19(1): ***The Article of Six Freedoms*:** All citizens shall have the right

(a) to freedom of speech and expression;
(b) to assemble peacefully and without arms;
(c) to form associations or unions;
(d) to move freely throughout the territory of India;
(e) to reside and settle in any part of the territory of India; and
(f) (omitted)
(g) to practise any profession, or to carry on any occupation, trade or business.

Sub clause (f) – Right to acquire, hold and dispose of property has been omitted by the 44th Amendment, 1978 with effect from (w.e.f.) 20.06.79.

Article 19(1)(a): This Article states that all citizens of India shall have the right to freedom of speech and expression.

Article 19(2): Nothing in sub clause (a) of clause (1) shall affect the operation of any existing law, or prevent the State from making any law, in so far as such law imposes reasonable restrictions on the exercise of the right conferred by the said sub clause in the interests of the sovereignty and integrity of India, the security of the State, friendly relations with foreign States, public order, decency or morality or in relation to contempt of court, defamation or incitement to an offence.

The State in this context includes not only the legislative authorities of the Union and the State, but also other local or statutory authorities of municipalities or local boards etc. within the territory of India or under the control of the Government of India. So, all of these authorities may impose restrictions on the freedom of press provided such restrictions are reasonable and can be related to Clauses 2 and 6 of Article 19.

Development of Meaning of the Freedom of the Press

1. Historically, the origin of the concept of the Freedom of the Press took place in England. Milton's '*Areopagitica*' was a protest addressed to the Parliament, which had taken up licensing, after the abolition of the Star Chamber. It was a result of such agitation that the Licensing Act of 1662 was eventually refused to be renewed by the House of Commons, in 1694, though the reasons were technical. The history of the Freedom of the Press in England is, thus, a triumph of the people against the power of the licensor. The Freedom of Press, in England, is measured by the freedom to write anything provided the law is not infringed. It is free from prior restraint to pre-censorship.
2. In 1776, the Virginia Bill of Rights asserted, "Freedom of the Press is one of the greatest bulwarks of liberty, and can never be restrained by despotic Governments."
3. The Federal Bill of Rights incorporated into the Constitution of United States by the First Amendment (1791) stated that 'Congress shall make no law... abridging the freedom... of the press.'

Need for Freedom of the Press

1. Ideologically, the indispensability of the Press for the proper functioning of democracy is so much embedded in the United States that Jefferson once said that if he had to choose between having 'a government without newspapers' on the one hand and 'newspapers without a government' on the other, he would have no hesitation in preferring the latter. This was the view, which eventually triumphed in the adoption of the first amendment to the American Constitution in 1791.
2. In the words of Blackstone, "The liberty of the press is indeed essential to the nature of a free state... the only plausible argument heretofore used for restraining the just freedom of the press, 'that it was necessary to prevent the daily abuse of it', will entirely lose its force, when it is shown... that the press cannot be abused to any bad purpose without incurring a suitable punishment: *whereas it can never be used to any good one, when under the control of an inspector*."

3. Public criticism is essential for the working of a democracy. Subject, of course, to the power of the State to punish for offences and incitement to commit offences through the Press, the Government should not suppress the freedom of a newspaper to publish any views or comments merely because they are critical of the Government.
4. In the case, *De Jonge vs. Oregon*, 1937 in the United States, Hughes, C.J. observed, "The very foundation of constitutional Government lies in the belief that changes, if desired, may be obtained by peaceful means…" Hence, 'The greater the importance of safeguarding the community from incitements to the overthrow of our institutions by force and violence, the more imperative is the need to inviolate the constitutional rights of free speech, free press and free assembly in order to maintain the opportunity for political discussion…'
5. In the case *Whitney vs. California*, 1927 in United States, Brandeis, J. quotes, "… fear breeds repression… repression breeds hate… hate menaces stable government; … path of safety lies in the opportunity to discuss supposed grievances and proposed remedies…"

The propositions arrived at by the American Supreme Court through the statements of Hughes, C.J. and Brandeis, J. were summarised as follows by the Supreme Court of India in the case *Express Newspapers vs. Union of India*, 1959; and held to be applicable in the interpretation of the Freedom of the Press in India as derived from Article 19(1)(a) of the Constitution:

(a) The freedom of the press rests on the assumption that the widest possible dissemination of information from diverse and antagonistic sources is essential for the welfare of the public;
(b) Such freedom is the foundation of free Government of free people;
(c) The purpose of such a guarantee is to prevent public authorities from assuming the guardianship of the public mind; and
(d) Freedom of the press involves freedom of employment or non-employment of the necessary means of exercising this right or, in other words, freedom from restriction in respect of employment in the editorial force.

'Freedom' means absence of control, interference or restriction. Hence, the expression 'Freedom of the Press' means the right to print and publish without any interference from the State or any public authority. But this freedom is not absolute; it is subject to the exceptions acknowledged in public interest, which in India are enumerated in Article 19(2) of the Constitution. But since, in India, freedom of expression is guaranteed by Article 19(1)(a) of the Constitution, and it has been held by the Supreme Court that the freedom of the Press is included in that wider guarantee, it is unnecessary to plead for freedom of the Press separately in this country.

Freedom of Press in India

Mahatma Gandhi, on the role of press said, "One of the objects of a newspaper is to understand the popular feeling and give expression to it; another is to arouse among people certain desirable sentiments; the third is to fearlessly expose popular defects."

In the context of freedom of press, the term 'press' is identified as the medium for dissemination of news, views and advertisements, namely radio, television, newspapers, books, periodicals, internet and others.

If we consult the history of press in India, we find that there is no document to prove that there was freedom of press in India before independence. The Act 11 of 1835 made by C.T. Metcalfe, the then Governor General, was the lone exception.

Article 19(1)(a) is the foundation of freedom of press in India, although the term 'press' is not directly mentioned in it.

Some people do point out that there is no statute as such to guarantee us the freedom of press in India. In contrast, they refer to the very First Amendment of the U.S. Federal Constitution, which specifically mentioned, "Congress shall make no law… abridging the freedom of press or of the press…"

To counter the above argument, it may be mentioned that in the USA too, most of the State Constitutions cite that, 'The State has the right to interfere if the freedom of speech or the press is abused' and 'the abuse of such freedom may be punished'.

There is no mention of freedom of press in Article 19(1)(a), but in various pronouncements, such as *Express Newspapers vs Union of India* (1958), *Bennett Coleman vs Union of India* (1973), *Indian Express Newspapers vs Union of India* (1986), the Supreme Court has upheld the freedom of press and has repeatedly and unambiguously declared that the press in India is free to collect, print, publish or circulate news and views.

The Supreme Court has maintained in various cases (*Romesh Thappar vs the State of Madras, Brij Bhushan vs the Union Territory of Delhi, Express Newspapers vs Union of India, Bennett Coleman Co. vs Union of India*) that the term 'freedom of expression' includes the term 'freedom of press', which includes freedom of printing, publishing, circulating and propagation.

In India, freedom of press has both positive and negative sides. On the positive side, Constitution allows the freedom and on the negative side, it imposes certain reasonable restrictions in the greater interest of the public and nation at large.

Thus, we can say that Indian journalists and the Supreme Court reinforced the freedom of press in India.

Judgements that Reinforced the Freedom of Press

1. *Sakal Papers (P) Ltd. vs Union of India*: The judgement mentioned, 'It is a

settled law that the right to freedom of speech and expression in Article 19(1)(a) includes the liberty of the press.'

2. *Romesh Thappar vs the State of Madras*: In this case, a notification banning the entry into or circulation, sale or distribution in Chennai of a newspaper named 'Crossroads' was held as invalid. The Court held that without liberty of circulation, the publication will be of little value.

The Chief Justice, Justice Patanjali Shastri observed, 'Freedom of speech and the press lay at the foundation of all democratic organisations, for without political discussions, no public education, so essential for the proper functioning of the process of popular government, is possible. A freedom of such amplitude might involve risks of abuse. But the framers of the Constitution may well have reflected with Madison, who was the leading spirit in the preparation of the First Amendment of the Federal Constitution, that it is better to leave a few of its noxious branches to their luxuriant growth than by pruning them away, to injure the vigour of those yielding the proper fruit.'

3. K.K. Birla vs the Press Council: In this case, Justice S.S. Chaddha said that the concept of freedom of press cannot be put in a narrow straightjacket. It is a living concept and cannot be confined in any narrow limits, which would restrict its growth.

4. *Indian Express Newspapers vs Union of India*: In this case, it has been held that the press plays a very significant role in the democratic machinery. The Courts have duty to uphold the freedom of press and invalidate all laws and administrative actions that abridge that freedom.

Freedom of press has three essential elements:

(a) Freedom of access to all sources of information;
(b) Freedom of publication;
(c) Freedom of circulation.

5. *Bennett Coleman Co. vs Union of India*: In this case, the validity of Newsprint Control Order, which fixed the maximum number of pages, was struck down by the Court holding it to be in violation of Article 19(1)(a) and not a reasonable restriction under Article 19(2).

Contents of the Freedom of the Press

Durga Das Basu, in the book, 'Law of the Press (Third Edition)', states that since freedom of expression includes the freedom to propagate one's own views as well as those of others and to communicate them to others, it follows that the freedom of the Press, (subject only to such restraints that are imposed by the State and are constitutionally permissible), includes the following rights:

1. To print and publish news and views;
2. To distribute and circulate such printed matter to any other party;
3. The freedom extends to the discussion and publication of views

related to all issues about which information is needed to enable the members of the society to cope with the exigencies of the period; and is not necessarily confined to political or public affairs;

4. A corresponding right to collect the information relating to public affairs or the right of access to the sources of such information;
5. To collect information from diverse and antagonistic sources, on a comparative basis, free from any monopolistic control from the Government.
6. The right to refuse any advertisement, including a Government advertisement. If, however, a newspaper accepts Government advertisement, it would be bound to abide by the terms and conditions of the contract or law relating to such contracts;
7. Freedom of choice in matter of employment or non employment of the necessary means of exercising the freedom of expression, including employment in the editorial force;
8. Immunity from any tax specially imposed on the Press or on advertisements in a newspaper, which was calculated to limit its circulation.

The Freedom of Press vs Defamation

Defamation is an injury into a person's reputation, which may constitute a criminal offence, punishable under Section 499 of the IPC; and also a civil wrong for which the person injured may bring an action for damages under Common law.

This wrong arises when a person publishes a false statement, which has a tendency to injure the plaintiff's reputation.

The Freedom of Press vs Right to Privacy

Since privacy is a recent development in the realm of law and the stream of its development is still flowing, it is difficult to give an exhaustive definition of what 'privacy' means in law. Loosely, it has been described as the right of a person 'to be let alone' or his right to repose in his private life and home.

Our Supreme Court has held that the individual's Right to privacy under Article 21 is to be balanced with the competing Freedom of press. Since Article 19(1)(a) is available against the State, so, the State cannot impose any prior restraint upon the Freedom of press on the ground that the relevant publication will offend the privacy of an individual or would defame a public official; the remedy in all such cases would be for the aggrieved person to lodge a complaint under the appropriate law after the offending matter is published.

In simple words, no person can publish anything concerning the privacy of any other person, his family, marriage, procreation, motherhood, child bearing, education and other related matters.

The Supreme Court of India, in the case of *R. Rajagopal vs State of Tamil* Nadu, stated that any publication with regard to above mentioned subjects becomes unobjectionable if such publication is based upon public records including court records. This is for the reason that once a matter becomes a matter of public record, the right to privacy no longer subsists and it becomes a legitimate subject for comment by the press and media among others.

The Supreme Court has further carved out an exception to the above mentioned rule, i.e., a female, who is a victim of sexual assault, kidnap, abduction or like offence should not be further subjected to indignity by mentioning her name or identity in the media.

The Supreme Court has further held that the right to privacy is also not available with respect to acts and conducts of public officials in discharge of their public duties.

The Freedom of Press vs Right to Fair Trial

In an article dated May 17, 2010, '*Freedom of the press and fair trial*' by the Reader's Editor of *The Hindu*, S. Viswanathan, said that the key concepts, such as free speech, freedom of the press, the right to life, the right to fair trial, and contempt of court have once again come to centre stage, thanks to a recent judgement and incidents of legal and judicial significance across the country. Human rights activists and progressive writers hailed the verdict when the Supreme Court of India quashed criminal proceedings against Tamil film actor Kushboo for her remarks on pre-marital sex, live-in relationships, and the need for sex education in schools in a 2005 interview to a Tamil weekly.

Understandably, the judgement came as a big relief to the actor, against whom as many as 23 complaints had been filed in several courts across the State under Sections 499 and 500 (criminal defamation) of the Indian Penal Code, obviously with the intention of harassing the popular actor. A couple of regional parties organised a demonstration in which women participated with brooms in hand. This forced Kushboo to come out with an apology to Tamils in a television broadcast. Several Tamil publications saw Kushboo's stand as an affront to Tamil sentiments.

What was Kushboo's alleged offence? All she did was comment on certain findings of a survey that the magazine had conducted. Asked about her views on a contention that there was increasing incidence of pre-marital sex among young girls, she cautioned them against sexually transmitted diseases. This perfectly sensible advice was misinterpreted by her detractors as a licence for immoral action and, believe it or not, an insult to the dignity of Tamil women. The judges rejected the complaints and upheld her right to free speech.

Another event that attracted intense media coverage was the IPL scandal that saw the ouster of a Union Minister of State and culminated in the suspension of IPL Commissioner and Chairman, Lalit Modi. With high news potential provided by the presence of a 'mysterious' woman player among the stakeholders of the Kochi franchise, the TV channels had a field day, with the print media not lagging far behind. All sorts of speculative stories revolving round the relationship between the Minister, Shashi Tharoor, and Sunanda Pushkar did the rounds in air and in print. The accent was on denigrating the character and competence of the businesswoman. This kind of 'investigative journalism' has nothing to do with the truth-telling function of the news media. What it does is to prejudice the course of public judgement and eventually justice.

The 'right to fair trial' is an integral part of the Indian criminal justice system. Along with the right to privacy, the right to fair trial flows from the broader fundamental right to life guaranteed by Article 21 of the Indian Constitution. The right to fair trial comprises many other rights that include the right to be presumed innocent unless or until proved guilty. These rights are no less important than the freedom of speech and expression guaranteed by Article 19(1)(a).

The Law Commission of India in its 200th report, released in August 2006 under the title, "Trial by Media: Free Speech and Fair Trial Under Criminal Procedure Code, 1973", elaborately deals with several aspects of the rights relating to freedom of speech, freedom of the press, and freedom of fair trial. Law Commission Chairman, Justice M. Jagannadha Rao says that the subject was taken up by the Commission *suo moto*, "having regard to the extensive prejudicial coverage of crime and information about suspects and accused, both in the print and electronic media."

"There is today a feeling," he explains, "that in view of the extensive use of the television and cable services, the whole pattern of publication of news has changed and several such publications are likely to have prejudicial impact on the suspects, witnesses and even Judges and, in general, on the administration of justice." He points out that under the Indian criminal justice system, a suspect or accused is entitled to a fair procedure and is "presumed to be innocent till proved guilty in a court" and no one "can be allowed to prejudge or prejudice his case by the time it goes to trial."

The Law Commission's report expresses concern over the fact that there is very little restraint in the media insofar as the administration of criminal justice is concerned. It reminds the media that while freedom of speech and expression is an important right, it is not absolute inasmuch as the Constitution itself has placed "reasonable restrictions" on it, with the restrictions encompassing the fair administration of justice as protected by the Contempt of Courts Act, 1971.

Explaining how media actions affect the administration of justice, the report says that "excessive publicity" about a suspect or an accused before trial prejudices a fair trial or results in characterising him as a person, who has committed the crime; and that this amounts to undue interference with the administration of justice, inviting proceedings for contempt of court against the media.

The underlying issue here is this: the media, while zealously protecting their entitlements and space, must accept social responsibility – the onerous obligation of upholding the larger interests of democracy, which means journalists do not have a licence to trample on the rights and dignity of others."

Extra Legal Restraint

1. The Press Council: The need for an institution to ensure a high standard of responsibilities on the part of the Press arises from the fact that the freedom of the Press is likely to be abused by what is called 'yellow journalism', i.e. the publication of matters, which debase public taste or indulge in intrusion into public lives even though such publication may not be punishable under the provisions of the existing law. Almost every modern country has, therefore, set up a body, which could serve as a watchdog over the standards of journalism and, at the same time, maintain the freedom of the Press against unwarranted government intrusion.

In India, the Press Council is a statutory body. It was first established by the Press Council Act, 1965, on the lines recommended by the first Press Commission (1954). Its functions are:

(a) To help newspapers and news agencies to maintain their independence.
(b) It has to ensure a high standard of public taste and responsibility in journalism, and for the purpose, it is empowered to build up a Code of Conduct for newspapers, news agencies and journalists in accordance with high professional standards.

2. **Self-censorship**: Censorship, which, when imposed by law, operates as a restriction upon the freedom of the Press, ceases to be so when it is self-imposed. In many countries, therefore, newspapers and journals have put their heads together to formulate a code of conduct or guidelines that they would observe to prevent abuses of the freedom of the Press. Though these voluntary guidelines do not operate as binding upon any of the units, they are usually compiled in order to avert a greater evil, namely, government intervention.

Self censorship imposed by voluntary restraint must be distinguished from guidelines issued by a Censor, an instance of which was seen in India during the 1975-76 Emergency.

4

Directive Principles of State Policy

The Directive Principles of the State Policy is an important feature of the constitution of India. The principal aim of these principles is to convert India into a welfare state. These policies are mentioned in Part IV of the constitution. The Directive Principles of the State Policy have been borrowed from the Irish constitution of 1937 which in turn has adopted them from the constitution of Spain.

Directive Principles of the State Policy covers articles 36 to 51 of the constitution of India.

Meaning and Objectives of the Directive Principles of the State Policy

Article 37 of the constitution of India says that the Directive Principles of the State Policy are fundamental in the governance of the country and it shall be the duty of the state to apply these principles in making laws. The Directive Principles of the State Policy are restatement of the ideals as laid down in the Preamble of the constitution of India. The centre and the states are to act in such a way so as to promote fraternity and equality and to guarantee justice and liberty to the people.

The Directive Principles of the State Policy: According to Dr. Ambedkar, constitute a very comprehensive social, economic and political programme for a modern democratic state. He said, "they lay down that our ideal is economic democracy." He further said, "where there is a grant of power in general terms for peace, order and good government, it is necessary that it should be accompanied by instructions relating to its exercise." The Directive Principles of the State Policy have been incorporated in the constitution of India to meet with the economic and social aspirations of the people of India. In this connection Dr. Ambedkar remarked, "How long shall we continue to deny equality in our social and economic life? If we continue to deny it for long, we will do so only by putting our political democracy in peril. We must remove this contradiction at the earliest possible moment or else those who suffer from inequality will blow off the structure of political democracy which this Assembly has so laboriously built up."

Part IV of the constitution of India is regarded as the sister part of Part III which deals with the fundamental rights of the Indian citizens. Political democracy must be based on social and economic order according to democratic principles that is in a political democracy the social position of every individual should be recognized on the basis of equality and at the same time they should have economic security. Part III of the constitution is meant for establishing political democracy but it is supplemented by Part IV which aims at establishing economic democracy. Hence these two parts of our constitution are like integral parts of the organic law of the land.

Dr. Kripesh Chandra Paul and *Durga Kanta Sarmah* in their individual textbooks written on the subject of Political Science give an elaborated description on the concept of Directive Principles of the State Policy. Their ideas have been adapted in this book for the better understanding of the students.

Directive Principles of the State Policy underline the philosophy of democratic socialism. It has a touch of Gandhian idealism also.

The objectives of the Directive Principles of the State Policy have come out very clearly in the words of M.C. Setalvad who says, "Although the Directive Principles of the State Policy confer no legal rights and create no legal remedies they appear to be like an instrument of instructions or general recommendations addressed to all authorities in the union reminding them of the basic principles of the new social and economic order which the constitution aims at building. These fundamental axioms of state policy, though of no legal effect, have serves as useful beacon lights to courts." The Directive Principles of the State Policy should act as a guide to all authorities functioning in India under the Constitution. The Directive Principles of the State Policy wants to achieve certain social, political, cultural and environmental goals of a welfare state. Their scope is very vast.

Differences between Fundamental Rights and Directive Principles

1. Fundamental rights are justiceable whereas the Directive Principles are non-justiceable.
2. Fundamental rights are not absolute as they are accompanied by some limitations. The Directive Principles are free from constitutional limitations.
3. Fundamental rights can be suspended during national emergency excepting the rights mentioned in Article 20 and 21 but the Directive

Principles are in a state of permanent suspended form unless they are implemented.

4. According to Gledhill, "Fundamental rights are injunctions to prohibit the government from doing certain things; the Directive Principles are affirmative instructions to the government to do certain things." In other words, the Fundamental rights are negative and the Directive principles are positive in character.
5. Aim of Fundamental rights is to establish political democracy and the aim of the Directive principles is to establish just, social, economic and political order.
6. Fundamental rights are Primary but the Directive principles are subsidiary in character. In case of the conflict between the two the rights shall prevail over the principles.
7. Fundamental rights can be enforced without new legislation but Directive principles cannot be implemented without new legislation.
8. Fundamental rights are political in character but Directive principles are dominated by economic principles.
9. Fundamental rights are meant for the people but Directive principles are meant for the state. They impose duties upon the state and the state has to follow them while governing the country.
10. Fundamental rights have limited the authority of the state but the Directive principles expanded the sphere of the activity of the state.
11. Fundamental rights are binding upon the state. It cannot do anything in violation of the rights but the Directive principles are optional in character. They may or may not be followed by the state.
12. Fundamental rights are based on individualism whereas the Directive principles are based on socialism.

Fundamental Rights and the Directive Principles are intimately connected and one cannot proceed without the other. For the collective good of the society individual rights will have to be scarified to a certain extent whenever necessary.

The Directive Principles of State Policy

The Directive Principles of State Policy may be classified into four categories on the basis of their objectives. These are:

1. Economic principles
2. Social principles
3. Gandhian principles
4. Principles for international peace and security

Now let us discuss each category as follows:

1. **Economic principles:** The state can ensure economic justice by providing:
   - Adequate means of livelihood for the citizens;
   - Equitable distribution of the ownership and control of the material resources of the community keeping in view the common good;
   - That concentration of wealth and means of production in the hands of a few is prevented because it is not in the inertest of the society;
   - Equal pay for equal work for both men and women;
   - That the health and strength of the workers; men and women and the tender age of children are not abused;
   - That citizens are not forced by economic necessity to enter vocations unsuited to their age or strength;
   - Protection of children and youth against exploitation and against moral and material abandonment;
   - Provision of public assistance in cases of unemployment, old age, sickness and disablement;
   - Inequities of income are minimized.
2. **Social principles:** The state can ensure social justice by:
   - Promoting educational and economic interest of the weaker sections of the society in general and of the scheduled castes and scheduled tribes in particular by preventing their exploitation in various forms;
   - Providing free legal aid to the poor so that justice is not denied to any citizen because of economic difficulties;
   - Eliminating inequalities in status, facilities and opportunities among different groups of people residing in different areas or engaged in different vocations;
   - Providing free and compulsory education for all people upto the age of fourteen;
   - Providing uniform civil code separating executive from judiciary.
3. **Gandhian principles:** These principles are:
   - Establishment of village panchayats as units of self government;
   - Promotion of cottage industries on an individual and cooperative basis in rural areas;
   - Making law for participation of workers in the management of undertakings, establishments and industries;
   - Raising the level of nutrition, standard of living of the people and the improvement of public health;
   - Prohibiting consumption of intoxicating drinks and drugs except for medical purpose;

- Organizing agriculture and animal husbandry on modern and scientific lines;
- Prohibiting slaughter of cows, calves and other milch and draught cattle;
- To protect and improve the environment, save the forests and wildlife of the country;
- To protect every monument or place of object of artistic or historical interest which is of national importance.

4. **Principles for international peace and security:** These principles are as follows:
   - Promote international peace and security;
   - Maintain just and honourable relations among nations;
   - Foster respect for international law and treaty obligations;
   - Encourage settlement of international disputes by arbitration.

Thus we conclude through the words of Dr. Ambedkar, "If these Directive Principles of State Policy are not socialistic in their direction and content, I fail to understand what more socialism there can be."

Constitutional Significance of the Directive Principles of State Policy

1. The Directive Principles of State Policy have great moral ideals. They appeal to the conscience of the law makers.
2. Directive Principles of State Policy cannot be enforced by the courts but they serve as ideals for the judges and influence their interpretation of laws. Since they are part of the constitution, it is the duty of the courts to protect them.
3. Directive Principles of State Policy are fundamental in the governance of the country. It is the duty of the state to apply these principles in making laws. Public opinion is the real force behind these principles. Dr. Ambedkar says that if any government ignores them, they will certainly have to answer for them before the electorate at the election time.
4. The Directive Principles of State Policy lay the corner stone of a welfare state.
5. The Directive Principles form an essential background for all state action. The success of the constitution depends on the successful implementation of the Directive Principles of State Policy.
6. The Directive Principles of State Policy have been embodied in the constitution so as to meet the aspirations of the people. The happiness and contentment of the people depends on the implementation of these principles as these principles meet most of their urgent needs.

7. The Directive Principles of State Policy constitute the very basis of a strong democracy. These are meant for the general well being of all classes of people.
8. The Directive Principles of State Policy though not binding upon the state yet, no government can ignore them because the people can judge the performance of any political party in the light of the implementation of these principles.

Criticism

1. Prof. K.T. Shah dubbed them as 'pious superfluities' and compared them with a 'cheque payable by a bank as per its convenience.' Sir Ivor Jennings describes them as 'little more than a manifesto of aims and aspirations.' Prof. K.T. Shah further remarks that the Directive Principles are a 'needless fraud' since it would provide an excellent window dressing without any stock behind that dressing. Prof. K.C. Wheare says, "If these declarations are, however, to be treated as 'words' they will bring discredit upon the constitution also."
2. As the directive principles are not justiceable, the state is not serious in the implementation of these principles. The greatest weakness is that these principles are not binding upon the authorities.
3. The public opinion is the only sanction behind the directive principles. It is said to be catalogue of good intentions but not of positive obligations.
4. Without missionary zeal of the administrative system the directive principles cannot be implemented.
5. Moreover there is lack of dedication on the part of various agencies who are responsible for the execution of these principles.
6. Lack of cooperation and vigilance on the part of the people is another factor for the failure of these principles.
7. Lack of resources is yet another factor for lack of implementation of these principles. And the resources which are available at the disposal of the state are often misused.

India cannot become a welfare state in the true essence until and unless the directive principles are implemented. All efforts should be made to make ordinary people economically secure because unless India becomes economically secure, it will lead to the failure of our political democracy. Mere slogans will not do. What is necessary at present is real action for the removal of difficulties which are faced by the people in their everyday lives; and this can happen only through the successful implementation of the Directive Principles of the State Policy endorsed in the constitution of India.

5

Emergency Provisions and their Effect on Press Freedom

The Part XVIII of the Indian Constitution deals with the Emergency provisions, which are also known as the Emergency powers of the President.

This Part deals with three kinds of Emergency provisions. They are:

1. National Emergency
2. Emergency due to breakdown of the Constitutional machinery in a State
3. Financial Emergency

National Emergency

National Emergency is dealt with in the Article 352 of the Indian Constitution.

This kind of Emergency can be made by the President at any time, when s/he is satisfied that the security of India or any part thereof has been threatened by war, external aggression or armed rebellion.

The 44th Amendment substituted the words 'armed rebellion' by 'internal disturbance', which was too vague and broad.

The 44th Amendment introduced a Clause 352(b) to the effect that the decision to issue such a proclamation has to be arrived at collectively by the Cabinet and not by the Prime Minister alone without consulting the Cabinet as in the case of the Emergency declared in 1975.

Every proclamation issued under Article 352 is to be laid before each house of the Parliament. It ceases to operate at the expiration of one month, unless, in the meantime, it has been approved by resolution of both the houses of the Parliament. If, however, at the time of the Proclamation, the Lok Sabha is dissolved without approving the Proclamation; and Rajya Sabha approves it, then the Proclamation ceases to operate after 30 days after the Lok Sabha sits again after fresh elections, unless, in the mean time, the new Lok Sabha passes a resolution approving the Proclamation.

The 44th Amendment laid down that a resolution approving the Proclamation has to be passed by each house by a majority of total membership of each house and not less than two-third of the members present and voting in each house.

Once approved by the Parliament, the Proclamation remains in force, unless revoked earlier, only for six months. For continuance beyond that period, Parliamentary approval is needed again. Thus, each time the Parliament approves the Proclamation; its life is extended for six months.

The 44th Amendment introduced that the President is obligated to revoke a Proclamation issued under Article 352(1) if the Lok Sabha passes a resolution disapproving the same. This resolution is passed by a simple majority of the members of the house present and voting.

National Emergency was proclaimed on the following events:

1. October 26, 1962 during the Chinese aggression in the North-East Frontier Agency (NEFA).
2. December 03, 1971 when Pakistan launched an undeclared war on India.
3. June 25, 1975 on the ground of an internal disturbance.

Effects

1. The Executive power of the Union can give direction to the State Executive.
2. Parliament's law making power will extend to subjects in the State list.
3. Parliament may, by law, extend the normal life of the Lok Sabha for a period not extending one year at a time and not extending, in any case, beyond a period of six months after the Proclamation has ceased to exist.
4. The federal provisions of the Constitution cease to function in the areas affected by the Proclamation.
5. The Fundamental Rights under Article 19 are suspended. The right to move to Court for implementation of Fundamental Rights conferred by Part III, except Article 20 and Article 21, can be suspended for the duration of the Emergency.

Emergency due to Breakdown of the Constitutional Machinery in a State

Emergency of this kind is dealt with in Article 355 of the Indian Constitution.

It is the duty of the Union to ensure that the Government of every State is carried on in accordance with the provisions of the Constitution. Article 356(1) states that the President is empowered to make a Proclamation, when he is satisfied that the Government of the State cannot be carried on in accordance with the provisions of the Constitution either on the report of the Governor of the State or otherwise.

The approval procedure is same as that of the National Emergency.

Effects

1. President may assume all or any of the functions of the State or he may vest all of those functions in any other Executive authority.
2. President may declare that the powers of the State Legislature shall be exercisable by the Parliament.
3. He may make any other incidental or consequential provisions necessary to give effect to the objects of the Proclamation.

Financial Emergency

Financial Emergency is dealt with in Article 360 of the Indian Constitution.

If the President is satisfied that a situation has arisen whereby the financial stability or credit of India or any part thereof is threatened, he may, by a Proclamation, make a declaration to that effect.

Effects

1. The Centre can give direction to any State to observe such canons of financial propriety as may be specified in the direction.
2. Direction for reduction of salary and allowances of all or any class of persons serving in the State.
3. It may require that all money bills or those, which involve expenditure from the State Consolidated Fund, shall be reserved for the President's consideration after being passed by the State legislature.
4. The President may also issue direction for reducing the salaries and allowances of persons serving in the Union including the Judges of the Supreme Court and High Courts.
5. The Proclamation of the Financial Emergency increases the supervision of the Centre on the States in financial matters.

Emergency Provisions and its Effect on Freedom of the Press

Durga Das Basu, in the book, 'Law of the Press (Third Edition)' gives a detailed description of how the Emergency provisions have an effect on the freedom of the Press. A summarized version of his work is stated as follows:

Suspension of Article 19 during Emergency

1. There is no provision in our Constitution for suspension of Fundamental Rights outside the Emergency provisions in Part XVIII. Two provisions of that Part are relevant in the present context – Articles 358 and 359.
2. Article 358 suspends the operation of Article 19 during the operation of a Proclamation of Emergency made under Article 352 on the ground of war or external aggression. The effect of Article 358 is that it suspends the restrictions on the powers of the State to make

any law in contravention of the provisions of Article 19 only during the pendency of the Proclamation. It does not lay down that the validity of any law, which had already been made, cannot be challenged on the ground of violating the provisions of Article 19. In other words:

(a) Laws or orders made prior to the coming into operation of the Proclamation of Emergency are not protected from the challenge of unconstitutionality on the ground of contravention of Article 19.

(b) But any law or order made after the coming into operation of the Proclamation of Emergency cannot be challenged, during the continuance of the Emergency, on the ground of contravention of Article 19. Even after the Emergency is over, the constitutionality of acts done or omitted to be done during the Emergency cannot be challenged on the same ground. The net result of Article 358 is, thus, to remove the fetters created on the legislative and executive powers by Article 19 and if the legislature makes laws or the executive commits acts, which are inconsistent with the rights guaranteed by Article 19, their validity is not open to challenge either during the continuance of the emergency or even thereafter.

(c) But as soon as the Proclamation ceases to operate, the legislative enactments passed and the executive actions taken during the course of the said Emergency shall be inoperative (except as to things already done or omitted during the period of the Proclamation of Emergency) to the extent to which they conflict with the rights guaranteed under Article 19, because as soon as the Emergency is lifted, Article 19, which was suspended during the Emergency, is automatically revived and begins to operate.

3. Article 359, on the other hand, does not purport expressly to suspend any of the fundamental rights. It authorizes the President to issue an Order declaring that the right to move any Court for the enforcement of such rights in Part III as may be mentioned in the Order and all proceedings in any Court for the enforcement of the rights so mentioned shall remain suspended for the period during which the Proclamation is in force or for any shorter period as may be specified in the Order. What the Presidential Order purports to do by virtue of the power conferred on the President by Article 359(1) is to bar the remedy to the citizens to move any Court for the enforcement of the specified rights.

4. The suspension of the fundamental right under Article 19 follows a Proclamation of Emergency under Article 352, without any further Presidential action (Article 352); but the right to enforce any other

fundamental right in the Courts does not so follow, but requires a specific Order of the President under Article 359 for that purpose.

5. It is to be noted that since the amendment of Article 359(1) by the Constitution (44th Amendment Act, 1978), Articles 20 and 21 cannot be included in an Order under Article 359(1). In the result, even during the subsistence of a Proclamation of Emergency under Article 352, a journalist, who may have been imprisoned or detained under any law of preventive detention, may challenge his imprisonment or detention on grounds available under Articles 20 and 21, even though his freedom of expression under Article 19 might have been suspended under Article 358 or the enforcement of the right under Article 19 has been barred by an Order under Article 359.
6. There is another provision, which has been imposed by the 44th Amendment Act, which states that neither the Proclamation of Emergency nor a Presidential Order shall *ispo facto* (meaning: by the fact itself or; by mere fact) suffice to confer immunity to a law made during an Emergency, either under Article 358 or Article 359, unless the law itself contains a recital to the effect that it relates to the Proclamation of Emergency.

Impact of Emergency on Press Freedom

1. On December 3, 1971, a Proclamation was issued in view of aggression by Pakistan. While this Emergency was continuing, a second Proclamation, on the ground of 'internal disturbance', was issued on June 26, 1975.
2. As a result Article 19 remained suspended by the operation of Article 358 and Order under Article 359 were also issued by the President barring the right to enforce in the Courts the fundamental rights under Articles 14, 21 and 22. On January 8, 1976, an Order under Article 19 was also issued, barring the right to move any Court for the enforcement of Article 19.
3. As a result of the foregoing constitutional suspensions consequential upon the Proclamation of Emergency, neither any legislation nor any executive order could be challenged on the ground of violation of Articles 19, 20 and 21, so that the freedom of the Press and of journalists lay completely at the mercy of the Government, without the risk of being challenged in a Court of law. Emboldened by this change in the constitutional background, the Government of India took the following repressive measures to curb the freedom of the Press.
   (a) Issued the Press Censorship Order on June 25, 1975, that is, immediately after the issue of the Proclamation, on the ground of 'internal disturbance'.

(b) Cancelled the declarations made under the Press and Registration of Books Act, 1867, relating to over 2,500 newspapers during the period of operation of the Emergency of June, 1975.

(c) Detained numerous journalists under the Maintenance of Internal Security Act or the Defence of India Rules.

(d) A specific Press law was enacted, namely, the Prevention of Objectionable Matter Act, 1976, empowering the Government to proceed directly against offending newspapers by way of forfeiture and the like.

(e) Article 31D was inserted in the Constitution itself by the 42nd Amendment Act, 1976, giving absolute power to the Government to deal with anti-national activities.

The Emergency declared in 1975 was a turning point in the history of Indian journalism. Indira Gandhi's government was marked by economic, social and political turmoil, much of which was blamed on the press. During the period of Emergency, she had introduced censorship and rigid restrictions on the Press.

One of the tools she used to harass the press was to cut off the power supply to Bahadur Shah Zafar Marg, New Delhi, which housed some of the largest publishing companies in India.

She ensured that even reports of the large scale arrests of top-ranking leaders of the opposition, and even dissidents within her own party, were not published.

The next 18 months saw the most humiliating period in the Indian press' history. During this time, several laws were amended and others passed, making it impossible for the press to criticize the government.

P.K. Ravindranath, in his book, 'Indian Regional Journalism', wrote that as many as 253 journalists were arrested and jailed all over the country. Government advertisements were withdrawn from over 100 newspapers and journals and 18 newspapers and periodicals were banned.

The rigid censorship had an adverse effect on the Government: it cut off all information on what was happening in the country and the genuine aspirations of the common people.

This gave birth to underground magazine reporting on the realities of India.

The Emergency saw the emergence of news magazines in a big way and of investigative reporters. Arun Shourie is known as the father of Indian investigative reporting.

The transformation of the publishing industry into a business began post 1977, after the Emergency was lifted.

Gossip and rumours abounded in the absence of authentic information and eroded the shrinking credibility of the ruling party and the Government.

The Janata Government, which came to power in the post-emergency elections of 1977, repealed most of the repressive laws. All the foregoing repressive measures were lifted on the eve of or after coming into power of Morarji Desai of the Janata Government.

(a) Both the Proclamations of Emergency of 1971 and 1975 were revoked towards the end of March, 1977.
(b) The Prevention of Objectionable Matter Act, 1976 was repealed in April, 1977.
(c) The Censorship Order was revoked on 22.03.1977.
(d) MISA, that is, Maintenance of Internal Security Act detenus were released.
(e) Article 31D of the Indian Constitution was omitted by passing the Constitution (43rd Amendment Act, 1977) in April, 1978.
(f) Articles 358 and 359 of the Constitution were amended in 1975 to control their arbitrary use; and Article 361 was inserted in order to give better protection to the reports of proceedings of the legislature.

The emergency left in its wake a plethora of scandals, gossips and unpleasant stories, which were like manna from heaven to the news hungry magazines, which exploited them to their best advantage and circulation soared to unheard of heights, bringing in more and more magazines, which flooded the market. Two of them, which have managed to forge ahead and establish themselves with unprecedented circulations, are *India Today* (1975) and *Sunday* (1970).

The journalist, who made the greatest impact on his readers, was Arun Shourie, who wrote for *India Today* and later became the Executive Editor of the *India Express*, which published his investigative stories. He exposed Emergency excesses and abuse of authority and his particular target was Indira Gandhi. Other investigative reporters were Aswin Sarin, Arun Sinha, Sheela Barse, Praful Bidwai and others.

In the first flush of success, the news magazines went all out to provide a diet of sensationalism and they specialised in 'stripping bodies and reputations'.

Conclusion

Rangaswami Parthasarthy, in his book, 'Journalism in India', writes that the declaration of Emergency in June, 1975, by the Government of Indira Gandhi came as a shocking blow to the Indian Press, which was its greatest victim.

There was a raging controversy (and it has continued even to this day) whether Indira Gandhi was justified in imposing the Emergency, but there was universal condemnation of the muzzling of the Press and drastic actions taken against some newspapers.

The worst form of pre-censorship was imposed on the Press during this period and even *The Hindu* had to scrap an editorial on the Proclamation of the Emergency as the censor refused to permit editorials on the Emergency. The do's and don'ts of unimaginative and authoritarian censorship made it almost impossible for the Press to function and even factual news and innocuous comments came under the axe.

J.N. Sahni wrote, "In the absence of news, the newspapers filled their columns with such vital topics" as the origin of the Ramayana and Mahabharata, the discovery of skull fossils of the ape man and the relative antiquity of Harappa and Mohenjo Daro.

Defending pre-censorship, Indira Gandhi told an interviewer, "To have had to impose regulations on newspapers does not make me happy. But some journals had shed all objectivity and independence and allied themselves totally with the opposition front and done everything to spread doom and defeatism. The Press was very much against us even before.... Some of the Press, here and abroad, are highlighting baseless charges of corruption. We have always looked into such matters and shall deal with them strictly."

The pre-censorship was imposed under Rule 48 of the Defence of India Rules 'in order to maintain public order.'

It prohibited all categories of news, comment and rumour relating to Emergency, arrests and detention unless pre-authorized in writing by an authorized officer from the Public Information Bureau in Delhi or by the Director of information of a State Government.

Guidelines for the Press, which were issued said that 'in the matter in which information is printed, published or disseminated, there can be an accretion of enormous strength to those, who are posing a threat to internal security.'

The Press was called upon for help 'in the fulfilment of the primary task of ridding the nation of the causes of the Emergency; by suppressing news themselves through moderation, particularly in illustration and headlines; by publishing nothing to excite disaffection towards government established by law in India; nothing to promote feelings of enmity between different classes of persons in India or likely to cause the cessation or slow down of work in any place, not anything objectionable already published in a foreign newspaper, nothing containing false allegations against leaders or denigrating the institution of Prime Minister; nothing to subvert the functioning of democratic institutions and nothing relating to agitations.'

On July 26, 1975, editors received even more detailed instructions according to which 'news was not to be published, which contributes to the scare and demoralisation about the general situation or public interest in all respects as determined by the Central Government; nothing, which will contribute even in a remote way to affect or worsen the law and order situation; nothing, which is likely to convey the impression of protest or disapproval of governmental measures.' These embargoes were extended to cartoons, letters to the editor and captions.

On December 8, 1975, three ordinances were issued banning the publication of 'objectionable matter', abolishing the Press Council and removing the freedom of the Press to report proceedings of the Parliament.

The Ordinance relating to publication of objectionable matter was made into a law on January 28, 1976. Among other things, it prohibited 'inciting any individual or class to disaffection, disharmony or ill-will or causing fear or alarm to any section of the public whereby any person may be induced to commit an offence against the State or public tranquillity.' They included anything defamatory (whether by word or sign) of the President, Vice President, Speaker of the Lok Sabha, State Governors, the Prime Minister and all the members of the Cabinet of Central and State Governments or deemed to be so by them. The law gave wide powers of search and seizure to the police and other petty officials. It provided for the forfeiture of securities of press deposits as safeguard against 'objectionable writing'. The Press Council was abolished, it was stated, because it had 'failed to curb tendentious and provocative writing'.

Sahni, on elaborating as to how the Press reacted to the draconian laws, writes, "The year 1976 will be specially remembered for a progressive voluntary blackout by the Press and a weakened submission by many editors to proprietors and to the establishment in a conspiracy of suppression.... While a lot will need to be written to explain the voluntary collapse, one may say that, all along, money has won and the conscience of the pen has lost. Reporters see things, but the pen does not see. Editors know things, but look ignorant. One cannot remember such transition in the behaviour and attitude of the Press anywhere, at any time, so willingly and voluntarily achieved.... There have been in the past repression, suppression and brain washing, but never a voluntary collapse of the mind, the desire to do more to suppress or eliminate than even demanded..."

However, there was at least one newspaper, which fought grimly and with determination the assault on the Press and became the special target of prosecution and vindictiveness. The '*Indian Express*', with its proprietor Ramnath Goenka and editor, V.K. Narasimhan wrote a glorious chapter in the battle for freedom of the Press and when the nightmare ended and the Press became free again, they were hailed as heroes.

All the restrictions on the Press were removed when the Janata Government came to power in 1977 and the Indian Press once again breathed freedom, never again to lose it. In words of Justice Grover, "The Indian Press today is as free as in any other free country in the world."

6

Amendment of the Constitution

The procedure for the amendment of the Constitution is its yard stick to judge whether the Constitution is rigid or flexible. The Constitution of India is federal in structure but the procedure as laid down in the Constitution for its amendment is neither rigid nor flexible.

There were two schools of thought whether the process of amendment should be flexible or rigid. The first school led by Sir Alladi Krishnaswami Ayyar and Prof. K.T. Shah held a view that the procedure for amendment of the Constitution should be rigid as it is federal in structure. The other school led by Jawaharlal Nehru and H.V. Kamath were in favour of a flexible Constitution if it has to survive because a rigid Constitution may prevent gradual innovation and may come in conflict with the will of the people.

The Drafting Committee of the Constitution of India made a compromise in adopting a method for the amendment of the Constitution. It is based on a formula 'evolved by D. Fulton in Canada. It provides different procedure for amendment attaching different categories of rigidity to different provisions of the Constitution. In India too the various articles of the Constitution have been divided into three categories and three different procedures have been provided for making changes in the Constitution.

The founding fathers of the Indian Constitution were very well guided by the maxim of Lord T.B. Macaulay that the basic law should be flexible enough so as to change with the call of time. Otherwise it would bring its own destruction in a revolution. The problem before the makers of the Constitution to devise such a process of amendment by which a comparative stability could be secured to the federal provisions of the Constitution while in other respect the Constitution could be made to respond to the needs for reform and progress under the new conditions. The framers of the Constitution of India devised a scientific formula for the amendment of the Constitution. It is conducive to the framework of a federal system. It is both viable and pliable not hampering the life of a vital and organic people. It is owing to this that our Constitution is said to represent a harmonious blending of the unitary and federal systems.

The procedure of the amendment of the Constitution is laid down in Article 368 of the Constitution of India.

There are three methods of amending the Constitution of India. They are explained as follows:

1. Simple or flexible method;
2. The flexible and rigid method; and
3. The rigid method.

Amending Process of the Indian Constitution

1. ***Simple or flexible method***: In this method a bill introduced in either house of the parliament must be adopted by the houses by a simple majority of the members present and voting and then be assented to by the President. This category includes provisions relating to the creation of a new state or altering the name and boundary of an existing state, creation or abolition of upper chamber in a state legislature, privileges of the members of parliament, quorum in the parliament and so on.

2. ***The flexible and rigid method***: Amendment under this method can be done by the unilateral action of the Parliament by a special majority. It is flexible because amendment can be done by the parliament alone. It is rigid for the reason that it requires a special majority of the parliament to amend the Constitution. An amendment of the Constitution may be initiated only by the introduction of a bill for the purpose in either house of parliament and when the bill is passed by each house by a majority of not less than two thirds of the members present and voting and by the majority of the total membership of the house, it shall be presented to the President for its assent. The President will give its assent and thereupon the Constitution shall stand amended in accordance with the terms of the bill. This category particularly includes fundamental rights and directive principles of state policy and so on. A major portion of the Constitution is covered by this method.

3. ***The rigid method***: Amendment under this method can be done by the bilateral action of the union and state legislatures. Part XX of the Constitution having Article 368 is very important. It deals with the procedure for the Constitutional amendment so far as the federal framework of the country is concerned. Here a bill must be passed by each house by a special majority of the total membership of that house and by a majority of not less than two thirds of the members present and voting. If such a bill is passed by a special majority in both the houses of Parliament then it shall be referred to the states for ratification. State legislatures will do the job of ratification by simple majority. If it is ratified by half of the states it shall be presented to the President for its assent. The President cannot refuse its assent to an amendment bill. No time limit is imposed on the President for its assent. This category includes provisions like the election of the President, extent of the executive powers of the union and states, representation of the states in Parliament and so on.

Drawbacks

1. It is complex because of the adoption of three specific methods.
2. Unless both the houses agree, the Constitution cannot be amended. There is no provision for a joint sitting of both the houses to resolve such a deadlog.
3. The procedure of amendment is violative of federal principles. Except parliament, neither the people nor the state legislatures can initiate a bill for amendment of any part of the constitution.
4. There is some vagueness in the procedures of amendment prescribed in the Article 368. It is not specifically stated whether the majority of total membership implies majority of the prescribed strength of each house or the majority of the actual membership at the time when voting takes place. The Constitution is also silent as to the time during which the President should give its assent. The President of India under this system gets a chance to keep his assent pending for a long time if he is convinced that the party in power has abused its majority in Parliament for its ulterior benefit.
5. The provision for the participation of the states in amendment of the constitution is not sufficient to project the interest of the states as amendment can be made even without sending the bill to certain states for ratification. The constitution has not made it obligatory to send a proposal for amendment to every state. There is no system of negative voting. If the party in power in the central government is also in power in more than half the states, it is possible to get the approval from the required number of the states even without sending the bill to the states in which parties other than the ruling one may be in power. The centre may also get an amendment bill ratified by the required majority of states by exerting influence on some of them.
6. There is no provision for the participation of union territories in the process of amendment of the constitution.

Merits

1. The procedures are of mixed nature and that is why it can adapt itself to various situations.
2. Because of its flexibity it can check the growth of revolutionary tendencies.
3. The mixed procedure is the main reason behind its success so far.
4. The procedures are in a position to meet with the aspirations of the people.
5. The flexibility of the constitution has made it possible to meet with the requirements of a dynamic and progressive nation.
6. There is no procedure that can alter the basic structure of the constitution by the simple will of the union parliament. This kind of rigidity in the amending procedure is extremely necessary for maintenance of its federal, republican and democratic character and for the unity and integrity of our nation.

Jawaharlal Nehru made an observation on the procedure for the amendment of the constitution. He said, "while we want this constitution to be as solid and permanent as we can make if there is no permanence in it." The constitution should never be amended to meet with partisan interest but only for the general welfare of the people of the country. The constitution should not stand in the way of the progress of the country. At the same time the fundamental values of the constitution be maintained by all means.

7

Public Interest Litigation

Black's Law Dictionary defines the term as a legal action initiated in a court of law for the enforcement of public interest or general interest in which the public or class of community have pecuniary interest or some interest by which their legal rights or liabilities are affected.

'*Pratiyogita Darpan*' which is a book on General Studies Indian Polity explained, "The judiciary formerly gave its judgments only when the Plaintiff and defendant asked for justice by presenting themselves in the Court. But this restriction was done away with a view to make expeditious justice available to the downtrodden, poor, backward, illiterate and handicapped persons. With this the judicial process was made simple and easy in matters of public interest.

In a PIL, the Court gives judgment on public interest on such matters as the basic needs of life, exploitation, environment, child labour, exploitation of women etc. if some person or institution just informs the Court. The Court investigates the matter and decides in the context of facts. Such cases constitute what is called PIL.

These cases can be presented only in the High Court or Supreme Court.

PIL was started by Justice P.N. Bhagawati and V.K. Krishna Iyer in the late 1970s. It was furthered by Justice Venkatachaliah, J.S. Verma, Kuldeep Singh and others. This measure has gone a long way in solving many problems of the people."

Sampat Jain in his book, '*Public Interest Litigation*', gives a detailed explanation of the term PIL. He writes, "Administrative inaction for the welfare of the poor and downtrodden has compelled the public spirited persons to obtain justice for the poor through extra ordinary jurisdiction of the High Courts and the Supreme Court which are the sentinels of fundamental rights. Such of the judges who have seen, experienced and witnessed the pinching poverty of poor persons of their country have come to the conclusion that economic and social justice cannot reach at the door steps of such poor persons in their lifetime unless the judiciary itself becomes active in matters of public interest."

Judicial activism and PIL are the two sides of the same coin. The aim of both is to improve the socio-economic conditions of the poor section by providing socio-economic justice to them in the areas where administrative machinery has failed to provide them justice in accordance with relevant provisions of law. The concept of PIL through Judicial activism is a reply to the administrative inaction in various fields in our country.

Prof. S.K. Agrawala, in his book '*Public interest litigation in India: a critque*', writes "If the state agencies misperform or do not perform at all, the 'Little Man' finds himself helpless. He does not have either the will or the wherewithal to stand up to the state agencies. How to make the state accountable for its actions or inaction and how to establish the Little Man to establish that accountability vis-à-vis his own rights and interests, have been matters of deep concern for the man of law and public affairs in all liberal democracies. PIL is a partial answer to this paradox. It is not the only answer."

The concept of PIL was explained by Justice V.R. Krishna Iyer for the first time in 1976 in Mumbai Kamgar Sabha Vs Abdulbhai as under, "Test litigations, representative actions, pro bono public and like broadened forms of legal proceedings are in keeping with the current accent on justice to the common man and necessary disincentive to those who wish to bypass the real issues on the merits by suspect reliance on peripheral, procedural shortcomings. Public interest is promoted by a spacious construction of locus standi in our socio-economic circumstances and conceptual latitudinarianism permits taking liberties with individualisation of the right to invoke the higher courts when the remedy is shared by a considerable number, particularly when they are weaker. Less litigation, consistent with fair process, is the aim of objective law."

PIL is the part of the process of participatory justice and standing in civil litigation of that pattern must have liberal reception at the judicial doorsteps.

Comprehensive outlook of the concept was given by Justice Bhagawati in *S.P. Gupta Vs Union of India* – "where a legal wrong or a legal injury is caused to a person or to a determinate class of persons by reason of violation of any constitutional or legal right or any burden is imposed in contravention of any constitutional or legal provision or any such legal wrong, or legal injury or illegal burden is threatened and such person or determinate class of persons is by reason of poverty, helplessness or disability or socially or economically disadvantaged position, unable to approach the court for relief, any member of the public can maintain an application for appropriate direction, order, writ in the High Court under Article 226 and in the case of breach of any fundamental rights of such person or determinate class of persons, in the Supreme Court under Article 32 seeking judicial redress for the legal wrong or injury caused to such person or determinate class of persons."

Fortifying the concept again in People's Union for Democratic Rights Vs Union of India, Justice Bhagawati observed – "The Court is moved for this purpose by a member of the public by addressing a letter drawing the attention of the Court to such legal injury or legal wrong. Court would cast aside all technical rules of procedure and entertain the letter as writ petition in the judicial side and take action upon it."

From the analysis of the above judgments of Justice Bhagawati, Sampat Jain in his book, '*Public Interest Litigation*', safely concluded that the concept of PIL will include the following points within its scope.

1. A legal wrong or legal injury is caused to:
   (a) a person
   (b) a determinate class of persons
2. Such legal wrong or legal injury is caused by the reason of:
   (a) violation of any constitutional or legal right
   (b) imposition of burden in contravention of any constitutional or legal provision or without authority of law.
3. On account of poverty, helplessness or disability or socially or economically disadvantaged position, a person or determinate class of people are unable to approach the Court for relief against such legal wrong or legal injury or illegal burden as stated above.
4. Any member of the public can maintain an application under Article 226 or 32 of the Indian Constitution and seek judicial redress o behalf of such person or determinate class of persons against the legal wrong or injury caused to them.
5. Instead of filing an application under Article 226 or 32, a member of public may address a letter to the Chief justice of High Court or Supreme Court to such a legal injury or legal wrong or illegal burden caused to the person(s).
6. The Court would cast aside all technical rules of procedure and entertain the letter as writ petition in the judicial side and take action upon it.

Limitations

The concept of PIL has certain limitations. The aim of PIL is to put the administrative machine in action which has adopted lethargic attitude in compliance with provisions of law. The judiciary can certainly issue direction which can be effectively implemented. Still a question remains to be answered whether the judiciary can give such direction to the executive where the availability of financial resources had a material bearing.

In state of *Himachal Pradesh Vs Umed Ram Sharma*, Justice R.S. Pathak held that the Court should be extremely slow and reluctant in issuing direction in matters of PIL where availability of financial resources and policy consolidation had a material bearing.

The parameter of PIL cases and Judicial Activism have not yet been settled and they vary from Bench to Bench. PIL has covered civil, criminal and constitutional matters. Judges have come forward for the rescue of labourers, children, prison inmates, tribals and sometimes public at large. Municipal Corporations and industries polluting the environment, statutory authorities, public bodies and the state governments who have not taken care of the roads, sanitation and public health have also become a subject of intervention by the Court through PIL cases. The consumer protection is another area which has developed through PIL.

It is not possible to prepare an elaborate list of areas which could be covered by the PIL. Neither, the Supreme Court nor the High Courts have laid down the periphery of PIL or the parameters of Judicial Activism in PIL cases.

8

Contempt of Court

The First Press Commission did not suggest any change in the provisions of the Contempt of Court Act, 1952.

The Sanyal Committee set up in 1961 made a comprehensive study of the law relating to contempt. Its recommendations resulted in the enactment of the Contempt of Court Act, 1971 and the repeal of the 1952 Act.

The Contempt of Court Act, 1971 was passed, as the Preamble says, to define and limit the powers of certain courts in punishing contempt of court.

The Indian Constitution through Article 129 vests the Supreme Court with the power to punish contempt of itself. It is the custodian of the administration of justice in the country and is expected to render justice without fear and favour.

Contempt of Court is also classified as direct and indirect, the test being whether the contempt is offered within or outside the courtroom. If it is outside the courtroom, it is indirect Contempt of Court. A direct Contempt of Court consists of words spoken or acts committed in the premises of the courtroom.

Under this classification are acts, such as attempting to influence the judge in his decision pending at the time of submission of a case; fighting in the court or in such close proximity of the court, as to be, in effect, within its immediate presence; threatening, assaulting or intimidating jurors, witnesses or the court officers while they attend on the court; or imputing that the judge is ignorant or unfair; or acting as an authority in law even though he is not licensed to practice law, have all been classified as direct Contempt of Court.

Pre-Independence Law

The Act of 1971 does not clarify what constitutes scandalising the court. Its predecessors, the Act of 1952 and the Act of 1926, did not even define contempt. However, courts in colonial India had adopted the idea of contempt even earlier from English common law and assumed powers for punishing it following the precedent of English courts. A couple of examples will illustrate the sensitivity of the colonial courts to any public criticism of judges and the judiciary.

The 'Bengalee' published an article in 1883 after the conclusion of a case criticising the *zubberdasti* (high handedness) of a judge of the Calcutta High Court in ordering a sacred Hindu Saligram to be physically produced in court. The court found the article to be contemptuous and defamatory of the judge, and sentenced the editor of the newspaper, Surendra Nath Banerjee, to prison.

The *Amrit Bazar Patrika* reported a speech made in 1935 in the Legislative Council, which contained some general criticism of the judges of the Calcutta High Court. The following extract from the report came in for scrutiny by the Court:

"We are glad to find that in the Bengal Legislative Council yesterday, there was a discussion about administration of the Calcutta High Court. Every word of Mr. N.K. Basu was true. It is so unfortunate and regrettable that at the present day, the Chief Justice and the Judges find a peculiar delight in hobnobbing with the Executive, with the result that the judiciary is robbed of its independence, which, at one time, attracted the admiration of the whole country. The old order of things has vanished away. We wish the Chief Justice and the Judges appreciate the sentiments of the public. The generation that has gone by should be an ideal to them."

While the Court could not take any action on the proceedings in the legislative council, it determined that the article in the *Amrit Bazar Patrika* was capable of "great public mischief" and sentenced the editor to prison for contempt of court.

The Promise of the Constitution

Article 19 of the Constitution of India guaranteed the right to freedom of speech and expression, but also allowed restrictions on this right to be imposed by law, including any Law of Contempt, provided only that the restrictions were reasonable. Articles 129 and 215 of the Constitution explicitly spelt out the power of the Supreme Court and High Courts to punish someone for contempt.

The law, when it was ready – The Contempt of Courts Act, 1952 that replaced the Act of 1926 – did not define 'contempt'. This omission on the part of the legislature was apparently deliberate, and designed to maintain the elastic character of the law, to enable its application over a wide field by the courts. Clearly, the immediate concern of the legislature of that period was to preserve continuity in the powers of the judiciary.

An interesting contempt prosecution from this period is that of the Telugu weekly, Praja Rajyam, published at Nellore, for an article it carried under the caption: "Is the Sub-Magistrate, Kovvur, corrupt?" The article stated that the person in question was known in the locality as a bribe taker; cited instances where he had either taken bribes or put parties to undue harassment; and concluded with the appeal: "Will the Collector enquire into the matter and allay the public of their fears?"

The Publisher and Managing Editor of the weekly appealed to the Supreme Court against a Madras High Court judgement finding him guilty of contempt. Dismissing the appeal (heard in 1952), a Constitution bench of the Supreme Court explained why the editor was indeed guilty of contempt:

"The article in question is a scurrilous attack on the integrity and honesty of a judicial officer. Specific instances have been given where the officer is alleged to have taken bribes or behaved with impropriety to the litigants, who did not satisfy his dishonest demands. If the allegations were true, obviously, it would be to the benefit of the public to bring these matters into light. But if they were false, they cannot but undermine the confidence of the public in the administration of justice and bring judiciary into disrepute.

- Disagreement is not contempt
- Free expression, without contempt

The appellant, though he took sole responsibility regarding the publication of the article, was not in a position to substantiate by evidence any of the allegations made therein. He admitted that the statement was based on hearsay. Rumours may have reached him from various sources, but before he published the article, it was incumbent upon him as a reasonable man to attempt to verify the information he received and ascertain, as far as he could, whether the facts were true or mere concocted lies. He does not appear to have made any endeavour in this direction. As the appellant did not act with reasonable care and caution, he cannot be said to have acted bona fide, even if good faith can be held to be a defence at all in a proceeding for contempt."

The judgement identified the issues that were important in the defence against contempt of scandalising the court – 'public interest', 'truth', and 'good faith'.

It took a decade for the Government to acknowledge, under pressure of public opinion, that the law of contempt was "somewhat uncertain, undefined, and unsatisfactory" and impinged upon the fundamental rights of the citizens – the right to personal liberty and the right to freedom of expression. The Sanyal Committee was set up in 1961 to examine the law and suggest reforms. It took another decade for the recommendations of this committee to be implemented in the Contempt of Courts Act, 1971.

The Act of 1971 offered some guidelines for reporting and comment on judicial proceedings that would not attract contempt charges. For example, "fair and accurate report of a judicial proceeding" and "fair comment on the merits of any case, which has been heard and finally decided", would not be contempt. The Act also provided that contempt would not be punishable unless it "substantially interferes, or tends substantially to interfere with the due course of justice". Notwithstanding these improvements, the definitions of contempt did not do away with the uncertainty, for example, 'scandalising the Court' was contempt, but what constituted 'scandalising the Court'?

Justice Krishna Iyer captured the problems inherent in the contempt law in a 1974 judgement, in these colourful phrases: "A vague and wandering jurisdiction with uncertain frontiers; a sensitive and suspect power to punish vested in the prosecutor; a law, which makes it a crime to publish regardless of truth and public good; and permits a process of *brevi manu* conviction, may unwittingly trench upon civil liberties."

These problems, he argued, imposed a special responsibility on the higher judiciary to be vigilant and protect free speech "even against judicial umbrage". The subsequent judgement of Justice Krishna Iyer in the Mulgaonkar case in 1978 (where contempt charges against the *Indian Express* were withdrawn) has been seen as the beginning of a liberal trend in the treatment of contempt by scandalizing the court. However, this is not the only or even the dominant trend.

Definitions

Section 2 of the Contempt of Court Act, 1971 says

(a) Contempt of Court—means civil contempt or criminal contempt;

(b) civil contempt—means wilful disobedience to any judgement, decree, direction, order, writ or other process of a court or wilful breach of an undertaking given to a court;

(c) criminal contempt—means the publication (whether by words, spoken or written, or by signs, or by visible representations, or otherwise) of any matter or the doing of any other act whatsoever which:

   (i) scandalises or tends to scandalise, or lowers or tends to lower the authority of any court; or

   (ii) prejudices, or interferes or tends to interfere with, the due course of any judicial proceeding; or

   (iii) Interferes or tends to interfere with, or obstructs or tends to obstruct the administration of justice in any other manner.

In simple words, Contempt of Court means:

1. Any act done or writing published, calculated to bring a court or a judge of the court into contempt or lower its authority is Contempt of Court.
2. Any act done or writing published, calculated to obstruct or interfere with the due course of justice or the lawful process of the court is Contempt of Court.

Exceptions

1. Section 3 of the Act says that innocent publication and distribution of matter is not contempt.
2. Section 4 says that a person shall not be guilty of contempt of court for publishing a fair and accurate report of a judicial proceeding or any stage thereof.
3. Section 5 says that a person shall not be guilty of contempt of court for publishing any fair comment on the merits of any case, which has been heard and finally decided.
4. Section 6 says that a person shall not be guilty of contempt of court in respect of any statement made by him in good faith concerning the presiding officer of any subordinate court to:
   (a) any other subordinate court, or
   (b) the High Court,

to which it is subordinate.

Explanation: In this section, 'subordinate court' means any court subordinate to a High Court.

5. Section 7 says that the publication of information relating to proceedings in chambers or in camera is not contempt except in certain cases.

Section 12 of the Act: Section 12 deals with the punishment for Contempt of Court, which could be a simple imprisonment for a term, which may extend to six months, or with fine, which may extend to two thousand rupees, or with both.

But, apology is readily accepted when offered at the earliest and in good faith.

[Though not stated in this section, it would be proper to quote Vir Bala Aggarwal and V.S. Gupta in the 'Handbook of Journalism and Mass Communication' that in case of a civil contempt, the contemptor cannot be sentenced even to a simple imprisonment. He can be detained in a civil prison for not more than six months, normally a fine would be considered sufficient to meet the ends of justice.]

Section 13: Contempt is not punishable in certain cases. Notwithstanding anything contained in any law for the time being in force, no court shall impose a sentence under this Act for a contempt of court, unless it is satisfied that the contempt is of such a nature that it '*substantially interferes, or tends substantially to interfere with the due course of justice*.'

This means that a person cannot be arbitrarily punished for an act which might seem like a contempt, but is actually not so, unless it substantially interferes, or tends substantially to interfere with the due course of justice.' In other words, to be Contempt of Court, the act of a person should substantially interfere, or tend to substantially interfere with the due course of justice.

Section 16: This section deals with Contempt by judge, magistrate or other person acting judicially. Subject to the provisions of any law for the time being in force, a judge, magistrate or other person acting judicially shall also be liable for contempt of his own court or of any other court in the same manner as any other individual is liable and the provisions of this Act shall, so far as may be, apply accordingly.

In other words, it means that law is the same for authorities in judiciary like judges or magistrates as it is for any other individual.

Section 20: This section deals with limitation for actions for contempt. No court shall initiate any proceedings for contempt, either on its own motion or otherwise, after the *'expiry of a period of one year'* from the date on which the contempt is alleged to have been committed.

Section 21: This section says that this Act does not to apply to Nyaya panchyats or other village courts, by whatever name known, for the administration of justice, established under any law.

Constitutionality of the Act

Article 129 of the Constitution of India declares the Supreme Court to be the Court of record and that it shall have all the powers of such a court including the power to punish for contempt of itself.

A similar declaration is made as regards a High Court by Article 215.

Article 19(2) does not apply to Members of Parliament within the premises criticizing a judgement; and is not counted as Contempt of Court.

Principles Common in Article 129 and Article 215

1. Both these articles are couched in the same language and the Supreme Court and the High Court have been placed on the same footing as a 'court of record' as regards the power to punish for contempt of itself.
2. In historical retrospect, at the outset, it was shown that this power was not created by the Constitution, but was derived by the Chartered High Court from Common law. It was adopted by the Constitution in Article 129 and Article 215 to remove any doubts and to save them from ordinary legislation.
3. The object of this power to punish is not the protection of the judges personally from imputations, but the protection of the public themselves from the mischief they will incur if the authority of the tribunal is impaired.
4. Even on the ground of interference with due course of justice, the Courts do not proceed by way of contempt 'unless there is real

prejudice, which can be regarded as substantial interference' as distinguished from a mere question of propriety.

5. This is an extraordinary power, which must be used sparingly, but where the public interest demands it, the Courts will not shrink from exercising it and imposing punishment even by the way of imprisonment; in cases where a mere fine may not be adequate.

Media and the Contempt of Court

Vir Bala Aggarwal and V.S. Gupta in the 'Handbook of Journalism and Mass Communication' state: Publication of anything, which tends to create in the minds of the people an apprehension about the integrity, ability or fairness of a judge or which tends to deter litigants from complete reliance upon the Court's administration of justice, amounts to contempt. Similarly, a publication which is likely to cause embarrassment in the judge's mind to the discharge of his official duty is a contempt of court.

Journalists, sometimes, investigate suspected crimes, malpractices and accumulate evidence. Publication of such material is often in the public interest. The law of contempt does not hinder publication of such accumulated evidence before the accused are arrested and charged. But once the judicial proceedings are set in motion, the Press should not publish the evidence.

When a person is being tried for an offence, if the Press has evidence that some other person is guilty of the crime, propriety would demand that the evidence in possession of the Press be placed before the Court. By adopting such a course, it will get the credit for its investigative effort, though the advantage of increased circulation through publication exclusively in its column will be lost.

However, the power to punish for scandalising the Court is to be used sparingly and in deference to the administration of justice only. It cannot be used for vindicating personal insult to judge. *Bona fide* criticism that is fair and reasonable criticism does not amount to contempt. But if improper motives are attributed to the judge, then it ceases to be *bona fide*. A judgment can be criticized as erroneous, but dishonesty on the part of the judge cannot be alleged. Trial by newspapers has been considered by Courts as interference with the proper administration of justice in pending cases.

However punishment can be awarded for interference with the due course of justice only if the interference is substantial. Similarly a person cannot be guilty of Contempt of Court for innocent publication or distribution during the pendency of civil or criminal proceedings of a matter, which would, otherwise, deem to constitute contempt.

Case Studies

1. In 1995, there was a Public Interest Litigation (PIL) filed in the

Supreme Court stating that the Punjab Police role was condemnable as it liquidated militancy by showing false encounters, which amounts to violation of Human Rights. The Supreme Court, in its observation, condemned the Punjab Police. On September 10, 1995, the Executive Editor of the *Hindustan Times*, Chandan Mitra wrote an article that Punjab Police had done a commendable job in dealing with the militancy and they should be lauded for it rather than condemned. He also added that the Supreme Court judges were in need of psychiatric treatment. The Editor, V.N. Narayanan, the *Hindustan Times*; President, Naresh Mohan; Printer and Publisher, Rakesh Sharma; and Executive Editor, Chandan Mitra were issued Contempt notice by Justice J.S. Verma and Justice B.N. Kripal.

The *Hindustan Times* published a front-page apology for writing in September 1995 that Supreme Court judges were "in need of psychiatric counselling" for passing strictures on Punjab Police officials. In a more detailed apology filed in the Court, the newspaper's executive editor and author of the piece, Chandan Mitra, said that he had made that "intemperate and unwarranted" comment because the assassination of Punjab Chief Minister, Beant Singh, "came as a great personal shock". Consequently, explained Mitra, that while writing the impugned piece, he was very uneasy and the objectionable sentence in his article was a result of this turmoil."

2. In the case *Chanchal Manohar Singh vs. High Court of Punjab and Haryana and Ors*. in 1996, Senior Reporter of *The Indian Express*, Chanchal Manohar Singh was sentenced to one month imprisonment and a fine of Rs. 2,000 by the Punjab and Haryana High Court. He was later pardoned as he submitted his apologies. But the Court made an important observation that the legal reporting assignment should only be given to those journalists, who have an experience in Court reporting and those, who have a good understanding of court and law procedures.

3. In 2002, the eminent writer, Arundhati Roy was booked for Contempt of Court. She led a dharna and raised slogans, in her *Narmada Bachao Andolan*, against the Supreme Court verdict for allowing the height of the dam to be maintained and giving a green signal to the project. She was issued a show-cause notice for Contempt of Court. She filed an affidavit as a reply in which she criticized the Court for issuing disturbing notice on the basis of an absurd, despicable, and entirely unsubstantiated petition. She further said that the notice indicated a disquieting inclination on the part of the Court to silence criticism and muzzle dissent and to harass those, who disagreed with it. By entertaining petition based on First Information Report (FIR), that even the local police does not see fit to act upon, the Supreme Court is doing its own reputation and credibility considerable harm.

The Court asked her to apologise, but she rather accepted the punishment of one day's imprisonment and a fine of Rs. 2,000.

4. Jayshree Khadilkar-Pande, editor of the popular Marathi daily, *Navakal*, and the first woman to be accorded the status of an International Grandmaster in chess, was served with a sentence for Contempt of Court on 12.07.2003 by the Bombay High Court.

Jailed on 16 July 2003, Jayshree spent six days behind bars. The issue was the editorials written by her father Neelkanth Khadilkar, wellknown proprietor and Executive Editor of *Navakal*, criticizing Justice B. N. Srikrishna while his inquiry into the 1992-93 communal riots was on. "The Bombay High Court filed a suit against us for contempt of court arguing that the said editorials referred to Srikrishna as Justice Srikrishna and the use of the prefix 'Justice' while criticising the Srikrishna commission lowers the dignity of the court," said Jayshree. She maintains their stand saying that since Srikrishna happens to be a justice, who was heading the commission, using the prefix is perfectly in order. "We respect the judiciary and had no intention to insult it," she said.

Because of his age, Neelkanth Khadilkar was not jailed; instead Jayshree opted to serve the sentence on his behalf. She claims to be the first editor to accept imprisonment rather than tender an apology to the court and be let off. All editors, who have so far been charged with contempt of court, have quietly apologised and spared themselves the pain of being in prison.

'Truth' as Defence

The most recent attempts to reform the contempt law started with the recommendation of the National Commission to Review the Working of the Constitution (NCRWC) in 2002 to allow 'truth' as defence in matters of Contempt of Court. While making this recommendation, the Commission observed:

> "Judicial decisions have been interpreted to mean that with the law, as it now stands, even truth cannot be pleaded as a defence to a charge of contempt of court. This is not a satisfactory state of law. It would, indeed be ironical if, in spite of the emblems hanging prominently in the court halls, manifesting the motto of *Satyameva Jayate*, in the High Courts and *Yatho dharma statho jaya* in the Supreme Court, the courts could rule out the defence of justification by truth."

The NCRCW recommendation was not particularly revolutionary. In the UK and Australia, truth as defence to a charge of contempt by scandalising had been available for several decades. The recommendation eventually resulted in a Bill to amend the law related to contempt.

The Parliamentary Standing Committee on Personal, Public Grievances, Law and Justice (Standing Committee) examined the Contempt of Courts

(Amendment) Bill, 2004 and provided several interesting insights in its report. The Government proposed to amend the 1971 Act by adding the clause: "The Court may permit, in any proceedings for contempt of court, justification by truth as a valid defence if it is satisfied that it is in public interest and the request for invoking the said defence is bona fide". However, the Standing Committee felt that the requirement that the 'truth' used as justification should be in public interest was an additional burden imposed on a person accused of contempt and would "virtually defeat the objective of the proposed legislation;" therefore, it recommended that the term 'in public interest' be deleted.

Debate on Contentious Issue of Contempt of Court

In 1970, the Marxist leader E.M.S. Namboordiripad was fined by the Supreme Court for what it described as scandalising the judges by alleging that they were "biased against the working classes". And, in 1988, the then Union Law Minister, P. Shiv Shankar faced contempt proceedings for alleging that "anti-social elements, FERA violaters, bride burners and a horde of reactionaries have found their haven in the Supreme Court."

But a bench headed by Justice Sabyasachi Mukherji, side stepping the Namboordiripad verdict, exonerated Shiv Shankar: "If anti-social elements and criminals have benefited by the decisions of the Supreme Court, the fault rests with the laws and the loopholes in the legislation. The speech of the minister read in its proper perspective did not bring the administration of justice into disrepute."

Former Supreme Court judge, O. Chinnappa Reddy, who retired in 1987, laments that the apex court did not "seize the opportunity" presented by the Shiv Shankar case to overrule the Namboordiripad verdict. It merely held that Shiv Shankar's speech did not constitute contempt. As a result, the bar put by the Namboordiripad case against any form of ideological criticism of the judiciary remains in force.

But far from overruling the Namboodiripad verdict, the Supreme Court has been increasingly looking beyond the Contempt of Courts Act and claiming undefined powers from the Constitution.

The Supreme Court also jailed a senior IPS officer of Haryana, M.S. Ahlawat, under Article 129 of the Constitution, which simply says that the apex court can "punish for contempt of itself."

Says senior advocate, F.S. Nariman: "It is unhealthy for our democracy that the Supreme Court has so far not specified what contempt powers it has assumed from the Constitution. As in every other sphere of law, the judges will, after all, have to adopt some self-imposed limitations in their contempt jurisdiction."

Reddy holds that the contempt law should be relaxed. Indeed, the definition of contempt, he says, should exclude "even criticism attributing improper motives to a judgement if made after inquiry and verification". In other words, if the criticism of a judge's motives is based on fact, it should not constitute contempt.

Another area related to contempt that has sparked off widespread debate is the Court's attitude towards the press. For instance, the bench dealing with the latest round of the Cauvery dispute – a case of great public interest in at least two states – warned the lawyers involved not to discuss the case on television. Since the media often takes the help of lawyers to unravel the intricacies of ongoing proceedings, senior Supreme Court advocate, Rajiv Dhavan feels that the judges are being "perhaps a little too sensitive" in this regard.

A contempt case filed by him, in fact, has been referred to a constitution bench to address a legal lacuna, which has a bearing on the freedom of the press. It was a petition filed in 1994 against VHP leader, Giriraj Kishore for casting aspersions on the integrity of Supreme Court judges in relation to the then pending Ayodhya case. *Indian Express* was also named as a contemnor for having reported Kishore's allegation. The newspaper argued that it could not be hauled up since it was merely doing its job of reporting what a public figure had said.

All the more so when *Indian Express* clarified in its columns that it did not subscribe to the VHP leader's statement. The judges directed that a larger bench be set up to decide whether a journalist enjoyed immunity against contempt in such a situation. The case, however, is yet to be listed before a constitution bench. Perhaps the strongest justification for relaxing contempt laws came as early as 1941 when the US Supreme Court ruled, in Bridges vs. State of California, that scandalising the court could not be a ground for contempt.

Justice Hugo Black, a champion of individual rights, observed: "The assumption that respect for the judiciary can be won by shielding judges from published criticism wrongly appraises the character of American public opinion. An enforced silence, however, limited solely in the name of preserving the dignity of the bench, would probably endanger resentment, suspicion and contempt much more than it would enhance respect." It's the spirit of Black's ruling, that legal experts say, should guide how the judiciary in India regards the issue of contempt.

Conclusion

In the law as it now stands, while a person accused of contempt can seek his defence in "truth", he must get the permission of court for this defence after satisfying that this truth will be in public interest and that he is acting bona fide, that is, with reasonable care and caution.

Other countries have progressed to a more liberal regime. In UK, prosecuting a person for contempt for scandalising the court is considered virtually obsolescent and the Courts have rarely used this power for several decades. In the US, the offense of scandalizing the court is unknown and US Courts initiate action for contempt only when they determine that there is 'clear and present danger' to the administration of justice.

In many other countries, like Norway and Sweden, there are no Contempt laws. If a judge is scandalized, it is for him to individually take action under the ordinary law. The dignity of the Court will in no way be offended by any comment on the judge. Noted Jurist K.K. Venugopal feels that steps are needed to rectify this situation.

Former judge of the Supreme Court, V.R.K. Iyer, says that there is a difference between Court and judge. He says that the law should seek to protect the Court as an institution, while judge as an individual could be open to criticism.

The editorial of *The Times of India* dated 08.03.2002 mentions, "The decision of the Supreme Court to symbolically punish author and activist Arundhati Roy to a day's imprisonment in Tihar jail in Contempt of Court raises more questions than it answers. To begin with whether an archaic legislation like the Contempt of Court Act is really consistent with the principles of free speech and even more pertinently, whether the interpretation by the Courts in recent times can pass the test of natural reason. Let us begin with the plain fact that Miss Roy committed a crime identical to the one for which she was hauled up by the Supreme Court; elsewhere in the democratic world, she would very likely have received no legal explanations much less a prison sentence. From Anglo American to Scandinavian, the Contempt of Court law has become a virtual dead letter in mature liberal democracies."

In our country, it is still too early to assess the impact of the recent changes in the law. However, what is clear is that only the judiciary, of its own accord, can make the move towards a more liberal interpretation of contempt that allows healthy criticism that can aid its own development as an institution.

9

Official Secrets Act, 1923

The first British Official Secrets Act (OSA) was enacted in 1911.

In India, the Official Secrets Act came into existence in 1923. The various Commissions and Committees including the First Press Commission Report (1954) and the Second Press Commission Report (1982) could not make any difference despite their recommendations that the Official Secrets Act be repealed.

Preamble of the Act

The Preamble of the Act says that it is an Act to consolidate and amend the laws relating to official secrets.

Salient Features of the Act

Section 1(2): This section mentions that the Act extends to the whole of India and applies also to servants of the Government and to citizens of India outside India.

Section 2: This section provides the definitions for better understanding of the Act.

In this Act, unless there is anything repugnant in the subject or context,

(1) any reference to a place belonging to Government includes a place occupied by any department of the Government, whether the place is or is not actually vested in Government;

(2) expressions referring to communicating or receiving include any communicating or receiving, whether in whole or in part, and whether the sketch, plan, model, article, note, document, or information itself, or the substance, effect or description thereof only be communicated or received; expressions referring to obtaining or retaining any sketch, plan, model, article, note or document, include the copying or causing to be copied of the whole or

any part of any sketch, plan, model, article, note or document; and expressions referring to the communication of any sketch, plan, model, article, note or document include the transfer or transmission of any sketch, plan, model, article, note or document;

(3) "document" includes part of a document;

(4) "model" includes design, pattern and specimen;

(5) "munitions of war" includes the whole or any part of any ship, submarine, aircraft, tank or similar engine, arms and ammunition, torpedo, or mine intended or adopted for use in war, and any other article, material or device, whether actual or proposed, intended for such use;

(6) "Office under Government" includes any office or employment in or under a department of the Government;

(7) "photograph" includes an undeveloped film or plate;

(8) "Prohibited place" means

(a) any work of defence, arsenal, naval, military or air force establishment or station, mine, minefield, camp, ship or aircraft belonging to, or occupied by or on behalf of Government, any military telegraph or telephone so belonging or occupied, any wireless or signal station or office so belonging or occupied and any factory, dockyard or other place so belonging or occupied and used for the purpose of building, repairing, making or storing any munitions of war, or any sketches, plants, models or documents relating thereto, or for the purpose of getting any metals, oil or minerals of use in time of war;

(b) any place not belonging to Government where any munitions of war or any sketches, models, plans or documents relating thereto, are being made, repaired, gotten or stored under contract with, or with any person on behalf of, Government, or otherwise on behalf of Government;

(c) any place belonging to or used for the purpose of Government, which is for the time being declared by the Central Government, by notification in the Official Gazette, to be a prohibited place for the purposes of this Act on the ground that information with respect thereto, or damage thereto, would be useful to an enemy, and to which a copy of the notification in respect thereof has been affixed in English and in the vernacular of the locality;

(d) any railway, road way or channel, or other means of communication by land or water (including any works or structures being part thereof or connected therewith) or any place used for gas, water or electricity works or other works for purposes of a public character, or any place where any munitions of war or any sketches, models, plans or documents relating thereto, are being made, repaired, or stored otherwise than on behalf of Government, which is for the time being declared by the Central Government, by notification in Official Gazette, to be a prohibited place for the purposes of this Act on the ground that information with respect thereto, or the destruction or obstruction thereof, or interference therewith, would be useful to an enemy, and to which a copy of the notification in respect thereof has been affixed in English and in the vernacular of the locality;

(9) "sketch" includes any photograph or other mode of representing any place of thing; and

(10)"Superintendent of Police" includes any police officer of a like or superior rank, and any person upon whom the powers of a Superintendent of Police are for the purposes of this Act conferred by the Central Government.

Section 3: This section deals with penalty for spying

(1) If any person for any purpose prejudicial to the safety or interests of the State

(a) approaches, inspects, passes over or is in the vicinity of, or enters, any prohibited place; or

(b) makes any sketch, plan, model, or note, which is calculated to be or might be or is intended to be, directly or indirectly, useful to an enemy; or

(c) obtains, collects, records or publishes or communicates to other person any secret official code or password, or any sketch, plan, model, article or note or other document or information, which is calculated to be or might be or is intended to be, directly or indirectly, useful to an enemy [or which relates to a matter the disclosure of which is likely to affect the sovereignty and integrity of India, the security of the State or friendly relations with foreign States], he shall be punishable with imprisonment for a term, which may extend, where the offence is committed in relation to any work of defence, arsenal, naval, military or air force establishment or station, mine, minefield, factory, dockyard, camp, ship or aircraft or otherwise in relation to the naval, military or air force affairs of Government or in relation to any secret official code, to fourteen years and in other cases to three years.

(2) On a prosecution for an offence punishable under this section 1, it shall not be necessary to show that the accused person was guilty of any particular act tending to show a purpose prejudicial to the safety or interests of the State, and, notwithstanding that no such act is proved against him, he may be convicted if, from the circumstances of the case or his conduct or his known character as proved, it appears that his purpose was a purpose

prejudicial to the safety or interests of the State; and if any sketch, plan, model, article, note, document or information relating to or used in any prohibited place, or relating to anything in such a place, or any secret official code or password is made, obtained, collected, recorded, published or communicated by any person other than a person acting under lawful authority, and from the circumstances of the case or his conduct or his known character as proved it appears that his purpose was a purpose prejudicial to the safety or interests of the State, such sketch, plan, model, article, note, document, [information, code or password shall be presumed to have been made], obtained, collected, recorded, published or communicated for a purpose prejudicial to the safety or interests of the State.

Section 4: This section says that communications with foreign agents amounts to be evidence of commission of certain offences.

Section 5: This section deals with wrongful communication etc. of information.

Section 5(4) mentions a person guilty of an offence under this section shall be punishable with imprisonment for a term, which may extend to three years, or with fine, or with both.

Section 6: This section mentions unauthorised use of uniforms; falsification of reports, forgery, personation, and false documents.

Section 6(3) provides that a person guilty of an offence under this section shall be punishable with imprisonment for a term, which may extend to [three years], or with fine, or with both.

Section 7: Interfering with officers of the police or members of the Armed Forces of the Union

(1) No person in the vicinity of any prohibited place shall obstruct, knowingly mislead or otherwise interfere with or impede any police officer, or any member of The Armed Forces of the Union, engaged on guard, sentry, patrol, or other similar duty in relation to the prohibited place.

(2) If any person acts in contravention of the provisions of this section, he shall be punishable with imprisonment, which may extend to three years, or with fine, or with both.

Section 8: This section deals with duty of giving information as to commission of offences.

(2) If any person fails to give any such information or attend as aforesaid, he shall be punishable with imprisonment, which may extend to [three] years, or with fine, or with both.

Section 9: Any person, who attempts to commit or abets the commission of an offence under this Act, shall be punishable with the same punishment, and be liable to be proceeded against in the same manner as if he had committed such offence.

Section 10: This section deals with the penalty for harbouring spies.

(1) If any person knowingly harbours any person whom he knows or has reasonable grounds for supposing to be a person, who is about to commit or who has committed an offence under section 3 or under section 3 read with section 9 or knowingly permits to meet or assemble in any premises in his occupation or under his control any such persons, he shall be guilty of an offence under this Section.

(2) It shall be the duty of every person having harboured any such person as aforesaid, or permitted to meet or assemble in any premises in his occupation or under his control any such persons as aforesaid, to give on demand to a Superintendent of Police or other police officer not below the rank of Inspector empowered by an Inspector-General or Commissioner of Police in this behalf, any information in his power relating to any such person or persons, and if any person fails to give any such information, he shall be guilty of an offence under this section.

(3) A person guilty of an offence under this section shall be punishable with imprisonment for a term, which may extend to three years, or with fine, or with both.

Section 12: Provisions of section 337 of Act 5 of 1898 to apply to offence under sections 3, 5 and 7 – The provisions of section 337 of the Code of Criminal Procedure, 1898 shall apply in relation to an offence punishable under section 3 or under section 5 or under section 7 or under any of the said sections 3, 5 and 7 read with section 9, as they apply in relation to an offence punishable with imprisonment for a term, which may extend to seven years.

Section 13: This section deals with the restriction on trial of offences.

(1) No Court (other than that of a Magistrate of the first class specially empowered in this behalf by the appropriate Government) which is inferior to that of a District or Presidency Magistrate shall try any offence under this Act.

(2) If any person under trial before a Magistrate for an offence under this Act at any time before a charge is framed claims to be tried by the Court of Session, the Magistrate shall, if he does not discharge the accused, commit the case for trial by that Court, notwithstanding that it is not a case exclusively triable by that Court.

(3) No Court shall take cognizance of any offence under this Act unless upon complaint made by order of, or under authority from the

appropriate Government, or some officer empowered by the appropriate Government in this behalf.

(4) For the purposes of the trial of a person for an offence under this Act, the offence may be deemed to have been committed either at the place in which the same actually was committed or at any place in India in which the offender may be found.

(5) In this Section, the appropriate Government means:

(a) in relation to any offences under section 5 not connected with a prohibited place or with a foreign power, the State Government; and

(b) in relation to any other offence, the Central Government.

Section 14: This section deals with the provision for exclusion of public from proceedings.

In addition and without prejudice to any powers, which a Court may possess to order the exclusion of the public from any proceedings if, in the course of proceedings before a Court against any person for an offence under this Act or the proceedings on appeal, or in the course of the trial of a person under this Act, application is made by the prosecution, on the ground that the publication of any evidence to be given or of any statement to be made in the course of the proceedings would be prejudicial to the safety of the State, that all or any portion of the public shall be excluded during any part of the hearing, the Court may make an order to that effect, but the passing of sentence shall in any case take place in public.

Case Studies

1. In June 2002, journalist Iftikhar Gilani was arrested for violating the OSA 1923. He was charged under the OSA, with a case under the Obscenity Act added to it. The first military report suggested that the information he was accused of holding was "secret" despite being publicly available. The second military intelligence report contradicted this, stating that there was no "official secret". Even after this, the government denied the opinion of the military and was on the verge of challenging it when the contradictions were exposed in the press. The military reported that, "the information contained in the document is easily available" and "the document carries no security classified information and the information seems to have been gathered from open sources." On January 13, 2003, the government withdrew its case against him to prevent having two of its ministries having to give contradictory opinions. Gilani was released the same month.

2. CBI booked journalist Santanu Saikia under OSA in 1999 after a three-year in-house probe to find out how the secret document on disinvestment had been leaked just a day before a Cabinet meeting. Although the prolonged

probe yielded no result and the CBI made no recovery from Saikia, a case was registered against him.

The main ground on which the court discharged Saikia was that the publication of the disinvestment document was unlikely to affect the sovereignty and integrity of India or the security of the state or friendly relations with foreign states.

3. Tarakant Dwivedi alias Akela, was arrested on May 18, 2011 for his article on how the weapons, purchased after the 26/11 terror attacks, were rotting in the armoury due to water leakage in monsoon. His article that was published on June 28, 2010 reported about how weapons procured by the Government Railway Police (GRP) and Railway Protection Force (RPF) officers were stored in a room with leakages at the Chhatrapati Shivaji Terminus armoury of the RPF. The court released Akela on a personal bond of Rs. 10,000 accepting the defence argument of bail.

The journalist was earlier booked on charges of trespass and related non-bailable sections under the Official Secrets Act.

GRP commissioner Tukaram Chavan told the *Hindustan Times*, "We had initially registered a case under Section 447 (punishment for criminal trespass) of the Indian Penal Code. However, after recording the statements of the concerned RPF officials, the investigating officer invoked Sections of the Official Secrets Act, 1923."

Local scribes had registered a strong protest against Akela's arrest and sought his immediate release.

A local magistrate's court granted bail to a Mumbai-based journalist arrested by the GRP under the Official Secrets Act.

Court Redefines 'Official Secret', Relief to Scribe

Abhinav Garg, TNN February 26, 2009 reported that, 'In a major boost to freedom of press, a Delhi court has ruled that the publication of a document merely labelled "secret" shall not render the journalist liable under the colonial relic, Official Secrets Act 1923.

Additional Sessions Judge Inder Jeet Singh discharged journalist Santanu Saikia in a case booked against him by the CBI 10 years ago for publishing the contents of a Cabinet note on disinvestment policy. The CBI case against Saikia, under OSA, had raised eyebrows because it was not uncommon for the media to do stories on the basis of Cabinet papers despite their being a classified secret.'

On his part Saikia, who argued the case himself in court, pointed out how an archaic Act – framed to nab spies – was being used to harass a journalist in the 21st century. He also argued that in the age of the Right to Information Act where courts and commissions are broadening the ambit of official documents accessible to citizens, a news report on disinvestment could in no way be seen as an offence inviting penalties as strict as those prescribed under OSA.

Official Secrets Act vs Right to Information

Ritu Sarin, in *Indian Express*, published an article on October 15, 2007 with the headline, 'Relevance of Official Secrets Act now limited, RTI Act will prevail if there's any direct conflict, says CIC.'

The report read:

Chief Information Commissioner, Wajahat Habibullah has said, he is "presuming" the Government is undertaking a review of the 1923 Official Secrets Act (OSA) – Major General (retired) V K Singh is its latest victim, booked for writing on corruption in the RAW – in view of the transparency regime ushered in by the 2005 Right to Information Act.

Speaking to *Indian Express*, Habibullah said: "I am very clear that when there is a direct conflict between the OSA and RTI Act, it is the RTI, which prevails. The OSA cannot be used in a manner in which it is inconsistent with provisions of the RTI Act."

"The OSA is a colonial law that protects the Government from the public. In a democracy, the public is the Government. Earlier, OSA was the guiding principle in terms of custody of information held by the Government. Now custody of information held by the Government has been given to the RTI Act," he said.

According to Habibullah, even on the question of supplying information or documents marked "secret" (thereby, bringing it under OSA), the competent authority or information officer could use discretionary powers to disclose details. This, he said, was relevant, for instance, to Section 8(j) of the RTI where a Central Public Information Officer can disclose personal information that has been sought, provided "public interest in disclosure outweighs the harm to the protected interests."

As per provisions of Section 8(d) and (e) of the RTI, in case the RTI request pertains to commercial information or information to a person in his fiduciary relationship, the competent authority, if convinced that "larger public interest" is served, may part with it. The "competent authority", Habibullah said, is the Department of Personnel and Training, which holds administrative supervision of the RTI.

"Even documents marked secret or confidential, which would normally attract provisions of the OSA, can be disclosed since the discretionary provision is there in the RTI Act. And if these requests are turned down, the applicant can always appeal to the CIC and argue about the public interest served. With such RTI provisions, the relevance of OSA has become very limited," he said. His comments are significant given the fact that the Second Administrative Reforms Commission has recommended scrapping of the OSA. The Ministry of Home Affairs is examining the recommendation.

An article in *The Indian Express*, published on 29th April 2012 named, 'National security vs. Right to know.' It highlighted these important points:

- There was a brief furore, in March 2012, on the leakage of a letter from the Army Chief to the Prime Minister, on the "state of preparedness" in the Indian Army was given wide publicity in the media. The debate focused on who "leaked" the letter, and with what motive rather than on the implications for the "security of the State". Not much light, however, has been thrown on the legal issues involved, in the context of the interface between the Official Secrets Act and the Right to Information Act.
- The Official Secrets Act 1923 (OSA) was enacted when India was under foreign rule, soon after the First World War.
- Indeed, the attempt made in 1997 to dilute the rigours of the Official Secrets Act but failed. Meanwhile, the Right to Information Act 2005, which, not by coincidence also originated from 1997, brought in the concept of transparency and openness in government practices and procedures.
- Going by the OSA as it stands now, the mere possession of a 'Top Secret' document by any unauthorised person, not to speak of its dissemination, is a punishable offence. Thus, nearly every media house, its anchor, and the media company's owner are clearly liable under the present draconian law, if the government were to prosecute them.
- The other argument trotted out, that ISI, CIA, Mossad, etc, were already aware of these "facts" is also not relevant. It's interesting to note that so many Indian commentators claim access to the inside information available in these foreign secret agencies.
- The media house, was legally bound to reveal the sources (Section 8 of OSA), and could not claim immunity, if a formal investigation were launched. It is well known that for many decades now, business houses have planted paid informants in strategic points in various ministries, it may not be a wild surmise that some media houses also have similar arrangements in key offices.
- In the case of the famous Pentagon Papers, where the issue went to the full bench of the US Supreme Court, it was held that the media had the right to publish sensitive information, even in the time of war. However in India, such is not the case, and immunity arguably is not available.
- There is no question that the OSA 1923 needs to be revised and sharply diluted. However, there would surely remain some ultra-sensitive areas, which would have to be protected in larger public interest. A case-by-case decision cannot be left to individual media houses, with their compulsions of TRP, "exclusives", "breaking-news" and "first-with-the-news". A line would have to be drawn but it is a moot question as to who will draw it, how the line will be guarded and what the sanction regime would be. There needs to be a national debate to delineate the line where RTI ends and a significantly attenuated OSA begins.

The newspaper DNA on October 15, 2011 published a report, 'Colonial era Official Secrets Act to be tweaked to get in tune with RTI'. The report highlights:

- The nodal M/o Home Affairs sought comments and views on the present status of the OSA from 20-odd ministries and key departments and how it can be amended to suit the needs of growing class of people raising clamour for transparency.
- Under flak for being over secretive in parting with even basic information that does not jeopardise national security, the Centre is mulling over changes in OSA, 1923, that contradicts provisions of the RTI Act, 2005.
- The DoPT is learnt to have told the MHA that RTI and OSA cannot exist together in their present forms as they contradict each other and if OSA cannot be repealed; at least amendments to the Act are a must to bring in transparency and accountability at large.
- Originally drafted as an anti-espionage act to suit the British interests, OSA is considered a powerful tool for the government that gives it powers to withhold information and punish even ordinary people.
- RTI Activist Venkatesh Nayak considers it as a welcome step and said, "The OSA has been used in two ways. Prior to the RTI Act, it was misused for withholding information from citizen and these days it is misused for putting journalists behind bars when they publish any information from sources that leak that from within the government. It will be good for Indian democracy if it happens".

Opinion: Former Judge of the Supreme Court, V.R.K. Iyer makes an observation regarding this Act and strongly advocates its abolition. He says, "Secrecy is the allergy of transparency. It is either a tragedy or a farce; or both." He further says that the role of the press is an important instrument in democracy. The journalist has to investigate and go beneath the surface to unearth wrongdoings. This Act poses a hindrance in their work.

Conclusion

Thus, we can see that the Official Secrets Act of 1923 is an archaic legislation, which has lost its charm further after the Right to Information Act of 2005, but still today, many of our journalists are being booked under the various provisions of this Act. There is a demand that this piece of legislation should be abolished, but no concrete step has been taken in this direction so far.

10

Right to Information (RTI)

The Right to Know has been given statutory form through the Right to Information Act, 2005. The Right to Information is based on the freedom of speech and expression. Without information and knowledge, one may not be able to speak and express freely.

The RTI Act 2005 is a historical legislation, which is needed for the existence of efficient and open government. To realize the Constitutional philosophy and to fulfil the commitment to the fairness in action, the RTI Act is a strong tool in the hands of public, empowering them to fix accountability to government action.

Introduction

Donald C. Rowat in the chapter, 'Laws on access to official documents' in the book 'Secrecy in Government' edited by T.N. Chaturvedi writes 'Sweden was the first country to provide freedom of information to its citizens far back in 1766. It was the outcome of an intense struggle during the last half of the 18th century between the two main political parties of Sweden; the Hats and the Caps. With the defeat of the Hats in 1765 after a long term in office, the Caps inserted the principle of public access in the Freedom of the Press Act as a reaction to their frustration over excessive administrative secrecy as well as press censorship under the regime of the Hats. Subsequently the principle was accepted as a part of the normal political life of Sweden.'

The RTI Act has been identified as a basic human right, which is required for the realisation of a true democratic and open government. The Right to access information held by public authorities is protected by Article 19 of the International Convention on Civil and Political rights.

In its very first session, in 1948, the UN General Assembly adopted Resolution 59(1) stating, 'Freedom of information is a fundamental human right…'

The RTI Act 2005 is a historic development, which is a culmination of very painstaking, thoughtful, dogged and relentless efforts over the last so many years by concerned citizens. Initial efforts to formulate the legal right to information began in 1989.

In the early 1990s, the Mazdoor Kisan Shakti Sangathana (MKSS) began a movement to bring in transparency in village accounts. Initially, MKSS lobbied government to obtain information, such as bills and vouchers relating to purchase and transportation of materials. This information was then crosschecked at *Jan Sunwais* (public hearings) against actual testimonies of workers. This was extremely successful in drawing attention to corruption and exposing leakages in the system. Success of MKSS became a source of inspiration for activists in India and led to the genesis of broader discourse on the RTI in India.

The RTI Act provides for setting out the political regime of the RTI for citizens to secure access to information under the control of public authorities in order to promote transparency and accountability in the working of every public authority.

History of RTI in India

Prof. Jaytilak Guha Roy, Indian Institute of Public Administration, gives a detailed history of the roots of RTI in India in his chapter on 'Transparency and Right to Information' in a book on 'Public Systems Management. Some of the important ideas can be divided chronologically for our convenience in understanding as under:

- ***Important Events in 1977***
  - (a) *First call for the Right to information for citizens*: In India, the first political commitment to the citizens' Right to information came up on the eve of the eve of the Lok Sabha elections in 1977 as a corollary to public resentment against suppression of information, press censorship and abuse of authority during the internal emergency of 1975-77 called by Mrs. Indira Gandhi.
  - (b) *Election manifesto of the Janata Party:* The Janata Party, in its election manifesto of 1977, promised 'an open government' and declared that 'it would not misuse the intelligence services and government authority for personal and partisan ends.'
  - (c) *Forming of the Working Group:* Sticking to its own commitment, the Janata government headed by Morarji Desai, constituted in 1977, a working group to ascertain if the Official Secrets Act, 1923 could be amended so as to facilitate greater flow of information to the public. After months of hard labour, the working group that comprised

officials from the Cabinet Secretariat and the Ministries of Home Affairs, Finance and Defence, recommended that the Act of 1923 should be retained without change. This 'no change' recommendation was not what people had expected.

(d) *Stagnant decision of the Working Group:* The very composition of the group, however, was indicative of the recommendation made by it. The bureaucracy by its nature, lives in secrecy, and hence any other recommendation would have been an exception. The country was ultimately back to square one, that is, India went back to the period of 1923.

- ***Important Events in 1989***

(a) *Renewal of commitment by National Front Government:* The events, which helped create political commitment to the RTI for the second time was when the National Front Government renewed its commitment to this right. Their decision was an outcome of people's frustration over the earlier government's reluctance to part with the information relating to Bofors and other deals.

(b) *Election manifesto of the National Front Government:* In its 1989 Lok Sabha Election Manifesto, the National Front committed itself to 'open government' and declared unequivocally that "People's Right to Information shall be guaranteed through constitutional provisions."

(c) *Reiteration of the commitment:* Reiterating this commitment, the then Prime Minister V.P Singh, in his first broadcast to the Nation in December 1989 said, "We will have to increase access to information. If the government functions in full public view, wrong doings will be minimized. To this end, Official Secrets Act will be amended and we will make the functioning more transparent. Right to Information will be enshrined in our Constitution."

(d) *Stagnancy in decision:* Despite such a strong commitment, there was actually mo headway towards transparency and openness in our governmental functioning due to early fall of the National Front government.

- ***Important Movements All Over India***

(a) The RTI movement initiated by Aruna Roy in Rajasthan was quite successful.

(b) A people's organisation called '*Mazdoor Kisan Shakti Sangathan*' did significant work in making the government respond to the demands of information and accountability. Through '*Jan sunwai*' or public hearings, people were able to speak up and air their grievances to the government functionaries. In fact, such movements by the people can effectively provide substance to the abstract notion of RTI and transparency.

(c) The RTI movement initiated in the state of Rajasthan in 1994, provided an opportunity to the people to demand information on spending in governmental activities, ensure accountability and redressal of grievances. The first "*Jan Sunwai*'was held in a village of Kotkirana in 1994. It gathered momentum with organising of *dharnas* in the state of Rajasthan which made the government agree that the people had the right to receive information about expenditure on development works in the villages. Later a Committee was set up at the Centre under the Chairmanship of Justice P.B. Sawant to draft a model Bill to be introduced in the Parliament and the states.

- ***Important Events in 1997***

(a) Working Group on Right to Information: In 1997, the Government of India had set up a Working Group on Right to Information and Promotion of Open and Transparent government. It was entrusted with the responsibility of examining the feasibility of introducing a RTI Act.

(b) Action Plan for Effective and Responsive Government: Later the Conference of Chief Ministers held in 1997, in its Action Plan for Effective and Responsive Government at the Central and state levels, reiterated the introduction of legislation on RTI as secrecy and lack of transparency was an inherent part of many governmental decision making activities.

(c) Coalition agenda for transparent government: Subsequently, the National Agenda of the multi-party coalition, that is, the National Democratic Alliance (NDA) declared, "Our first commitment to the people is to give a stable, honest, transparent and efficient government capable of accomplishing all-round development. For this the government shall introduce time-bound programme for administrative reforms..."

- ***Important Events after 2000***

(a) In pursuance with this commitment, the NDA government introduced the Freedom of Information (FOI) Bill, 2000 in the Parliament.

(b) Meanwhile, instead of waiting for a central legislation, half a dozen states had enacted their own laws on RTI. These include Goa (1997), Tamil Nadu (1997), Rajasthan (2000), Maharashtra (2000), Karnataka (2000), and Delhi (2001). Beisides, Madhya Pradesh had issued wide ranging administrative directives on dissemination of information upto the level of Gram Panchayats.

(c) The Rajasthan RTI Act, 2000 clearly laid down the procedure for supply of information, grounds on which some information can be withheld, procedure for appeal in case of non-receipt of information etc.

(d) The Delhi RTI Act 2001 also indicated the obligations on public authorities to provide information, procedure for supply of information, restrictions on parting with information etc. Interestingly all states that had enacted their own RTI laws were non-NDA partners when the Act was passed.

(e) However, despite the passing of these Act, the concerned citizens and civil society organisations still complained about the denial of information on important issues relating to public interest.

- ***Controversy Over the FOI Bill***

The proposed FOI Bill by the NDA government evoked a lot of controversy on various issues, of which, some of them are mentioned as follows:

- The bill exempted from disclosure of 'information engaged in confidence between the central and state governments or any of their authorities or agencies'. This was too wide a clause to cover a lot of such information which should otherwise be available to people.
- A major lacuna of the bill was that it did not specifically provide for penalties against the officials who, in violation of the law, would either refuse to provide information or give false, misleading or incomplete information.
- In this age of economic liberalisation, when the governments are keen on outsourcing many of their traditional functions to private agencies and allowing foreign direct investments in telecom, power, banking and other major sectors, the bill, however did not apply to private sector.
- The most serious shortcoming of the bill was that it provided for appeals only within the government bodies.

- ***Passing of the FOI Bill***

It is pertinent to note that the Supreme Court has already declared the Right to Information as a Fundamental right. Pursuant to this declaration and also in response to the petitions filed by the Common Cause and the Centre for Public Interest Litigation, the Supreme Court reportedly decided to scrutinize the proposed FOI Bill to ascertain whether the government had given enough power to the citizens to know what they want to know about governance. This was indeed a welcome step against the backdrop of lack of political will to recognize people's right to know. Meanwhile, the FOI Bill had been somewhat hurriedly passed by the Lok Sabha on 4th December 2002 without plugging the various loopholes.

- ***Change of Name from Freedom of Information Act to Right to Information***

The Congress government had tabled the RTI Bill in Parliament on December 23, 2004. The National Advisory Council (of the Congress Government) had recommended 36 amendments to the Freedom of Information Act 2002 including changing its name to the RTI Act, which would emphasize the fundamental nature of the right.

- ***The Right to Information Act gets passed and enforced***

The Parliament passed the Right to Information Bill on 11th May 2005 with 146 amendments and it came into effect from 12th October 2005.

Salient Features of the Act

Section 2: Section 2(f) states that "information" means any material in any form, including records, documents, memos, e-mails, opinions, advices, press releases, circulars, orders, logbooks, contracts, reports, papers, samples, models, data material held in any electronic form and information relating to any private body, which can be accessed by a public authority under any other law for the time being in force.

Section 2(i) states that "record" includes:

(a) any document, manuscript and file;
(b) any microfilm, microfiche and facsimile copy of a document;
(c) any reproduction of image or images embodied in such microfilm (whether enlarged or not); and
(d) any other material produced by a computer or any other device;

Section 2(j) states that "right to information" means the right to information accessible under this Act which is held by or under the control of any public authority and includes the right to:

(i) inspection of work, documents, records;
(ii) taking notes, extracts or certified copies of documents or records;
(iii) taking certified samples of material;
(iv) obtaining information in the form of diskettes, floppies, tapes, video cassettes or in any other electronic mode or through printouts where such information is stored in a computer or in any other device;

Section 5: Section 5 deals with Public Information Officers and Assistant Public Information Officers

Section 5(1) states that every public authority shall, within one hundred days of the enactment of this Act, designate as many officers as the Central Public

Information Officers or State Public Information Officers, as the case may be, in all administrative units or offices under it as may be necessary to provide information to persons requesting for the information under this Act.

Section 5(2) states that every public authority shall designate an officer, within one hundred days of the enactment of this Act, at each sub-divisional level or other sub-district level as a Central Assistant Public Information Officer or a State Assistant Public Information Officer, as the case may be, to receive the applications for information or appeals under this Act for forwarding the same forthwith to the Central Public Information Officer or the State Public Information Officer.

Section 6: Section 6 deals with the application procedure for requesting the information.

Section 6(1) states that a person, who desires to obtain any information under this Act, shall make a request in writing or through electronic means in English or Hindi or in the official language of the area in which the application is being made, accompanying such fee as may be prescribed, to:

(a) the Central Public Information Officer or State Public Information Officer, as the case may be, of the concerned public authority;
(b) the Central Assistant Public Information Officer or State Assistant Public Information Officer, as the case may be, specifying the particulars of the information sought by him or her.

Section 6(2) states that an applicant making request for information shall not be required to give any reason for requesting the information or any other personal details except those that may be necessary for contacting him.

Section 7: Section 7 deals with the time limit to get the information. We can summarize the Section as:

1. 30 days from the date of receipt of application.
2. 48 hours for information concerning the life and liberty of a person.
3. 5 days shall be added to the above response time, in case the application for information is given to the Assistant Public Information Officers.
4. If the interests of a third party are involved, then the limit will be 40 days (maximum period plus the time given to the party to make representation.)

Section 8: This section deals with information that is exempted from disclosure. They are:

(a) information, disclosure of which would prejudicially affect the sovereignty and integrity of India, the security, strategic, scientific or economic interests of the State, relation with foreign State or lead to incitement of an offence;

(b) information, which has been expressly forbidden to be published by any court of law or tribunal or the disclosure of which may constitute contempt of court;
(c) information, the disclosure of which would cause a breach of privilege of Parliament or the State Legislature;
(d) information including commercial confidence, trade secrets or intellectual property, the disclosure of which would harm the competitive position of a third party, unless the competent authority is satisfied that larger public interest warrants the disclosure of such information;
(e) information available to a person in his fiduciary relationship, unless the competent authority is satisfied that the larger public interest warrants the disclosure of such information;
(f) information received in confidence from foreign Government;
(g) information, the disclosure of which would endanger the life or physical safety of any person or identify the source of information or assistance given in confidence for law enforcement or security purposes;
(h) information, which would impede the process of investigation or apprehension or prosecution of offenders;
(i) cabinet papers including records of deliberations of the Council of Ministers, Secretaries and other officers;
(j) information, which relates to personal information the disclosure of which has no relationship to any public activity or interest, or which would cause unwarranted invasion of the privacy of the individual unless the Central Public Information Officer or the State Public Information Officer or the appellate authority, as the case may be, is satisfied that the larger public interest justifies the disclosure of such information.

Section 12: Section 12 deals with the Central Information Commission.

Section 12(2) states that the Central Information Commission shall consist of:

(a) the Chief Information Commissioner; and
(b) such number of Central Information Commissioners, not exceeding ten, as may be deemed necessary.

Section 12(3) states that the Chief Information Commissioner and Information Commissioners shall be appointed by the President on the recommendation of a committee consisting of:

(i) the Prime Minister, who shall be the Chairperson of the committee;
(ii) the Leader of Opposition in the Lok Sabha; and
(iii) a Union Cabinet Minister to be nominated by the Prime Minister.

Section 15: Section 15 deals with the State Information Commission.

Section 15(2) states that the State Information Commission shall consist of:

(a) the State Chief Information Commissioner, and
(b) such number of State Information Commissioners, not exceeding ten, as may be deemed necessary.

Section 15(3) states that the State Chief Information Commissioner and the State Information Commissioners shall be appointed by the Governor on the recommendation of a committee consisting of:

(i) the Chief Minister, who shall be the Chairperson of the committee;
(ii) the Leader of Opposition in the Legislative Assembly; and
(iii) a Cabinet Minister to be nominated by the Chief Minister.

Section 24: Sections 24(1) states that nothing contained in this Act shall apply to the intelligence and security organisations specified in the Second Schedule, being organisations established by the Central Government or any information furnished by such organisations to that Government: Provided that the information pertaining to the allegations of corruption and human rights violations shall not be excluded. Such information shall be provided within forty-five days from the date of the receipt of request.

Sections 24(4) states that nothing contained in this Act shall apply to such intelligence and security organisations being organisations established by the State Government, as that Government may, from time to time, by notification in the Official Gazette, specify: Provided that the information pertaining to the allegations of corruption and human rights violations shall not be excluded. Such information shall be provided within forty-five days from the date of the receipt of request.

These 22 organizations are:

1. Intelligence Bureau, Ministry of Home Affairs; 2. Directorate of Revenue Intelligence, Ministry of Finance; 3. Central Economic Intelligence Bureau, Ministry of Finance; 4. Directorate of Enforcement, Ministry of Finance; 5. Narcotics Control Bureau; 6. Aviation Research Centre; 7. Special Frontier Force; 8. Border Security Force, Ministry of Home Affairs; 9. Central Reserve Police Force, Ministry of Home Affairs; 10. Indo-Tibetan Border Police, Ministry of Home Affairs; 11. Central Industrial Security Force, Ministry of Home Affairs; 12. National Security Guard, Ministry of Home Affairs; 13. Research & Analysis Wing of The Cabinet Secretariat; 14. Assam Rifles, Ministry of Home Affairs; 15. Sashastra Seema Bal, Ministry of Home Affairs; 16. Special Protection Group; 17. Defence Research and Development Organisation, Ministry of Defence; 18. Border Road Development Organisation; 19. Financial Intelligence Unit, India; 20. Directorate General

Income Tax (Investigation); 21. National Technical Research Organisation; and 22. National Security Council Secretariat.

Criticism

Prof. Jaytilak Guha Roy has made critical assessment as under:

- Experience reveals that mere enactment of Right to Information legislation would not be enough to provide open and transparent public administration.
- It would just be the beginning of a long and costly process.
- The first and foremost task would be to suitably review and revise such legislations as the Official Secrets Act, 1923 and the Indian Evidence Act, 1872, so as to replace the inhospitable or negative provisions therein with suitable provisions, encouraging dissemination of information and limiting the clauses relating to withholding of information. Section 5 of the Official Secrets Act, for example is regarded as 'catch-all provision', as it covers all kinds of secret official information irrespective of the effect or consequence of disclosure. Again Section 123 of the Indian Evidence Act provides that no one shall be permitted to give any evidence from unpublished official records, relating to any affairs of the state, except with the permission of the head of the department who will file or withhold such permission as he or she thinks fit. Even the courts can be denied documents if the government holds that they relate to affairs of the state.
- The non inclusion of the Chief Justice of India in the Committee for recommendation of the appointment of Chief Information Officers and Additional Information Officers. This has been criticized as heavily weighted towards the Central government.
- Several prominent members of the Civil Society have expressed their apprehension over the government policy to appoint retired civil servants as Chief Information Officers and Additional Information Officers.
- Likewise the Commission of Enquiry Act, 1952 would also need to be thoroughly scanned and suitably amended so as to make it obligatory for the governments to present the reports of all such commissions before the legislatures within the stipulated time. The amendment should also provide for publication of these reports within a fixed time from the date of presentation in the legislatures.
- In this context, the following observation of Justice Krishna Iyer (1985) is worth consideration, "When Commissions prolong their

enquiries and produce reports, which are shelved for long in government pegion-holes, matters of public interest suffer, face-out and the people are stultified by denial of information..." in most of these legislations, governments enjoy the option to accept or reject the report, which means that the administration may use Enquiry Commissions as crisis tactics, the end product being conveniently discarded if unfavourable. Thus, unless governments become really interested and wish to prove their bonafides as democracy promoters from the angle of freedom of information, the strategy of constituting Commissions may prove to be informational treachery.

- Suitable amendments in the conduct rules are also to be made to enable them to disseminate to the people as much information as possible. Rule 11 of the Central Civil Services (Conduct) Rules 1964, for instance, forbids a government servant to communicate to any person, including a fellow government servant about any official document or any part thereof or any information acquired by him during the course of his or her official duties. A violation of this rule will subject the civil servant to disciplinary action over and above punishment under any such law as the Official Secrets Act, 1923.
- The government should also put an end to its stringent and unnecessary classification of information. This calls for a well planned and enlightened information policy as an important part of government's public relation policy.
- Hence apart from modification of the conduct rules and the statutes like the Official Secrets Act, specific guidelines concerning dissemination of official information to the public would also have to be laid down and made applicable to all ministers and departments of the central and the state governments.

Conclusion

We conclude with the words of Prof. Jaytilak Guha Roy that the most challenging task for operationalising the Right to Freedom of Information would be to bring about major changes in our administrative system so as to evolve and facilitate an altogether new culture of openness in place of existing age-old secrecy. The revamping of our administrative system in this direction requires multi-pronged measures, which includes:

- Formulation of a comprehensive training policy with a view to inculcating right attitudes among the public functionaries in the context of open government.
- Institution of an effective system of reward for enthusiastic service rendered by public functionaries with regard to the dissemination of

information as also punishment for those who would be found withholding information in an arbitrary and capricious manner.'

Section 5 of the Official Secrets Act, 1923 made it a crime to communicate, possess or even receive official secret information of any kind. The big question now is whether with the coming in of the Central RTI Act of 2005, the Official Secrets Act of 1923 has been overridden?

Chapter VI, Article 22 states that the provisions of the RTI Act shall have effect notwithstanding any other law for the time being in force or in any instrument having effect by virtue of any other law than this Act.

A plain reading of this provision leads one to believe that the Official Secrets Act has totally overridden the RTI Act, 2005, however, a cautious reading of the Act reveals that there are several provisions for exemptions and exceptions.

The real difference, however, is in the shift of culture of the two regimes. While the Official Secrets Act had legally perpetuated a culture of secrecy; the RTI Act brings in an era of transparency and accountability.

Ex Chief Information Officer, Wajahat Habibullah says that he is clear that when there is a direct conflict between Official Secrets Act and the RTI Act, it is the RTI Act that prevails. The OSA cannot be used in a manner in which it is inconsistent with the RTI Act.

Mr. Habibullah said that the OSA had always been undemocratic and draconian and the RTI Act would rectify these shortcomings.

The OSA 1923 allowed the government to deny public access to many documents on the grounds of secrecy. The colonial legacy of stringent control over information continued to dominate the official approach for almost 60 years even after India became independent. The advent of the RTI Act on 15 June 2005 at one stroke superseded most provisions of the Official Secrets Act.

As of now, both the RTI Act and the Official Secrets Act have their relevance and importance in their own unique ways.

The proper implementation of the RTI would require an efficient information management system with the help of sophisticated information technology. With the increasing use of information technology in our government departments and offices, it should not be very difficult in the near future to evolve an effective and useful system of information management in the government.

Thus the mere conferment of the RTI without changing the prevalent style of governance would make the entire exercise futile. The prevalent style is very secretive in nature and overrides our democratic principles. The present scenario, characterised by the lack of political will and the reluctant attitude of bureaucracy to recognize the people's right to information, the role of civil society organisations would be crucial and significant in ushering in a new era of open, transparent and accountable governance.

11

Right to Privacy

The Indian Constitution does not explicitly guarantee the Right to Privacy as a fundamental right.

The Right to privacy is a rapidly developing concept. It was Thomas Cooley, an American scholar, who, about a century ago, described the Right to privacy as a right to be left alone.

The Right to privacy has been recognized by the International Convention of Human Rights, 1948. Article 12 of the Universal Declaration of Human Rights states, "No one shall be subjected to arbitrary interference with his privacy, family, home or correspondence nor to attack upon his honour and reputation. Everyone has the right to the protection of the law against such interference or attacks."

The power to make these laws is derived from the constitution. "Privacy" is not a subject in any of the three lists in Schedule VII of the Constitution of India. That is the State list, the Union list or the Concurrent list. Thus, only the Indian Parliament is competent to legislate on privacy since it can be interpreted as any other matter not enumerated in List II and List III. Till date, there is no specific enactment on Privacy.

Judicial activism has brought the Right to Privacy within the realm of Fundamental Rights. Article 141 of the Constitution states that "the law declared by the Supreme Court shall be binding on all courts within the territory of India." Therefore, the decisions of The Supreme Court of India become the Law of the Land.

The Supreme Court of India has come to the rescue of the common citizens, time and again by construing the Right to privacy as a part of the Fundamental rights to protection of life and liberty under Article 21 of the Constitution, which states, 'No person shall be deprived of his life or personal liberty, except according to procedure established by law.'

Media and the Right to Privacy

Recently there has been an increasing unrest at the media's willingness to intrude on the private lives of individuals. Using examples of dubious undercover journalism, such as when veteran Bengali superstar Suchitra Sen was hospitalized; of charade sting operations, like that carried out on school teacher, Uma Khurana; and of irresponsible reporting, as with the Aarushi murder case, critics argue that the media have become exploitative, publishing sensationalist stories rather than those that can be said to be in the 'public interest'. Biased or corrupted media, they suggest, can often persecute individuals in the name of journalism. Whilst some call for more robust action from the Press Council of India, or the introduction of a binding code of conduct from the Information and Broadcasting Ministry, others are pushing for a more robust law to protect the right to privacy.

Ratan Tata in reference to Radia Tapes scandal said that, "I have the right to privacy and media cannot violate it." Tata group Chief Ratan Tata submitted to Supreme Court that despite being a public figure, he has the Right to privacy and the media cannot violate it by publishing or telecasting his private conversation contained in the Radia tapes. His counsel, Mukul Rohatgi said before a bench headed by Justice G.S. Singhvi that Mr. Ratan Tata contended that as Corporate Lobbyist Nira Radia's phone was tapped for probing the alleged tax evasion, but the tapes cannot be used for any other purpose.

Case Studies

The Supreme Court has reiterated the Right to Privacy in the following cases:

Kharak Singh vs State of UP: In this case, the appellant was being harassed by police under Regulation 236(b) of UP Police Regulation, which permits domiciliary visits at night. The Supreme Court held that the Regulation 236 is unconstitutional and violative of Article 21. It concluded that the Article 21 of the Constitution includes 'right to privacy' as a part of the right to 'protection of life and personal liberty'. In fact, it was the minority view expressed by Justice Subba Rao that equated 'personal liberty' with 'privacy', and observed, that "the concept of liberty in Article 21 was comprehensive enough to include privacy and that a person's house, where he lives with his family, is his 'castle' and that nothing is more deleterious to a man's physical happiness and health than a calculated interference with his privacy."

Gobind vs State of Madhya Pradesh: This is another case on domiciliary visits. The Court in this case observed that, "domiciliary visits and picketing by the police should be reduced to the clearest cases of danger to community security and not routine follow-up at the end of a conviction or release from prison or at the whim of a police officer. In truth, legality apart, these regulations ill accord with the essence of personal freedoms and the State will do well to revise these old police regulations verging perilously near unconstitutionality."

The Court also mentioned, "... privacy-dignity claims deserve to be examined with care and to be denied only when an important countervailing interest is shown to be superior. If the Court does find that a claimed right is entitled to protection as a fundamental privacy right, a law infringing it must satisfy the compelling State interest test…"

State vs Charulata Joshi: The Supreme Court held that "the constitutional right to freedom of speech and expression conferred by Article 19(1)(a) of the Constitution, which includes the freedom of the press, is not an absolute right. The press must first obtain the willingness of the person sought to be interviewed and no court can pass any order if the person to be interviewed expresses his unwillingness."

R. Rajagopal vs State of Tamil Nadu: The Supreme Court held that the petitioners have a right to publish what they allege to be the life-story/autobiography of Auto Shankar insofar as it appears from the public records, even without his consent or authorization. But if they go beyond that and publish his life story, they may be invading his right to privacy, and then they will be liable for the consequences in accordance with law. Similarly, the State or its officials cannot prevent or restraint the said publication.

Justice B.P. Jeevan Reddy observed that the right to privacy is implicit in the right to life and liberty guaranteed by the citizens of this country by Article 21. It is the right to be let alone. He also added, "A citizen has a right to safeguard the privacy of his own, his family, marriage, procreation, motherhood, child bearing and education among other matters. None can publish anything concerning the above matters without his consent – whether truthful or otherwise and whether laudatory or critical. If he does so, he would be violating the right to privacy of the person concerned and would be liable in an action for damages…"

People's Union for Civil Liberties (PUCL) vs Union of India: The Supreme Court held that the telephone tapping by Government under Section 5(2) of Telegraph Act, 1885 amounts infraction of Article 21 of the Constitution of India. Right to privacy is a part of the right to 'life' and 'personal liberty' enshrined under Article 21 of the Constitution. The said right cannot be curtailed "except according to procedure established by law."

If one follows the judgements given by the Hon'ble Supreme Court, three themes emerge:

(1) That the individual's Right to privacy exists and any unlawful invasion of privacy would make the 'offender' liable for the consequences in accordance with law;
(2) That there is constitutional recognition given to the Right of privacy, which protects personal privacy against unlawful governmental invasion;
(3) That the person's 'right to be let alone' is not an absolute right and may be lawfully restricted for the prevention of crime, disorder or protection of health or morals or protection of rights and freedom of others.

The Right to Privacy and Norms of Journalistic Conduct

The articles of Press Council of India's Norms of Journalistic conduct that deals with the right to privacy are:

Article 6. Right to Privacy

(i) The Press shall not intrude or invade the privacy of an individual, unless outweighed by genuine overriding public interest, not being a prurient or morbid curiosity. So, however, that once a matter becomes a matter of public record, the right to privacy no longer subsists and it becomes a legitimate subject for comment by the Press and the media, among others.

Explanation: Things concerning a person's home, family, religion, health, sexuality, personal life and private affairs are covered by the concept of privacy excepting where any of these impinges upon the public or public interest.

(ii) *Caution against Identification:* While reporting crime involving rape, abduction or kidnap of women/females or sexual assault on children, or raising doubts and questions touching the chastity, personal character and privacy of women, the names, photographs of the victims or other particulars leading to their identity shall not be published.

(iii) Minor children and infants, who are the offspring of sexual abuse or 'forcible marriage' or illicit sexual union, shall not be identified or photographed.

Article 7. Privacy of Public Figures

(i) Right to Privacy is an inviolable human right. However, the degree of privacy differs from person to person and from situation to situation. The public person, who functions under public gaze as an emissary/representative of the public cannot expect to be afforded the same degree of privacy as a private person. His acts and conduct as are of public interest ('public interest' being distinct and separate from 'of interest to public') even if conducted in private may be brought to public knowledge through the medium of the press. The press has, however, a corresponding duty to ensure that the information about such acts and conduct of public interest of the public person is obtained through fair means, is properly verified and then reported accurately. For obtaining information in respect of acts done or conducted away from public gaze, the press is not expected to use surveillance devices. For obtaining information about private talks and discussion while the press is expected not to badger the public persons, the public persons are also expected to bring more openness in their functioning and co-operate with the press in its duty of informing the public about the acts of their representatives.

(ii) The interviews/articles or arguments pertaining to public persons, which border on events that are in public knowledge, if reported correctly, cannot be termed as intrusion into private life. There is a very thin line between public and private life and public persons should not to be too skinned to criticism

(iii) Newspapers are allowed latitude in criticising persons, who are in seats of power, because their conduct discloses public interest provided their criticism is not motivated to gratify private spite of opponent/rival of public figure.

Article 8. Recording interviews and phone conversation

(i) The Press shall not tape-record anyone's conversation without that person's knowledge or consent, except where the recording is necessary to protect the journalist in a legal action, or for other compelling good reason.

(ii) The Press shall, prior to publication, delete offensive epithets used by a person whose statements are being reported.

(iii) Intrusion through photography into moments of personal grief shall be avoided. However, photography of victims of accidents or natural calamity may be in larger public interest.

The Right to Privacy and Freedom of Speech and Expression

In India, the Supreme Court has held that the right to privacy has two fold sources:

1. Common law;
2. Constitutional law

Common law: Under this head, the English Common law of Torts and a privacy action for damages for unlawful invasion of privacy, or defamation applies.

To such action, the Printer and Publisher of a journal, magazine or book may be liable if he publishes, for advertising or non-advertising purposes, any matter concerning the private life of a citizen, example, his family, marriage, procreation, motherhood, child bearing, education, without such person's consent, subject to the following exceptions:

(i) When the publication is based upon public records, including court records because right to privacy no longer subsists once a matter becomes a matter of public record.

(ii) When the offending publication relates to the acts and conduct relevant to the discharge of official duties of a public servant, unless the publication is proved to be false or actuated by malice or reckless disregard for truth.

Constitutional law: The Right to freedom of speech and expression and the Right to privacy are intricately connected. Right to freedom of speech and expression is guaranteed by Article 19 (1)(a) of the Indian constitution, which, at the same time, is limited by certain reasonable restrictions under Article 19(2).

Our Supreme Court has held that the individual Right to privacy under Article 21 is to be balanced with the competing Freedom of press. Since Article 19(1)(a) is available against the State, so, the State cannot impose any prior restraint upon the Freedom of press on the ground that the relevant publication will offend the privacy of an individual or would defame a public official; the remedy in all such cases would be for the aggrieved person to lodge a complaint under the appropriate law after the offending matter is published.

The Supreme Court of India, in the case of R. Rajagopal vs State of Tamil Nadu, stated that any publication in regards to above mentioned subjects becomes unobjectionable if such publication is based upon public records including court records. This is for the reason that once a matter becomes a matter of public record, the right to privacy no longer subsists and it becomes a legitimate subject for comment by the press and media among others.

The Supreme Court has further carved out an exception to the above mentioned rule, i.e., a female, who is a victim of sexual assault, kidnap, abduction or a like offence, should not be further subjected to indignity by mentioning her name or identity in the media.

The Supreme Court has further held that the right to privacy is also not available with respect to acts and conducts of public officials in discharge of their public duties.

The Right to Privacy and Defamation: Privacy is protected by laws relating to defamation under Section 499 of the IPC. Defamation is making known through words, spoken or written or through signs or visible representation, an imputation, which is intended to harm the reputation of a person. However, it must be pointed that persons, who are in public life, cannot claim privacy to the same extent as ordinary citizens. Sometimes, a case can be met out that such exposures have been done in good faith and in the public interest or for the public good.

But care should be taken that the reports or photos published are not obscene, do not offend morality or decency and, above all, do not affect public order. Further, the reports need to be substantially correct. So, it is not defamatory to comment on or criticize the conduct of a public figure in the discharge of his public duties.

The Right to Privacy and the Right to Publish: There is a conflict between the Right to privacy and the Right to publish. Yet both are equally precious in a free society. Journalists, therefore, have to tread warily lest they be hauled up by the law for infringement of privacy. They have to act in good faith and in public interest. Journalists must not forget that they have no legal basis to keep their sources of information to themselves. Sources have to be disclosed when asked for, either by the police, or by the Court of law. In most cases, however, the law respects the confidentiality of the sources of a journalist unless public interest and justice are involved.

The Right to Privacy and Sting Operation: Cameras and microphones reduced to the size of a matchstick head can record visuals and pick up sound waves; and transmit them to eavesdroppers. There are infra red techniques through which one can watch and photograph what is happening in the adjoining room. Due to these developments, an individual has become vulnerable with regard to his privacy.

The Right to Privacy and Yellow Journalism: In India, many news channels, magazines and tabloid newspapers, etc. thrive on yellow journalism. The people in India do not file suits against such stories and sue them in the Court because the legal process is slow, but foreign countries have very stringent laws for violation of Right to privacy. The Courts in foreign countries take a serious view of such violations and give exemplary punishments by way of heavy fines and imprisonment.

Conclusion

After the leakage of the Radia tapes, the government has made proposals on two important areas. They are:

1. Proposal to come out with a privacy law;
2. Proposal to make Right to privacy a fundamental right.

The Indian Express on December 19, 2010 published an article with the headline, 'After Radia tapes, Government works on a privacy law.' The points to be highlighted from the article are:

- Worried about the negative impact of the leakage of intercepted conversations, the Centre has begun working on codifying privacy laws in the country. The new law will frame rules for monitoring phone and the Internet and for providing a redressal mechanism in case of breach of privacy.
- The Union Law Ministry is working on a framework of what could be done under the Constitution to protect an individual's privacy. Sources said that the Law Minister, M Veerappa Moily had asked his officers to prepare a blueprint for codification of privacy laws.
- Prime Minister Manmohan Singh had, while defending the government agencies' right to resort to phone tapping to deal with issues like crime and tax evasion, acknowledged that such steps must be well regulated and not misused. "We are aware of the nervousness in some sections of the corporate sector about phone tapping. While these powers are needed, they have to be exercised with utmost care and under very defined rules, procedures and mechanisms so that they are not misused," he had said.

- The Law Ministry intends to propose a vastly amended Communications Convergence Bill 2001, which was introduced in the Parliament in 2001 and is still pending. The Ministry is likely to propose that Communications Commission of India (CCI), a super-regulator envisaged in the original Bill, be given wide-ranging powers to take up complaints by citizens against invasion of privacy in the name of law enforcement.
- The Law Ministry also favours bringing in a stand-alone legislation on data protection to ensure confidentiality of all information transmitted through computer networks and telephones as per international standards. Anybody, either in the government or outside, who leaks personal data, including intercepted conversations, of an Indian citizen must be held accountable and measures will be suggested to ensure that intercepted data doesn't find its way into the public domain.

The Times of India on June 04, 2011 published an article with the headline, 'After Radia tapes, Government works on a privacy law.' The points to be highlighted are:

- The law ministry is working on a proposal to make right to privacy a fundamental right.
- The right to privacy would include the right to confidentiality of communication, confidentiality of private or family life, protection of his honour and good name, protection from search, detention or exposure of lawful communication between individuals, privacy from surveillance, confidentiality of banking, financial, medical and legal information, protection from identity theft of various kinds, protection of use of a person's photographs, fingerprints, DNA samples and other samples taken at police stations and other places and protection of data relating to individual.
- If the legislation is passed, it would address several concerns expressed by some sections of the civil society. For instance, there has been outrage over the 'compromise' of an individual's privacy in a project like UID, where all personal data will be available at the click of a mouse.

Hence, from the above two news reports, it can be expected that in the near future our Right to privacy is strengthened further if the proposals are given a concrete shape and turned into reality.

Unit 2: Media Laws

12

Civil and Criminal Law of Defamation

Introduction

Defamation has been described by the Second Press Commission as 'a tale of two interests', which are:

(a) The interest of the individual in his reputation,
(b) The interest of the society that information should pass freely.

Defamation can be constituted in two ways:

Libel: Libel is a written defamation or statement that tends to damage a person's reputation or good name that brings the person into hatred, contempt or ridicule or injures his business or occupational pursuits.

Libel can again be classified into two types:

(i) *Libel per se:* some words are always libellous. Falsely written accusations, such as labelling a person as a thief, swindler or imposter automatically constitutes libel.
(ii) *Libel per quod:* words that seem perfectly innocent in themselves can become libellous under certain circumstances. A wrong report that Mr. X was seen eating non vegetarian food in a party may be harmless unless Mr. X happens to be associated with an International Organisation for Vegetarians.
  (a) *Slander*: It is defamation caused through spoken words. But when a defamatory statement is broadcast, it is considered as libel even though technically the words are not written.

Civil Law of Defamation: Since defamation is an injury to a person's reputation, which is considered as his property, it constitutes an objectionable wrong and gives rise to the civil remedy of damages.

The civil law of defamation in India is not yet codified and still rests on English Common Law.

The Civil law being uncodified, in a civil suit for damages, the Court has to apply the corresponding rules of English Common Law, in so far as consistent with principles of justice, equity and good conscience.

In a civil action for defamation, the intention of the defendant is, in general, immaterial and it is no defence in a civil action that the defendant did not intend to defame the plaintiff. Good faith is not a good defence except in cases of qualified privilege.

What is defamation?

1. Defamation is an injury to a man's reputation. The right to reputation is an absolute right and anybody, who touches the reputation of another, is said to do so at his peril.
2. The wrong of defamation consists in the publication of a false and defamatory statement respecting another person without lawful justification or excuse.
3. In a civil action, intention of the defendant, in general, is immaterial.
4. The test of the defamatory nature of a statement is its tendency to excite against the plaintiff the adverse opinions or feelings of other persons.

Four conditions of defamation:

1. The statement must be defamatory.
2. The statement must refer to the plaintiff.
3. The statement must be published by the defendant.
4. The statement must be false.

Vir Bala Aggarwal and V.S. Gupta, in the *Handbook of Journalism and Mass Communication*, write;

In order to win a libel suit brought against the media, the person must prove five things:

1. That he or she has actually been defamed and harmed by the statements,
2. That he or she has been identified (although not necessarily by name),
3. That the defamatory things have been published,
4. That the media were at fault, and
5. In most instances, that what was published or broadcast was false.

Liability of the press republication:

1. Every repetition of a defamatory matter is a new publication and a distinct cause of action. A man, who receives from the hands of

another a libel on any person, is not justified in publishing it. 'Tale bearers are as bad as tale makers.'

2. The principle behind such strict liability is that every republication of a libel is a new libel, and each publisher is answerable for his act to the same extent as if the calumny originated with him. It is, therefore, no defence to an action for libel that the defendant received libellous statement from another whose name he disclosed at the time of publication. In short, if one chooses to repeal a calumny, one must take the responsibility for doing so.
3. Except in the case recognized by law to be privileged of reports of parliamentary or judicial proceedings, a newspaper or other organ of the press does not enjoy any special privilege in the law of defamation merely because it publishes matters in which the public are interested. A journalist like everyone else is subject to the ordinary law in the absence of statutory exception.

Defence to an action for defamation

1. *Justification*: Truth is the best defence against libel. However, knowing the truth is one thing, proving it is another. There is no defamation if what is reported is proven to be true. But since it is extremely difficult to prove the truth of a statement, this defence is seldom used.
2. *Fair comment*: Fair comment is a defence on a matter of public interest.
3. Privilege
   (a) Absolute privilege:
   - Statements made in the course of Parliamentary proceedings.
   - Statements made in the course of Judicial proceedings.
   - Any communication relating to affairs of State made by one officer of State to another in the course of duty is also absolute privilege on the ground of public policy.

   (b) Qualified privilege:
   - Statements made in performance of a duty where there is a confidential relation between two persons, such as creates a special duty of giving information; communication made by one to the other are privileged, even when no inquiry is made. Examples would be communication between a solicitor and client or father and daughter, etc.
   - Statements made in protection of an interest.
   - Fair reports of public proceedings, judicial proceedings,

parliamentary proceedings or public meetings etc. are also privileged.

Who may sue?
The person defamed; Corporation; Unincorporated association

Who may be sued?
Author; Corporation; Editor; Printer; Proprietor; Publisher

The Criminal Law of Defamation

It is codified in Section 499 of the Indian Penal Code (IPC). It constitutes a criminal offence if the conditions of the Section 499 are satisfied.

For the very reason that the criminal law of defamation is codified exhaustively, in Section 499 of the IPC, rules of English Common law cannot be imported to invent exceptions, which are not expressly enacted in the 10 exceptions of Section 499.

An essential ingredient of an offence of defamation under Section 499 of the IPC is that the imputation must be published 'intending to harm, or knowing or having reasons to believe that such imputation will harm.'

Good faith on the part of the accused is a good defence in criminal prosecution.

Section 499 of the IPC: Whoever by words either spoken or intended to be read, or by signs or by visible representations, makes or publishes any imputation concerning any person intending to harm, or knowing or having reason to believe that such imputation will harm, the reputation of such person, is said, except in the cases hereinafter excepted, to defame that person.

The four explanations:

Explanation 1: It may amount to defamation to impute anything to a deceased person, if the imputation would harm the reputation of that person if living, and is intended to be hurtful to the feelings of his family or other near relatives.

Explanation 2: It may amount to defamation to make an imputation concerning a company or an association or collection of persons, as such.

Explanation 3: An imputation in the form of an alternative or expressed ironically, may amount to defamation.

Explanation 4: No imputation is said to harm a person's reputation, unless that imputation directly or indirectly, in the estimation of others, lowers the moral or intellectual character of that person, or lowers the character of that person in respect of his caste or of his calling, or lowers the credit of that person, or causes it to be believed that the body of that person is in a loathsome state, or in a state generally considered as disgraceful.

The ten exceptions:

First Exception: Imputation of truth, which public good requires to be made or published.

It is not defamation to impute anything, which is true concerning any person, if it be for the public good that the imputation should be made or published. Whether or not it is for the public good is a question of fact.

Second Exception: Public conduct of public servants.

It is not defamation to express in good faith any opinion whatever respecting the conduct of a public servant in the discharge of his public functions, or respecting his character, so far as his character appears in that conduct, and no further.

Third Exception: Conduct of any person touching any public question.

It is not defamation to express in good faith any opinion whatever respecting the conduct of any person touching any public question, and respecting his character, so far as his character appears in that conduct, and no further.

Fourth Exception: Publication of reports of proceedings of courts.

It is not defamation to publish a substantially true report of the proceedings of a Court of Justice, or of the result of any such proceedings.

Fifth Exception: Merits of case decided in Court or conduct of witnesses and others concerned.

It is not defamation to express in good faith any opinion whatever respecting the merits of any case, civil or criminal, which has been decided by a Court of Justice, or respecting the conduct of any person as a party, witness or agent, in any such case, or respecting the character of such person, as far as his character appears in that conduct, and no further.

Sixth Exception: Merits of public performance.

It is not defamation to express in good faith any opinion respecting the merits of any performance, which its author has submitted to the judgement of the public, or respecting the character of the author so far as his character appears in such performance, and no further.

Seventh Exception: Censure passed in good faith by person having lawful authority over another.

It is not defamation in a person having over another any authority, either conferred by law or arising out of a lawful contract made with that other, to pass in good faith any censure on the conduct of that other in matters to which such lawful authority relates.

Eighth Exception: Accusation preferred in good faith to authorised person.

It is not defamation to prefer in good faith an accusation against any person to any of those, who have lawful authority over that person with respect to the subject matter of accusation.

Ninth Exception: Imputation made in good faith by person for protection of his or other's interests.

It is not defamation to make an imputation on the character of another provided that the imputation be made in good faith for the protection of the interest of the person making it, or of any other person, or for the public good.

Tenth Exception: Caution intended for good of person to whom conveyed or for public good.

It is not defamation to convey a caution, in good faith, to one person against another, provided that such caution be intended for the good of the person to whom it is conveyed, or of some person in whom that person is interested, or for the public good.

Section 500 of the IPC: This Section codifies the punishment for the offence of criminal defamation.

It states, 'Whoever defames another shall be punished with simple imprisonment for a term, which may extend to two years, or with fine, or with both.'

13

Indian Penal Code, 1860

(Sections 124A, 153A, 153B, 292, 293)

History of the Indian Penal Code

Krishna Deo Gaur, in his book 'Textbook on the India Penal Code', gives a detailed history of the Code. He writes that at the time when British came to India, the criminal law in existence was the Mohammedan law. This law, which had replaced the Hindu law, continued to be the basic law in the Mofussil, until the enactment of the Indian Penal Code (Act XLV of 1860).

To streamline the legal system in the then British India, the Governor General of India in Council appointed the 'Law Commissioners' in 1834 to inquire into the then existing state of law and to suggest a comprehensive Penal Code for India. The First Law Commission of India was, thus, constituted in 1834. Lord Macaulay was its President and Macleod, Anderson and Millet were appointed as Commissioners to prepare the Penal Code for India. The Commission submitted a Draft Code on October 14, 1837, which was circulated for ascertaining views of judges and law advisors. In 1845, the Second Law Commission was constituted with the same members, as the terms of the First Commission expired, which submitted the reports in two parts – one in 1846 and the other in 1847. The Draft Code again underwent a thorough revision by Benthune and Peacock, who were the Law Members of the Governor General's Council and it was submitted to the Legislative Council in 1856. The Code was finally passed after a thorough discussion and after receiving the assent of the Governor General in Council on October 6, 1860. The Indian Penal Code (Act XLV of 1860) came into force on January 1, 1862.

The Indian Penal Code is a comprehensive piece of legislation. The Code embodies the general penal law of the country and is the sole authority in respect to the general conditions of liability, the definitions of the specific offences in the Code and the conditions of exemptions from criminal liability. Some crimes are cognizable while some are not. Some offences are non-bailable while for some, the offender can avail bail.

The India Penal Code provides punishment for offences against the State, offences affecting the well being of the society, offences affecting human body, property, reputation and the like. The Code also codifies social offences like those relating to public tranquillity, elections, public justice, religion and the like.

It is important to note that the provisions relating to the Indian Penal Code have been adopted and implemented in most of the countries of the Commonwealth in South Asia, South East Asia, Middle East and Africa, which are incorporated with slight modifications to suit the local conditions and requirements of the concerned country. For instance, the Penal Codes of Malaysia, Singapore, Sri Lanka, Bangladesh, Nigeria, Somali, Sudan, Kenya, Tanzania, Uganda and many others have been modelled in the pattern of the Indian Penal Code and applied.

In the state of Jammu and Kashmir, the IPC is known as the Ranbir Penal Code (RPC).

Section 124A: *Sedition*: Whoever by words, either spoken or written, or by signs, or by visible representation, or otherwise, brings or attempts to bring into hatred or contempt, or excites or attempts to excite disaffection towards the Government established by law in India, shall be punished with imprisonment for life, to which fine may be added, or with imprisonment, which may extend to three years, to which fine may be added, or with fine.

Explanation 1: The expression "disaffection" includes disloyalty and all feelings of enmity.

Explanation 2: Comments expressing disapprobation of the measures of the Government with a view to obtain their alteration by lawful means, without exciting or attempting to excite hatred, contempt or disaffection, do not constitute an offence under this section.

Explanation 3: Comments expressing disapprobation of the administrative or other action of the Government without exciting or attempting to excite hatred, contempt or disaffection, do not constitute an offence under this section.

Constitutionality of Section 124A

The constitutionality of this Section has been upheld by the Supreme Court as a reasonable restriction in the interest of public order, after narrowly interpreting its text according to which it would be no offence merely to cause ill feeling or absence of affection against the government; it would be so only if it is intended or has a tendency to create public disorder or incite violence.

The Right to Comment and Criticize: The Freedom of Press includes the right to criticize and comment on the government's administration and policies, provided such criticism does not endanger any of the social interests safeguarded by Clause 2 of Article 19 of the Constitution of India some of which are security of state, public order, etc.

Procedure

No Court can take cognizance of an offence under Section 124A of the IPC without the previous sanction of the Central or State government, as required by the Section 196 (1)(A) of the CrPC, 1973.

V. Venkatesan wrote the cover story in *Frontline*, January 15-28, 2011 with the headline, 'The sedition law' wherein the important points he stated are:

- Section 124A of the Indian Penal Code (IPC), dealing with sedition, has an interesting history. It did not form part of the IPC originally, when it was enacted in 1860, although it was proposed to be included by the draft prepared by the Indian Law Commissioners in 1837. It was omitted from the IPC for some unknown reason. In 1870, it was inserted by the IPC (Amendment) Act. This provision was later on replaced by the present Section 124A by an amending Act of 1898.
- The difference between the old Section 124A and the present one is that in the former, the offence consisted in exciting or attempting to excite feelings of "disaffection", but in the latter "bringing or attempting to bring into hatred or contempt the Government of India" has also been made punishable.
- Indeed, the Supreme Court came very close to hold this provision unconstitutional in Kedarnath vs. The State of Bihar (AIR 1962 SC 955). The court, in this case, considered two possible interpretations of this provision. It held that if sedition is understood to mean incitement of disorder or tendency or likelihood of public disorder or reasonable apprehension thereof, the section will lie within the ambit of permissible legislative restrictions mentioned in clause (2) of Article 19, which guarantees freedom of expression. If, on the other hand, it is to be held that even without any tendency to disorder or intention to create disturbance of law and order by the use of words, written or spoken, which merely create disaffection or feelings of enmity against the government, the offence of sedition is complete, then such an interpretation would make the section unconstitutional.
- Consistent with the legal principle that the court should prefer an interpretation, which would render a provision constitutional, the court held that the section aims at rendering penal only such activities as would be intended or have a tendency to create disorder or disturbance of public peace by resort to violence.

Case Studies

1. *Lokmanya Bal Gangadhar Tilak:* He was tried twice under this Section in 1898 and 1906. The second instance was when on April 30, 1908, two young revolutionaries Prafulla Chaki and Khudiram Bose threw a bomb onto a carriage in Muzzafarpur in order to kill the Chief Prisidency Magistrate

Douglas Kingsford, but by mistake, killed two women in the carriage instead. Chaki commited suicide before he was caught, while Bose was hanged. In his newspaper, *'Kesari'*, Tilak defended the two young men and called for immediate swaraj. This was followed by the immediate arrest of Tilak by the British on charges of sedition. The Parsi judge, Dinshaw. D Davar trying the case, termed Tilak's articles in '*Kesari*' as "seething with sedition" and accused him of glorifying violence and approving of murder. By the end of the case, Tilak was sentenced to a jail term from 1908 to 1914 in Mandalay in Burma.

2. *Mahatma Gandhi:* He was booked for sedition in 1922 and was sentenced to six years of imprisonment for his writings in '*Young India*'.

3. *Aseem Trivedi:* Charged with sedition, cartoonist Aseem Trivedi was sent to jail for two weeks by a Mumbai court, but was released on bail after police said it did not require his custody anymore two days after his arrest that sparked an outrage.

Trivedi did not apply for bail in the case until the sedition charge, for which maximum punishment is life imprisonment, was dropped, even as the Maharashtra government sought to distance itself from the case.

He was arrested in Mumbai on Saturday under IPC Section 124 (sedition), section 66 A of Information Technology Act and section 2 of Prevention of Insults to Nation Honour Act.

The Kanpur-based artist was accused of putting up banners mocking the Constitution during a rally of anti-corruption crusader Anna Hazare in Mumbai late last year and posting the same on his website.

One cartoon titled, 'Gang rape of Mother India' shows 'Mother India' dressed in a tri-colour sari, with politicians and bureaucrats about to assault her, with a gleeful beast standing by described as 'Corruption'. One cartoon shows India's national emblem, the Ashoka Lions, with foxes rather than lions. In the inscription on the emblem, the words 'Satyamev Jayate' are replaced with 'Brashtamev Jayate' (meaning corruption alone triumphs) and a danger sign.

Trivedi was arrested on the basis of a complaint filed by a member of Republican Party of India, Amit Katarnayea.

4. *Binayak Sen*: An Indian pediatrician, public health specialist and activist, Dr. Binayak Sen is the national vice-president of the People's Union for Civil Liberties.

Dr. Binayak Sen was accused of sedition by the Chhattisgarh government. He, however, was granted bail on April 15, 2011, by the Supreme Court of India, which said that no evidence of sedition was produced against the accused by the Chhattisgarh government.

On 24 December 2010, the Additional Sessions and District Court Judge, B P Varma, Raipur, found Binayak Sen, Naxal ideologue Narayan Sanyal and Kolkata businessman Piyush Guha, guilty of sedition for helping Maoists in their fight against the state.

In May 2007, Dr. Sen was detained for allegedly supporting the outlawed Naxalites, thereby violating the provisions of the Chhattisgarh Special Public Security Act 2005 (CSPSA) and the Unlawful Activities (Prevention) Act 1967.

The evidence presented against him included his meetings with the jailed Naxalite leader Narayan Sanyal and certain documents allegedly supporting his links with the Naxalites.

5. *Arundhati Roy:* Noted writer Arundhati Roy was sought to be charged with sedition for advocating independence for the Kashmir region.

Arundhati Roy, Hurriyat leader Syed Ali Shah Geelani and others were booked on charges of sedition by Delhi Police for their "anti-India" speech at a seminar in 2010.

The filing of the FIR came following a directive from a local court on a petition filed by Sushil Pandit, who alleged that Geelani and Roy made anti-India speeches at a conference on "Azadi – the Only Way" on October 21, 2010.

Geelani shared the dais with Roy and pro-Maoist leader Varavara Rao among others.

Reacting to the court order, Roy said that perhaps they should "posthumously file a charge against Jawaharlal Nehru" and cited 14 instances where the first Prime Minister said that "the question of accession in any disputed territory or state must be decided in accordance with the wishes of people."

6. *Praveen Togadia:* "Fireband leader Praveen Togadia was, in 2003, slapped with the charge of sedition by the Rajasthan government after which an Ajmer court denied bail and extended his judicial remand. The charges included an attempt "to wage a war against the nation."

Togadia, who was jailed on charges of defying the prohibitory orders and ban on distribution of tridents, also faced a charge under Section 121-A of IPC (waging war or attempting anti-national activity).

In a sharp reaction, senior VHP leader Acharya Giriraj Kishore alleged that the sedition charge was levelled as an afterthought and the Rajasthan government had intentionally applied it so that Togadia was not given bail.

7. *Simranjit Singh Mann:* Simranjit Singh Mann, president of the Shiromani Akali Dal, Amritsar, was arrested from Sangrur district of Punjab in connection with four different cases of sedition registered against him.

Mann had raised pro-Khalistan slogans on June 6, 2005 in the golden temple complex on the 21st anniversary of Operation Blue Star. Mann admitted that he had helped Bhindranwale and his men by distributing arms, while he was posted in Faridkot as a senior superintendent of police in the early 1980s.

"The offences committed by him are serious and seditious in nature and he should be prosecuted for the offences. He distributed arms to terrorists and committed heinous crimes. He had also made provocative speeches in Anandpur Sahib and Damdama Sahib as well. He was booked under 124 A of IPC for waging war against the state," a senior Punjab police officer had said.

Mann was named in the assassination of former Prime Minister Indira Gandhi, but investigations could not substantiate the charges and, hence, he was not prosecuted in that case.

Criticism: *The Hindu* on March 13, 2011 published a report, 'Section 124-A of IPC unconstitutional' wherein eminent scientists, human rights activists, advocates and writers, who participated in a seminar on the law of treason and sedition felt that Section 124-A of the Indian Penal Code (IPC) was unconstitutional, draconian and should be got rid of.

Former Director of the Centre for Cellular and Molecular Biology (CCMB) P.M. Bhargava, former Director of the National Institute of Nutrition (NIN) Mahtab S. Bamji, rights activists Viajayalaxmi, Jasveen Jairath, writer Nikhileshwar, lawyers Mihir Desai, Sagar, I. Mallikarjuna Sharma and others spoke at the meet organised as part of the "Free Binayak Sen Campaign".

They stressed the need for generating awareness and debate on the law of sedition. Several European and North American countries have already done away with such sections in their laws. Dr. Bhargava said that there was a strong case for filing public interest litigation (PIL) against Section 124-A, as it was unconstitutional.

A larger bench of the Supreme Court should look into it as the law of sedition was coming in conflict with other articles of the Constitution. An advocate from Mumbai, Mihir Desai said that the rights activist, Binayak Sen was wrongly framed and convicted on the charges of sedition, though he had never incited violence through his speech or action.

Section 153A: Promoting enmity between different groups on ground of religion, race, place of birth, residence, language etc., and doing acts prejudicial to maintenance of harmony—(1) Whoever

(a) by words, either spoken or written, or by signs or by visible representations or otherwise, promotes or attempts to promote, on grounds of religion, race, place of birth, residence, language, caste or community or any other ground whatsoever, disharmony or feelings of enmity, hatred or ill-will between different religious, racial, language or regional groups or castes or communities, or

(b) commits any act, which is prejudicial to the maintenance of harmony between different religious, racial, language or regional groups or castes or communities, and which disturbs or is likely to disturb the public tranquillity, or

(c) organizes any exercise, movement, drill or other similar activity intending that the participants in such activity shall use or be trained to use criminal force or violence or knowing it to be likely that the participants in such activity will use or be trained to use criminal force or violence, or participates in such activity intending to use or be trained to use criminal force or violence or knowing it to be likely that the participants in such activity will use or be trained to use criminal force or violence, against any religious, racial, language or regional group or caste or community and such activity for any reason whatsoever causes or is likely to cause fear or alarm or a feeling of insecurity amongst members of such religious, racial, language or regional group or caste or community, shall be punished with imprisonment, which may extend to three years, or with fine, or with both.

(2) Offence committed in place of worship, etc. – Whoever commits an offence specified in sub-section (1) in any place of worship or in any assembly engaged in the performance of religious worship or religious ceremonies, shall be punished with imprisonment, which may extend to five years and shall also be liable to fine.

Procedure

1. Under the first schedule of the CrPC 1973, an offence under Section 153 A is:
   (i) Triable by a Magistrate of the First class
   (ii) Non bailable
   (iii) Cognizable
2. Section 196(1)(A) of the CrPC 1973 provides that no Court shall take cognizance of an offence under Section 153A or 153B of the IPC except with previous sanction of the Central or state government.

Case Studies

1. *L.K. Advani and twenty others*: *India Today* on December 6, 2012 published a report, Babri Masjid demolition case: SC directs expeditious hearing' wherein it stated: 'The CBI had charge-sheeted Advani and 20 others under sections 153A IPC (promoting enmity between classes), 153B (imputations, assertions prejudicial to national integration) and 505 (false statements, rumours, etc. circulated with the intent to cause mutiny or disturb public peace).'

This was in relation to the Babri Masjid Demolition case, which were later quashed off.

Besides Advani, others were Kalyan Singh, Uma Bharti, Satish Pradhan, CR Bansal, MM Joshi, Vinay Katiyar, Ashok Singhal, Giriraj Kishore, Sadhvi Ritambhara, VH Dalmia, Mahant Avaidhynath, RV Vedanti, Param Hans Ram Chandra Das, Jagdish Muni Maharaj, BL Sharma, Nritya Gopal Das, Dharam Das, Satish Nagar and Moreshwar Save.

Section 153B: Imputations, assertions prejudicial to national integration:

(1) Whoever, by words either spoken or written or by signs or by visible representations or otherwise:

(a) makes or publishes any imputation that any class of persons cannot, by reason of their being members of any religious, racial, language or regional group or caste or community, bear true faith and allegiance to the Constitution of India as by law established or uphold the sovereignty and integrity of India, or

(b) asserts, counsels, advises, propagates or publishes that any class of persons by reason of their being members of any religious, racial, language or regional group or caste or community be denied, or deprived of their rights as citizens of India, or

(c) makes or publishes and assertion, counsel, plea or appeal concerning the obligation of any class of persons, by reason of their being members of any religious, racial, language or regional group or caste or community, and such assertion, counsel, plea or appeal causes or is likely to cause disharmony or feelings of enmity or hatred or ill-will between such members and other persons, shall be punished with imprisonment, which may extend to three years, or with fine, or with both.

(2) Whoever commits an offence specified in sub-section (1), in any place of worship or in any assembly engaged in the performance of religious worship or religious ceremonies, shall be punished with imprisonment, which may extend to five years and shall also be liable to fine.

Procedure

3. Under the first schedule of the CrPC 1973, an offence under Section 153 A is:

(i) Triable by a Magistrate of the First class
(ii) Non bailable
(iii) Cognizable

4. Section 196(1)(A) of the CrPC 1973 provides that no Court shall take cognizance of an offence under 153B of the IPC except with previous sanction of the Central or state government.

Section 292: Sale, etc., of obscene books, etc.—(1) For the purposes of sub-section (2), a book, pamphlet, paper, writing, drawing, painting representation, figure or any other object, shall be deemed to be obscene if it is lascivious or appeals to the prurient interest or if its effect, or (where it comprises two or more distinct items) the effect of any one of its items, is, if taken as a whole, such as to tend to deprave and corrupt persons, who are likely, having regard to all relevant circumstances, to read, see or hear the matter contained or embodied in it.

(2) Whoever—

(a) sells, lets to hire, distributes, publicly exhibits or in any manner puts into circulation, or for purposes of sale, hire, distribution, public exhibition or circulation, makes, reduces or has in his possession any obscene book, pamphlet, paper, drawing, painting, representation or figure or any other obscene object whatsoever, or

(b) imports, exports or conveys any obscene object for any of the purposes aforesaid, or knowing or having reason to believe that such object will be sold, let to hire, distributed or publicly exhibited or in any manner put into circulation, or

(c) takes part in or receives profits from any business in the course of which he knows or has reason to believe that any such obscene objects are, for any of the purposes aforesaid, made, produced, purchased, kept, imported, exported, conveyed, publicly exhibited or in any manner put into circulation, or

(d) advertises or makes known by any means whatsoever that any person is engaged or is ready to engage in any act, which is an offence under this section, or that any such obscene object can be procured from or through any person, or

(e) offers or attempts to do any act, which is an offence under this section, shall be punished on first conviction with imprisonment of either description for a term, which may extend to two years, and with fine, which may extend to two thousand rupees, and, in the event of a second or subsequent conviction, with imprisonment of either description for a term, which may extend to five years, and also with fine, which may extend to five thousand rupees.

Exception

This section does not extend to –

(a) any book, pamphlet, paper, writing, drawing, painting, representation or figure:
   (i) the publication of which is proved to be justified as being for the public good on the ground that such book, pamphlet, paper, writing, drawing, painting, representation or figure is in the interest of science, literature, art or learning or other objects of general concern, or
   (ii) which is kept or used bona fide for religious purposes;

(b) any representation sculptured, engraved, painted or otherwise represented on or in:
   (i) any ancient monument within the meaning of the Ancient Monuments and Archaeological Sites and Remains Act, 1958 (24 of 1958), or
   (ii) any temple, or on any car used for the conveyance of idols, or kept or used for any religious purpose.

Ingredients of Offence

1. Knowledge of the object being obscene is not required.
2. Intention is an ingredient, but it may be inferred from circumstances.

Procedure

1. Section 95(1) of the CrPC empowers the state government to forfeit, search for and seize obscene publications coming under Section 292 and 293.
2. Section 108 (i)-(ii) of the CrPC empowers a Magistrate, having jurisdiction to draw up a proceeding under Section 108, calling upon a person to execute a bond for his good behaviour, on receiving information that he makes, publishes etc., obscene matters falling under Section 292 of the IPC.
3. The offences under Sections 292 and 293 of the IPC are, under the first schedule of the CrPC 1973 are non-cognizable and bailable.

Case Studies

1. Ranjit D. Udeshi vs State of Maharashtra on 19 August 1964: The appellant, a bookseller, sold a copy of the unexpurgated edition of "Lady Chatterley's Lover". He was convicted under Section 292, Indian Penal Code. In his appeal to the Supreme Court, he contended that:

(i) the section was void because it violated the freedom of speech and expression guaranteed by Art. 19(1)(a) of the Constitution of India;
(ii) even if the section was valid, the book was not obscene and;
(iii) it must be shown by the prosecution that he sold the book with the intention to corrupt the purchaser, that is to say, that he knew that the book was obscene.

The Court dismissed the appeal by holding that the laws relating to obscenity were a reasonable restriction on the right to freedom of expression in that they uphold public decency and morality.

2. *Jagdish Chavla and others vs. the State of Rajasthan, 1999*: In the case of '*Jagdish Chavla and others vs. the State of Rajasthan*', 1999 CR LJ 2562 (Raj), the accused was caught viewing an obscene film on the television with the help of a VCR, which along with the cassette was seized and a case under section 292 of the IPC was registered. The accused filed a petition in the High Court for quashing of the proceedings and it was held that simply being in possession of a blue film could not make a person guilty under section 292, unless it was further proved that the purpose of keeping the same was selling or letting it on hire. Therefore, without proving the purpose of keeping the same no offence mentioned in section 292 was made out and the proceedings were quashed. The law, therefore, excludes from liability (under

section 292) the mere possession of obscene material for one's own personal use without any intention to perform any of the purposes specified in section 292.

Section 293: Sale, etc., of obscene objects to young person: Whoever sells, lets to hire, distributes, exhibits or circulates to any person under the age of twenty years any such obscene object as is referred to in the last preceding section, or offers or attempts so to do, shall be punished on first conviction with imprisonment of either description for a term, which may extend to three years, and with fine, which may extend to two thousand rupees, and, in the event of a second or subsequent conviction, with imprisonment of either description for a term, which may extend to seven years, and also with fine, which may extend to five thousand rupees.

Criticism of the Indian Penal Code

The structure and the categories listed under the Indian Penal Code have always been intended to be versatile enough to cover all possible situations of crimes and breach of laws. In spite of the striving efforts of the law makers as well as enforcers, the Indian Penal Code has been constantly tested and put under a critic's scanner at various instances. A section of the Indian Penal Code – Section 377 had to do with the rights of the sexual minorities in India. This had been harsh especially for those suffering from ghastly sexual diseases, like HIV/AIDS. Thus, due to the increasing pressure from the human rights activists, this section had to be reformed and was successfully executed. Another section 309 penalizes a person, who unsuccessfully commits a suicide. This is not at all humane as what actually is needed in this case is to provide the person with proper counselling in order to counter the root cause of this kind of a harsh step. Thus, this section, that reflected a colonial outlook that impaired the citizens of it's rights, has been done away with. There also used to be a section numbered 497 that inflicted punishment, even for sexual acts initiated with the consent of the two parties. This was highly unprogressive and was strongly objected. This has also been altered.

All in all, the Indian Penal Code of the present day has done away with almost all of it's flaws and has evolved into a modern law enforcing document, that takes into consideration the humane side of the personalities of culprits as well. This has escalated the Indian system of Law to greater heights and has led to a firm respect for it in every citizen of the country.

14

Criminal Procedure Code, 1973

(Sections 93, 95, 96, 108, 144,196, 327)

HISTORY OF THE CRIMINAL PROCEDURE CODE 1973

There was no uniform law of criminal procedure for the whole of India. For the guidance of the Courts, there were special Acts, which were applicable in erstwhile provinces and the Presidency towns. The Acts, which were applicable in the Presidency towns, were first consolidated by the Criminal Procedure Supreme Court Act (16 of 1852). The Acts, which were applicable in the provinces, were consolidated by the Criminal Procedure Code (25 of 1861). Criminal Procedure Supreme Court Act was replaced by the High Court Criminal Procedure Act (12 of 1865). And the Criminal Procedure Code was replaced by Act 10 of 1872. A uniform law of procedure for the whole of India was consolidated by the Code of Criminal Procedure, 1882 (10 of 1882). It was replaced by Code of Criminal Procedure, 1898 (5 of 1898). This Code of 1898 has been amended by various amending Acts. To make the criminal procedure more comprehensive, a Law Commission was asked to undertake a detailed examination of the Code of Criminal Procedure, 1898. The Commission submitted its report on February 19, 1968. In the meanwhile, the Law Commission was reconstituted and the reconstituted Commission made a detailed study of the Code of 1898 and submitted its report on September, 1969. Thereafter, a Draft Bill was introduced in the Rajya Sabha on December 10, 1970. The Bill was referred to a Joint Select Committee of both the Houses of Parliament. Incorporating the recommendations of the Joint Select Committee, the Code of Criminal Procedure Bill was taken up for consideration by the Parliament. The Bill having passed by both the Houses of the Parliament received the assent of the President on January 25, 1974. It came on the Statute Book as Code of Criminal Procedure, 1973.

Section 93: When search warrant may be issued:

(1) (a) Where any Court has reason to believe that a person to whom a summon or order under section 91 or a requisition under sub-section (1) of section 92 has been, or might be, addressed, will not or would not produce the document or thing as required by such summons or requisition, or

(b) Where such document or thing is not known to the Court to be in the possession of any person, or

(c) Where the Court considers that the purposes of any inquiry, trial or other proceeding under this Code will be served by a general search or inspection, it may issue a search warrant; and the person to whom such warrant is directed, may search or inspect in accordance therewith and the provisions hereinafter contained.

(2) The Court may, if it thinks fit, specify in the warrant the particular place or part thereof to which only the search or inspection shall extend; and the person charged with the execution of such warrant shall then search or inspect only the place or part so specified.

(3) Nothing contained in this section shall authorise any Magistrate other than a District Magistrate or Chief Judicial Magistrate to grant a warrant to search for a document, parcel or other thing in the custody of the postal or telegraph authority.

Conditions for issue of Search Warrant:

1. A search warrant may be issued by the Court only in any of the three specified circumstances:
   (i) Where the Court has reasons to believe that summons for production of a document or thing will not be obeyed;
   (ii) Where the document or thing is not known to be in the possession of any person or Court;
   (iii) Where a general search or inspection is considered necessary for the purpose of trial or inquiry or other proceedings under the code whether pending or in contemplation.
2. Since a search warrant is a drastic invasion upon the privacy of a individual, the Code subjects the power to certain limitations:
   (i) The document or thing must be distinctly specified;
   (ii) The Magistrate must exercise his judicial discretion and shall not issue the search warrant unless the condition specified above is present.
   (iii) The search should be made in the presence of two or more respectable witnesses of the locality and the list of things seized in the course of such search and of the places in which they are expected to be found shall be prepared by the searching officer

and signed by such witnesses. The occupant of the place searched or some person on his behalf shall be permitted to appear and a copy of the list prepared and signed by the witnesses shall be delivered to such occupant or person on his behalf.

Section 95: Power to declare certain publications forfeited and to issue search warrants for the same:
Where

(a) Any newspaper, or book, or
(b) Any document.

Wherever printed, appears to the State Government to contain any matter the publication of which is punishable under section 124A or section 153A or section 153B or section 292 or section 293 or section 295A of the Indian Penal Code (45 of 1860), the State Government may, by notification, stating the grounds of its opinion, declare every copy of the issue of the newspaper containing such matter, and every copy of such book or other document to be forfeited to Government, and thereupon any police officer may seize the same wherever found in India and any Magistrate may by warrant authorise any police officer not below the rank of sub-inspector to enter upon and search for the same in any premises where any copy of such issue or any such book or other document may be or may be reasonably suspected to be.

Scope: Power to forfeit objectionable publication:

The power under this section can be used to proceed against a publication, which contains a matter punishable against any of the following offences:

Section 124A *(Sedition)*: Section 153A (Promoting enmity between classes); Section 153B (Matter prejudicial to national integration); Section 292 and Section 293 (Obscene publication); Section 295A (Malicious insult to religion or religious beliefs of any class).

Section 96: Application to High Court to set aside declaration of forfeiture:

(1) Any person having any interest in any newspaper, book or other document, in respect of which a declaration of forfeiture has been made under section 95, may, within two months from the date of publication in the Official Gazette of such declaration, apply to the High Court to set aside such declaration on the ground that the issue of the newspaper, or the book or other document, in respect of which the declaration was made, did not contain any such matter as is referred to in sub-section (1) of section 95.
(2) Every such application shall, where the High Court consists of three or more Judges, be heard and determined by a Special Bench of the High Court composed of three Judges and where the High Court

consists of less than three Judges, such Special Bench shall be composed of all the Judges of that High Court.

(3) On the hearing of any such application with reference to any newspaper, any copy of such newspaper may be given in evidence in aid of the proof of the nature or tendency of the words, signs or visible representations contained in such newspaper, in respect of which the declaration of forfeiture was made.

(4) The High Court shall, if it is not satisfied that the issue of the newspaper, or the book or other document, in respect of which the application has been made, contained any such matter as is referred to in sub-section (1) of section 95, set aside the declaration of forfeiture.

(5) Where there is a difference of opinion among the Judges forming the Special Bench, the decision shall be in accordance with the opinion of the majority of those Judges.

Scope: The person gives the person interested in the publication, which has been forfeited, a right to apply to the High Court to set aside the order of the forfeiture.

Section 108: Security for good behaviour from persons disseminating seditious matters:

(1) When Judicial Magistrate of the first class receives information that there is within his local jurisdiction any person who, within or without such jurisdiction:

(i) Either orally or in writing or in any other manner, intentionally disseminates or attempts to disseminate or abets the dissemination of:
   (a) any matter the publication of which is punishable under section 124A or section 153A or section 153B or section 295A of the Indian Penal Code (45 of 1860), or
   (b) any matter concerning a Judge acting or purporting to act in the discharge of his official duties, which amounts to criminal intimidation or defamation under the India Penal Code (45 of 1860),

(ii) makes, produces, publishes or keeps for sale, imports, export conveys, sells, lets to hire, distributes, publicly exhibits or in any other manner puts into circulation any obscene matter such as is referred to in section 292 of the Indian Penal Code (45 of 1860), and the Magistrate is of opinion that there is sufficient ground for proceeding, the Magistrate may, in the manner hereinafter provided, require such person to show cause why he should not be ordered to execute a bond, with or without sureties, for his good behaviour for such period, not exceeding one year, as the Magistrate thinks fit.

(2) No proceedings shall be taken under this section against the editor, proprietor, printer or publisher of any publication registered under, and edited, printed and published in conformity with, the rules laid down in the Press and Registration of Books Act, 1867 (25 of 1867), with reference to any matter contained in such publication except by the order or under tile authority of the State Government or some officer empowered by the State Government in this behalf.

Conditions for the application of Section 108

This section provides for demanding a bond for maintaining good behaviour on the following conditions:

(i) The power is conferred only on a Judicial Magistrate of the First Class;

(ii) He can act only if he receives information about the presence within his local jurisdiction of a person, who is involved in the dissemination of any matter concerning any of the offences specified in Clause (i) of sub-section (1) or is responsible for an obscene matter in any manner as specified in Clause (ii).

(iii) Such offences are:

- (a) under sections 124A, 153A, 153B, 295A, of the IPC
- (b) Offences under Sections 499, 503 of the IPC, concerning a Judge and relating to the purported discharge of his official duties.
- (c) Offences under section 292 of the IPC

(iv) In the case of a matter falling under Clause (i), the dissemination must be intentional, though the offender under section 153A itself may be committed without any malicious intention.

(v) Such offence may be committed within or without the local jurisdiction of the Magistrate.

(vi) But no action can be taken, without an order by or under the authority of the State government (i.e. without its prior sanction), where such person is the proprietor, printer or publisher of a publication registered under the Press and Registration of Books Act, 1867, and it has been edited, printed and published in conformity with the provisions of that Act.

(vii) The Magistrate can take action only if, with reference to the information received, he forms the opinion that there is sufficient ground for proceeding under this section. In order to form such opinion, he has to determine two questions:

- (a) Whether such person has been party to dissemination of objectionable matter as enumerated in sub-section (1), and
- (b) Whether there is a fear of repetition of such offence or his part, so as to necessitate binding him down for good behaviour.

Though the Magistrate acts primarily on the information received, he must apply his mind to the antecedents of the person and the surrounding circumstances, so as to form his opinion as to the need for taking action under this section.

Section 144: Power to issue order in urgent cases of nuisance of apprehended danger

(1) In cases where, in the opinion of a District Magistrate, a Sub-divisional Magistrate or any other Executive Magistrate specially empowered by the State Government in this behalf, there is sufficient ground for proceeding under this section and immediate prevention or speedy remedy is desirable, such Magistrate may, by a written order stating the material facts of the case and served in the manner provided by section 134, direct any person to abstain from a certain act or to take certain order with respect to certain property in his possession or under his management, if such Magistrate considers that such direction is likely to prevent, or tends to prevent, obstruction, annoyance or injury to any person lawfully employed, or danger to human life, health or safety, or a disturbance of the public tranquillity, or a riot, of an affray.

(2) An order under this section may, in cases of emergency or in cases where the circumstances do not admit of the serving in due time of a notice upon the person against whom the order is directed, be passed *ex parte*.

(3) An order under this section may be directed to a particular individual, or to persons residing in a particular place or area, or to the public generally when frequenting or visiting a particular place or area.

(4) No order under this section shall remain in force for more than two months from the making thereof: Provided that, if the State Government considers it necessary to do so for preventing danger to human life, health or safety or for preventing a riot or any affray, it may, by notification, direct that an order made by a Magistrate under this section shall remain in force for such further period not exceeding six months from the date on which the order made by the Magistrate would have, but for such order, expired, as it may specify in the said notification.

(5) Any Magistrate may, either on his own motion or on the application of any person aggrieved, rescind or alter any order made under this section, by himself or any Magistrate subordinate to him or by his predecessor-in-office.

(6) The State Government may, either on its own motion or on the application of any person aggrieved, rescind or alter any order made by it under the proviso to sub-section (4).

(7) Where an application under sub-section (5) or sub-section (6) is received, the Magistrate, or the State Government, as the case may be, shall afford to the applicant an early opportunity of appearing before him or it, either in person or by pleader and showing cause against the order; and if the

Magistrate or the State Government, as the case may be, rejects the application wholly or in part, he or it shall record in writing the reasons for so doing.

Applicability of Section 144 to the Press

1. Section 144 is a general provision and is not directed specifically against the Press. But it may be applicable against the Press if the conditions laid down in the Section are satisfied. The primary condition is that there must be urgency in the circumstances calling for an exercise of the power conferred by the Section. This urgency is not the same thing as in the state of Emergency.
2. Section 144 is applicable even in normal times when there is no proclamation of Emergency. The urgency referred here is the urgency of the situation, for example, such as breach of public order, which needs immediate prevention. This would enable the Magistrate to even make *ex parte* order according to the gravity of the situation.
3. Section 144 empowers the specified Executive Magistrate to issue temporary order (*inter alia*) in urgent cases of apprehended danger. It has been held that under this section, it is competent for a Magistrate to impose pre censorship on a newspaper or journal, i.e., to direct the editor, or publisher of a newspaper to abstain from publishing, without previous scrutiny of the Magistrate, or some other specified officer, any matter in such newspaper, which may cause disturbance of public tranquillity, such as communal riot or affray.

Conditions precedent for exercise of the power under Section 144

An order under this Section can be made only if the following conditions are satisfied:

(i) The order can be made only by a District Magistrate, a Sub-divisional Magistrate or any other Executive Magistrate specially empowered by the State Government in this behalf.

(ii) Such Magistrate must be satisfied that there is sufficient ground for proceeding under this Section and immediate prevention is desirable to prevent a disturbance of the public tranquillity or danger to human life or safety. But the power may be exercised not only where present danger exists, but also where there is a reasonable apprehension of danger, for which no overt act is necessary.

(iii) The Magistrate must record an order stating the material facts and also his finding that were sufficient grounds for proceeding under this section.

Penalty for breach of an order under Section 144

1. The punishment for violating an order issued by a competent

Magistrate under Section 144 is provided in Section 188 of the IPC, which deals with 'disobedience to an order duly promulgated by a public servant'.

2. The ingredients of the offence under Section 188 are:
   (a) The Magistrate, who issued the order in question, must have been overpowered by law to issue it;
   (b) The order must be lawful;
   (c) The order must have been disobeyed;
   (d) The accused must have had knowledge of the promulgation of the order;
   (e) His disobedience either causes or tends to cause a riot or affray, or danger to human life or safety. Here, it is not necessary that the offender should intend to produce harm, or contemplate his disobedience as likely to produce harm. It is sufficient that he knows of the order, which he disobeys and that his disobedience produces or is likely to produce harm.

Defence: In defence to a prosecution under Section 188 of the IPC, it is open to the accused to plead in his defence that the order under Section 144 is not legally valid.

Case Studies

1. *India Today*, on June 5, 2011 published a report, 'Ramdev fallout: Section 144 of CrPC imposed in New Delhi', which read:

In an effort to pre-empt any protest by supporters of Baba Ramdev, Delhi Police imposed prohibitory orders on June 5 for a week in New Delhi district where such agitations are apprehended. "We have imposed section 144 of CrPC in New Delhi district till June 11," a senior police official said.

The decision to impose prohibitory orders came in the backdrop of some followers of Ramdev camping at Jantar Mantar after they were ousted from the Ramlila Maidan where their congregation was disrupted by a mid-night police action.

The official said that the police anticipate protests at India Gate, Boat Club or Jantar Mantar, places which fall in New Delhi district. Police stormed the site of Baba Ramdev's hunger strike a little past midnight, firing tear gas shells and resorting to lathi charge on his supporters. "The prohibitory orders were issued following reports indicating that such conditions now exist that unrestricted holding of public meetings, processions and demonstrations in the area are likely to cause obstruction to traffic, danger to human safety and disturbance of public tranquility," the official said.

Police have banned holding of any public meeting, assembly of five or more persons, carrying of fire-arms, banners, placards, lathis, spears, swords, sticks and brickbats, shouting of slogans, making speeches, processions and demonstrations and picketing or dharnas.

2. *The Times of India*, on August 17, 2011, published a report, 'City no stranger to section 144 of CrPC' wherein the city referred to Varanasi. The report read:

Many city residents were surprised at Delhi police's 'overboard drive' to highlight the issue of enforcing prohibitory orders under section 144 of CrPC in a specific area to restrict anti-corruption crusader Anna Hazare from beginning his hunger strike at JP Park. The district administration of Varanasi, which is a highly sensitive city, keeps such orders promulgating round the year.

When *Times of India* tried to take stock of the records of the district administration of the last 12 months, it was found that the section 144 enforced in the district on July 16, 2010, continued till September 3, 2010. After it, the prohibitory orders were enforced again from September 4, 2010, to October 30, 2010. Again on November 1, 2010, this order became effective in the district till December 26. On the very next day, the same order was made effective till February 21. The prohibitory orders became effective again on February 22 and continued till April 15. On April 16, the district administration promulgated section 144 and it continued till June 12. The same orders were made effective from June 13 till August 5, and against from August 6 till September 25. In the latest prohibitory orders issued under section 144 by the ADM (city) M P Singh, it was mentioned, "In festivals like Janmashtami, Eid, Vishwakarma Puja, exams at different institutions, programmes by political and religious organisations, anti-social and mischievous elements could cause disturbance. To check the activities of such elements in order to maintain law and order and peace, enforcing prohibitory orders is a must."

As per this order, moving with arms and ammunition, especially at public places, distribution of hand bills to cause disturbance, forcing closure of shops, use of loud speakers, storage of explosives and materials for destruction, gathering of five or more persons at a place, disturbing traffic, operating photocopy machines near any examination centre and some other activities are prohibited.

In case of violation of these orders, action under section 188 of the IPC was prescribed in the order issued by the city ADM. The content in almost all the orders issued for promulgating section 144 in the district remains the same. But this order is mainly followed by those organisations, which hold any sit-in stir or demonstration or those, who execute their plan after seeking permission from the district administration only. However, the orders prohibiting people from carrying arms and ammunition at public places and use of loud speakers are often violated in the city. When some police officials were contacted to know what action has been taken under section 188 in case of violation of the orders issued under section 144, no cop was able to give a proper reply. The senior officials surely mentioned that initiating action under section 151 (breech of peace) was more convenient for the police in case of such violations due to typical technicalities of section 188.

3. *Frontier India News Network* on January 3, 2013 published a report with the headline, 'Section 144 at India Gate during anti-rape protests invoked without proper procedures: Delhi High Court' that read as follows:

In a judgement, the Delhi High Court has pulled up Delhi police for imposing Section 144 CrPC (probationary orders) during the protests against the government's inability to provide sufficient security in wake of the Delhi Gang Rape incident. The police had brutally beaten up peaceful protesters including women. While P. Chidambaram, the Congress Member of Parliament had justified Section 144 as routine in a August 2012 Parliament debate when the nation stood up with Gandhian Anna Hazare for his arrest under the section, the Delhi HC said that the legal provisions of Section 144 of CrPC may lose their sanctity if invoked without procedures.

The rights of movement and speech and expression cannot be invoked, observed bench consisting of Chief Justice D. Murugesan and Justice V.K. Jain. The judges were addressing the Public Interest Litigation (PIL) filed by lawyer Anand K. Misra, who alleged that the government imposed section 144 CrPc in an arbitrary manner without proper procedures.

Appearing for Delhi police, Additional Solicitor General Siddharth Luthra opposed the plea saying the guidelines for imposition of prohibitory orders under Section 144 of CrPC (which deals with the power to issue order in urgent cases of nuisance or apprehended danger) cannot be framed as all cases are 'distinguishable' and contain different facts.

Misra contended that the whole capital was already traumatised over the gang-rape and many women had gathered at India Gate to protest over the insufficient security measures by the government, but imposition of prohibitionary orders arbitrarily was wrong and illegal.

4. *The Economic Times*, on January 6, 2013 published a report, 'Dissecting Section 144: Have prohibitory orders become a tool used in daily police work?' wherein it stated:

Between December 23 and 31, the Delhi Police issued five orders under section 144 of the Criminal Procedure Code (CrPC), covering the capital's most well-known landmarks: Rashtrapati Bhavan, Parliament House, India Gate, Rajpath as well as the PM's house.

Each one of those orders was the same – all of them prohibited the "holding of any public meeting", the "assembly of five or more persons" as well as the carrying of arms, banners and placards, or the shouting of slogans in these areas. Used to clamp down on protesters, the orders were widely criticised and a public interest litigation against them is currently pending in the Delhi High Court.

Section 144, or the "prohibitory order" as it's otherwise called, has an old and notorious history. Introduced into Indian law through the first ever CrPC in 1861, it was used frequently during the British Raj to clamp down on nationalist protests. But it survived independence and found its way, little changed in basics, into today's criminal code. It not only survived, it thrived.

During the nine days that those five prohibitory orders on "unlawful assembly" were issued, the Delhi Police issued 18 other prohibitory orders under section 144. The content of those orders and others issued in the past few years provides an insight into the kinds of security threats that the capital faces–or the threats that the Delhi Police think the capital faces.

Wide Powers

Much of the debate around section 144 revolves around the idea of "unlawful assembly"—put simply, the banning of any kind of protests whatsoever in areas where section 144 comes into play. But the ambit of section 144 is actually much wider-indeed the letter of the law doesn't even talk about protests or demonstrations (though it does mention "riot").

The law, in fact, kicks in when a local magistrate foresees any danger to life, or a "disturbance of the public tranquillity, or a riot", or even wants to prevent any "obstruction, annoyance or injury to any person lawfully employed". In such cases, he or she can ask anyone to abstain from a certain act, or indeed, to take an action that can ward off that danger. Such orders can be directed to a specific person or even to the public at large.

SECTION 144: What it says and **WHAT IT MEANS**

3 — **Such orders** are issued for two months at a time and powers are supposed to be used in cases of urgency and when a quick response is needed

4 — **The Supreme Court** has ruled that section 144, if used appropriately, is not unconstitutional. Powers are supposed to be used in an emergency

1 — **Usually seen as a law** to ban protests in a certain area, the ambit of section 144 of the Criminal Procedure Code is actually much wider

2 — **First Introduced in 1861,** the law gives powers to a magistrate to order a person to abstain from an act, which could obstruct or cause annoyance or injury to any person "lawfully employed", or pose a "danger to human life, health or safety, or a disturbance of the public tranquillity"

The general nature of section 144 and the wide powers it gives a local magistrate (in Delhi, these powers are conferred on the police), have made it a target of sharp criticism for well over a century. It was used to clamp down on pretty much every nationalist agitation, including some of the most famous ones, such as that against the salt tax, and issued against Jawarharlal Nehru, Mahatma Gandhi and Madan Mohan Malaviya, to name just a few.

Post-independence-era governments adapted it smoothly to their needs – it was served on everyone from Ram Manohar Lohia to V.P. Singh to Baba Ramdev and justified by all governments, from Congress to communist, often comprised of the very same politicians, who were targeted by such orders during the colonial era.

Given the wide use of section 144, it is little surprise that the Supreme Court has been often asked to rule it unconstitutional – the court instead upheld it in 1970, but laid down standards for its use. "The gist of action under section 144 is the urgency of the situation, its efficacy in the likelihood of being able to prevent some harmful occurrences. As it is possible to act absolutely and even *ex parte* it is obvious that the emergency must be sudden and the consequences sufficiently grave," a constitutional bench said.

As recently as last year, in a case involving the imposition of section 144 on agitations headed by Baba Ramdev at Delhi's Ramlila Maidan, a Supreme Court bench said: "It must be borne in mind that the provisions of section 144 CrPC are attracted only in emergent situations. in case of a mere apprehension, without any material facts to indicate that the apprehension is imminent and genuine, it may not be proper for the authorities to place such a restriction upon the rights of the citizen."

So how have the Delhi Police used their powers under section 144? Have they used them only in "emergent situations"?

From Liquor Shops to BPOs

To answer that question, *ET Magazine* compiled a list of the prohibitory orders issued by the Delhi Police under section 144 between 2008 and 2012. Prohibitory orders are published in the daily bulletins issued by the police and available on their official website. However, it's not clear whether the bulletins carry copies of all such orders passed in the National Capital Region, and include copies of those orders, which may be issued to specific individuals, rather than the public at large. So our list is not necessarily complete.

But even if our list is partial, it throws up several interesting findings. First, the big numbers. A total of 1,317 orders under section 144 were issued between May 2008 and December 2012. While in 2009, the number of orders issued was 145, it progressively increased to 535 in 2012. However, due to administrative changes in the kinds of officers empowered to issue such orders, the data before 2011 (in terms of the number of orders) are not comparable

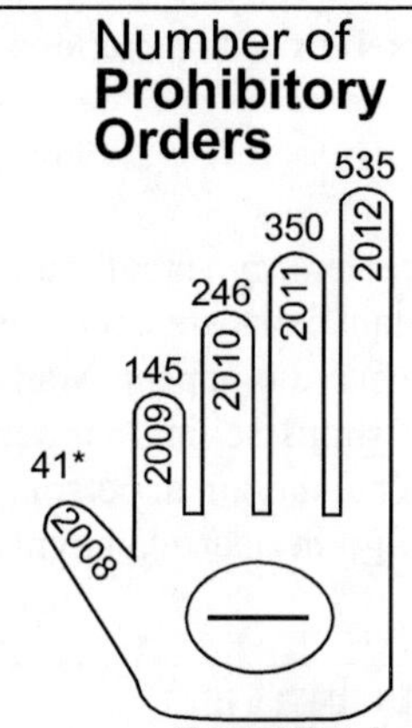

Grand Total
1,317
Source: Delhi Police Bulletins

*Note: Data for 2008 only between May and December Data before 2011 not Comparable with later years

with later years. But even between 2011 and 2012, the number of prohibitory orders rose by 52 per cent.

Of the 885 orders issued in 2011 and 2012, only about five per cent or so concern themselves with the issue of unlawful assembly as was the case with the orders imposed at India Gate during the recent protests. Another six per cent or so don't ban protests outright but, interestingly, ban the carrying of live fire in any form – flame torches and candles, for instance, during protests or demonstrations.

But the largest number of prohibitory orders don't concern themselves with protests at all, but with imposing regulations upon certain categories of the population – 15 per cent of the orders in 2011 and 2012, for instance (the largest number), is imposed on liquor shops and vends requiring them to install CCTV cameras to cover the area just outside the shop. The aim? To crack down on people, who drink in public outside the liquor vend itself. Managers of the vends are also required to inform the police if they witness any public drinking outside the shop.

Each of these orders is issued separately in specific areas of the city under the jurisdiction of an Assistant Commissioner of Police (ACP). Since these orders cannot be issued for more than two months, the ACP in question often reissues the same order afresh as soon as the two-month validity of the previous order comes to an end.

In the subdivision of Rohini in Delhi, for example, an order covering liquor vends was issued on March 2012, ran till May and was subsequently reissued to run till July, and then renewed successively till September and November 2012, and then till January this year. Multiply that pattern across all such subdivisions in Delhi, and the number of prohibitory orders mounts very quickly.

The next biggest category of orders was imposed on BPOs and companies in general, requiring them to take steps to ensure the safety of women employees, who travel back from work late at night – the orders require keeping a database of drivers, ensuring that women do not travel on their own at night and are escorted by male colleagues or a guard to their front door. A third set of orders was imposed on landlords, requiring them to register details of tenants with the police (and requiring tenants to register themselves with the cops as well).

Riotous Situations

Prohibitory orders were imposed on second-hand car dealers, cyber cafes and private courier companies too – requiring them to maintain exhaustive records of their customers, including keeping copies of identification papers. Many prohibitory orders ban *paan* and cigarette shops and shops selling aerated water from staying open beyond 1 am, since they "attract gathering of persons, who cause annoyance to the neighbourhood and indulge in quarrels having the potential of escalation into riotous situations".

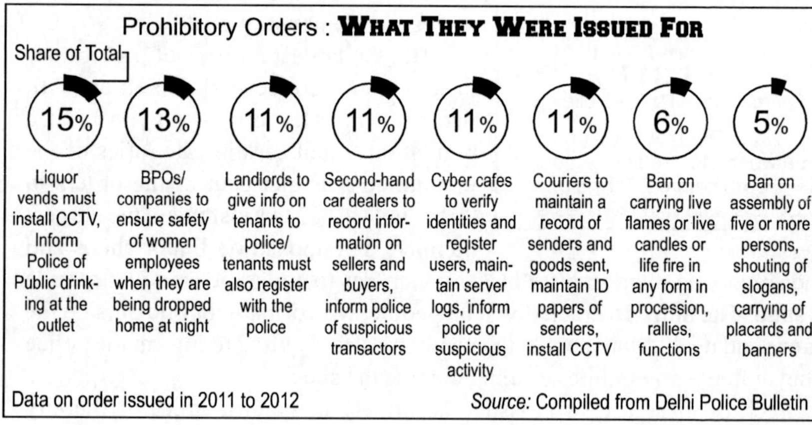

Prohibitory orders issued during the kite-flying season ban the sale of certain types of kite string or "manja" coated with metallic dust, which conduct electricity and which, if they get entangled in power lines, can result in those lines going down, or the electrocution of the kite flyer.

What the data makes clear is that far from being a power to be used only in an emergency, the prohibitory order has, to an extent, become a tool used in daily police work. Far from being a rarity, they are, in fact, issued in the hundreds every year (more than one a day in 2012), and barely register in the public consciousness—until of course they do.

5. *The Hindu*, on March 31, 2013 published a report, 'Police asked to explain rationale behind imposing prohibitory orders'. The report read:

A court in New Delhi on Saturday directed the Delhi Police to furnish all information on what necessitated imposition of prohibitory orders in a case in which Arvind Kejriwal and his supporters were charge-sheeted for allegedly rioting in Central Delhi on August 26 last year during protests against "corruption" in coal block allocation.

While ordering further investigation in the case, Metropolitan Magistrate Jay Thareja said that in the recent past, the Supreme Court and the Delhi High Court had been critical of misuse of power by the Delhi Police under Section 144 of the Criminal Procedure Code, which forbids unlawful assembly.

In its judgement in the Ramlila Maidan midnight crackdown incident involving Baba Ramdev's supporters, the Supreme Court had said that Section 144 must be invoked only in emergency situations having grave consequences. In a May 2011 order, the Delhi High Court had criticised the Delhi Police for "passing of repetitive orders" under Section 144 and had disposed of the writ petition after the police submitted in an affidavit that the "repeated use of power under Section 144 CrPC has been discontinued in the New Delhi district." Mr. Thareja said that the views expressed by the Supreme Court and the Delhi High Court made it imperative for the State to explain the circumstances under which ACP Bhoop Singh passed the order imposing Section 144 CrPC on August 6, 2012, and to disclose if this was part of a series of repetitive orders. The Court also asked the Investigating Officer to ascertain the circumstances and the reports ACP Bhoop Singh reviewed, which necessitated passing of the August 6 order.

While the prosecution had argued that at the stage of framing of charge, it was sufficient for the Court to be satisfied that ACP Bhoop Singh's order was present on the Court record, defence counsel Somnath Bharti argued that it was unfair that the State was withholding the information on the basis of which Mr. Singh passed the order.

Advocate Prashant Bhushan, an accused in the case, had argued that keeping Section 144 CrPC imposed over Central Delhi for a long period was a violation of the citizens' fundamental right to protest in a democracy.

Further, the Delhi Police were asked to submit video-graphic evidence they had in their possession and also obtain video footage available with TV news channel reporters, who had covered the protests. The defence had argued that this would help the Court establish *prima facie* the veracity of the charges that the Delhi Police wanted framed on the accused.

In his order, Mr. Thareja said that the facts stated in the police charge-sheet "encapsulate an interesting interplay between the duty of the State to maintain law and order and the right of the citizens to move freely within the territory of India and their rights to express themselves by protesting against the Government".

6. *The Times of India*, on October 15, 2013 published, 'Section 144 clamped at meat complex', which was a report from Ponda, Goa. The report read:

Anticipating communal tension and breach of public peace and tranquillity over the slaughtering of animals during the Eid festival on October 16 at Goa meat complex, Mharvasaddo-Usgao, the Ponda sub-divisional magistrate (SDM) has imposed Section 144 of Criminal Procedure Code (CrPC) from Monday midnight.

Section 144 will be in force in and around the GMC compound wall and within a radius of one km from the same, for a period of seven days until the midnight of October 22. Any person contravening this order shall be punishable under Section 188 of the Indian Penal Code, the order warns. Ponda sub-divisional magistrate (SDM) Johnson Fernandes has issued the order late Monday afternoon following demonstrations against slaughtering from some non-governmental organizations (NGOs) near the meat complex.

Some animal lovers, along with members of various non-governmental organizations, sat below a tree on the roadside at a distance of 30 mts from the side gate of the meat complex on Monday afternoon and demonstrated by reciting bhajans with the help of a tambora, tal, mridang, etc. and by displaying some anti-slaughter banners on the tree. The order also states that a report from Ponda police inspector reveals that large number of animals are being slaughtered at the meat complex's abattoir during Eid.

The slaughtering is being monitored by the high court of Bombay at Panaji, and in furtherance to the directives issued by the court, a committee has been constituted to monitor the entry of cattle brought for the slaughtering, the SDM has noted.

Section 196: Prosecution for offences against the State and for criminal conspiracy to commit such offence:

(1) No Court shall take cognizance of:
  (a) any offence punishable under Chapter VI or under section 153A, of Indian Penal Code, or Section 295 A or sub section (1) of section 505 of the Indian Penal Code (45 of 1860) or
  (b) a criminal conspiracy to commit such offence, or
  (c) any such abetment, as is described in section 108A of the Indian Penal Code, except with the previous sanction of the Central Government or of the State Government.

(1A) No Court shall take cognizance of:
  (a) any offence punishable under section 153B or sub-section (2) or sub-section (3) of section 505 of the Indian Penal Code (45 of 1860), or
  (b) a criminal conspiracy to commit such offence, except with the previous sanction of the Central Government or of the State Government or of the District Magistrate.

(2) No Court shall take cognizance of the offence of any criminal

conspiracy punishable under section 120B of the Indian Penal code, other than a criminal conspiracy to commit an offence punishable with death, imprisonment for life or rigorous imprisonment for a term of two years or upwards, unless the State Government or the District Magistrate has consented in writing to the initiation of the proceedings: Provided that where the criminal conspiracy is one to which the provisions of section 195 apply, no such consent shall be necessary.

(3) The Central Government or the State Government may, before according sanction under sub-section (1) or sub-section (1A) and the District Magistrate may, before according sanction under sub-section (1A) and the State Government or the District Magistrate may, before giving consent under sub-section (2), order a preliminary investigation by a police officer not being below the rank of Inspector, in which case such police officer shall have the powers referred to in sub-section (3) of section 155.

Section 327: Court to be open

(1) The place in which any Criminal Court is held for the purpose of inquiring into or trying any offence shall be deemed to be an open Court, to which the public generally may have access, so far as the same can conveniently contain them:

Provided that the presiding Judge or Magistrate may, if he thinks fit, order at any stage of any inquiry into, or trial of, any particular case, that the public generally, or any particular person, shall not have access to, or be or remain in the room or building used by the Court.

(2) Notwithstanding anything contained in sub-section (1), the inquiry into and trial of rape or an offence under section 376, section 376A, section 376B, section 376C or section 376D of the Indian Penal Code shall be conducted in camera:

Provided that the presiding judge may, if he thinks fit, or on an application made by either of the parties, allow any particular person to have access to, or be or remain in, the room or building used by the court.

(3) Where any proceedings are held under sub-section (2), it shall not be lawful for any person to print or publish any matter in relation to any such proceedings, except with the previous permission of the court.

15

Intellectual Property Rights

The Intellectual Property (IP) is the creation of human intellect. It refers to the ideas, knowledge, invention, innovation, creativity, research, etc. all being the product of human mind and are similar to any property, whether movable or immovable, wherein the proprietor or the owner may exclusively use his property at will and has the right to prevent others from using it without his permission. The rights related to intellectual property are known as 'Intellectual Property Rights' (IRP).

Intellectual Property Rights, by providing exclusive rights to the inventor or creator, encourages more and more people to invest time, efforts and money in such innovations and creations.

The protection of intellectual property rights in India until recent times was at a very nascent stage. After the signing of certain conventions and international treaties, IPR protection has gradually been strengthened. There is now a well-established statutory, administrative and judicial framework to safeguard IPRs, whether they relate to patents, trademarks, copyright or industrial designs. Thus, the importance of IP in India is well established at all levels – statutory, administrative and judicial. India ratified the agreement establishing the World Trade Organisation (WTO). This agreement, inter alia, contains an agreement on Trade Related Aspects of Intellectual Property Rights (TRIPS), which came into force from 1 January 1995. It lays down minimum standards for protection and enforcement of IP rights in the member countries, which are required to promote effective and adequate protection of the IP rights with a view to reduce distortion and impediments to international trade. The obligation under the TRIPS Agreement relate to provisions of minimum standard of protection within the legal systems and practices of the member countries.

The Agreement provides for norms and standards in respect of the following areas of IP:

- Copyright
- Trade Marks
- Geographical Indications
- Industrial Designs
- Layout of designs of integrated circuits
- Protection of undisclosed information (Trade secrets)
- Patent
- Plant varieties

Intellectual Property

It is the creative ideas and expressions of human mind or intellect possessing commercial value. It can be tangible or intangible.

The WIPO (World Intellectual Property Organisation) 1967, one of the specialized agencies of UN provided that IP rights shall include rights related to:

- Literary, artistic and scientific work;
- Performance of performing artists, programmes and broadcast;
- Invention in all fields of human endeavour;
- Scientific discoveries;
- Industrial designs;
- Trade Marks, Service Marks and Commercial names and designations;
- Protection against unfair competition and all other rights resulting from intellectual activity in the industrial, scientific, literary or artistic fields.

The Intellectual Property Rights laws in India include five broad categories: Trademarks, Copyrights, Patents, Industrial Designs and Geographical Indications.

India provides protection to IPR in accordance with its obligations under the TRIPS Agreement of the WTO, as adopted in the respective legislations.

India is also a signatory to a number of Conventions and, hence, the protection under IPR matches the international system at certain level. Conventions are named hereunder:

- Berne Convention, 1971
- Universal Copyright Convention, 1979
- Vienna Classification, 1973
- Paris Convention for the Protection of Industrial Property, 1979
- Geneva Convention for the Protection of Rights of Producers of Phonograms, 1971

Other than the civil remedies and compensation, the Police and enforcement authorities are also empowered to take action against infringement of IPRs.

Petitions are filed for infringement of IPRs and are tried in the judicial courts like other suits.

Appeals are also filed in the judicial courts against the administrative decisions relating to IPR.

Significance of Intellectual Property Rights

IP rights give the inventors/authors the exclusive right and monopoly over the invention/technology developed and also the right to exclude others from exploiting the same from commercial use. The purpose of safeguarding IP rights is to make money out of new ideas created. It provides better relation or invention over Research and Development (R&D). Once the IP rights are granted, the owner can exploit it commercially by utilising it himself, assigning it to someone else, licensing it to others to utilize it or can sell it outright.

Indian Laws on Intellectual Property Rights

1. Copyright: The Copyright Act in India was enacted in the year 1957. It has been amended five times since then, once each in the years 1982, 1984, 1992, 1994 and 1999. Though the amendment in the year 1994 was quite comprehensive, only minor changes were introduced through the amendment made in the year 1999 to bring the Act in conformity with the TRIPS Agreement.

Prior to the Act of 1957, the Law of Copyrights in the country was governed by the Copyright Act of 1914. This Act was essentially the extension of the British Copyright Act, 1911 to India.

The copy right ensures that computer programmes will be protected as literary works under the Berne Convention and outlines how databases should be protected. It also expands international copyright rules to cover rental rights. Authors of computer programmes and procedures of sound recordings must have the right to prohibit the commercial rental of their works to the public. A similar exclusive right applies to films where commercial rental has led to widespread copyright infringement, affecting copyright-owners' potential earnings from their films. The performers must also have the right to prevent unauthorized recording, reproduction and broadcast of live performances for not less than 50 years. Producers of sound recordings must have the right to prevent the unauthorized reproduction of recordings for a period of 50 years.

India's copyright law, laid down in the Indian Copyright Act, 1957 as amended by Copyright (Amendment) Act, 1999, fully reflects the Berne Convention on Copyrights, to which India is a party.

Additionally, India is party to the Geneva Convention for the Protection of rights of Producers of Phonograms and to the Universal Copyright Convention. India is also an active member of the World Intellectual Property Organization (WIPO), Geneva and UNESCO.

The copyright law has been amended periodically to keep pace with changing requirements. The recent amendment to the copyright law, which came into force in May 1995, has ushered in comprehensive changes and brought the copyright law in line with the developments in satellite broadcasting, computer software and digital technology. The amended law has made provisions for the first time, to protect performer's rights as envisaged in the Rome Convention.

Several measures have been adopted to strengthen and streamline the enforcement of copyrights. These include the setting up of a Copyright Enforcement Advisory Council, training programmes for enforcement officers and setting up of special policy cells to deal with cases relating to infringement of copyrights.

2. Trade Marks: Trade mark means a mark or a symbol being represented graphically, which is capable of distinguishing the goods or services of one person from the others and can include shape of goods, their packaging, colours, etc.

Such distinguishing marks constitute protectable subject matter under the provisions of the TRIPS Agreement. The Agreement provides that initial registration and each renewal of registration shall be for a term of not less than seven years and the registration shall be renewable indefinitely. Compulsory licensing of trade marks is not permitted.

Unregistered trademarks can be protected through common law remedy of "passing off" only and infringement actions are not possible. Hence, to get maximum protection for any trade, it is necessary to register their trade name and marks.

Keeping in view the changes in trade and commercial practices, globalisation of trade, need for simplification and harmonisation of trademark registration systems, etc., a comprehensive review of the Trade and Merchandise Marks Act, 1958 was made and a Bill to repeal and replace the 1958 Act has since been passed by the Parliament and notified in the Gazette on 30.12.1999. This Act not only makes Trade Marks Law, TRIPS compatibility, but also harmonises it with international systems and practices. Work is underway to bring the law into force.

In India, the Trademarks related laws fall under two legal provisions:

- The Trade Marks Act, 1999
- The Trade Marks Rules, 2002

The Trade Marks Act, 1999: The Trade and Merchandise Marks Act was passed in the year 1958 and has served its purpose over the last four decades. It was felt that a comprehensive review of the existing law be made in view of the developments in trading and commercial practices.

Accordingly, the Trade Marks Bill, 1999 was introduced in the Parliament. The Trade Marks Act, 1999 is more compliant with the TRIPS Agreement. Major change has taken place in The Trade Marks Act, 1999, which has come into force from 15 September 2003. It includes the following:

- It has enlarged the definition of trade mark. It now includes shape of goods, packaging and combination of colours, which can be adopted as a trade mark;
- The Act provides for registration of trade mark for services in addition to goods;
- It provides for a single Register of Trade Marks with simplified procedures for registration;
- The Act has simplified the procedure for registration of registered user (licensing of registered trade mark);
- Provides for registration of collective marks owned by association of persons;
- Provides for establishment of an Intellectual Property Appellate Board for speedy disposal of appeal from Registrar orders and decision, which earlier lie before the High Courts;
- Transferred the final authority for registration of certification of trade marks to the Registrar;
- Provides for enhanced punishment for the offences relating to trade marks on par with the Copyright Act, 1957 to prevent the sale of spurious goods;
- Prohibits the use of someone else's trade marks as part of corporate names or name of business concern;
- Provides for filing of a single application for goods or services falling in more than one class (multi class filing);
- Increased the period of registration and renewal from seven years to ten years;
- Has made some trade mark offences cognizable;
- The Act has amplified the powers of the court to grant *ex parte* injunction in certain cases;
- There are other related amendments to simplify and streamline the administration of the trade marks law and procedures in the country;
- The 1999 Act makes the service marks also registrable;
- The Act provides that the Registrar shall classify goods and services

in accordance with their international classification for registration of trade marks.

The Trade Marks Rules, 2002: The Central Government being empowered by section 157 of the Trade Marks Act, 1999, made Trade Marks (Application and Appeals to the Intellectual Property Appellate Board) Rules, 2003 with effect from 5 December 2003. The procedure for applications, forms of appeals to the Intellectual Properties Appellate Board and the procedure of verification of such applications were made as provision in the First Schedule to this Rule.

3. Patent: A patent is a legal monopoly, which is granted for a limited time by a country to the owner of an invention. Merely holding a patent does not give the owner the right to use or exploit the patented invention. That right may still be affected by other laws, such as health and safety regulations, food and drugs regulations or even by other patents. A patent, in the eyes of the law, is a property right that can be given away, inherited, sold, licensed and even abandoned. As it is conferred by the government, the government can, in certain cases, revoke the patent (even after the grant of patent or even if it has been sold or licensed to another in the meantime).

A Patent gives an inventor the right for a limited period of time to stop others from making, using, selling or importing the patented invention without the permission of the inventor. That is why a patent is called a "negative right".

Patents are generally concerned with functional and technical aspects of products and processes and must fulfil specific conditions to be granted.

Most patents are for incremental improvements in known technology – evolution rather than revolution. The technology does not have to be complex. Patent rights are territorial; an Indian patent does not confer any rights outside India. Patent rights last for 20 years in India and also in most countries outside India. Depending on where you wish your patent to be in effect, you must apply to the appropriate body. In India, it is The Indian Patent Office.

The registration and protection of Patents in India is governed by Patents Act, 1970 (Patents Act), which has been amended from time to time. The Indian Patent Act, 1970 repeals the Indian Patent and Designs Act, 1911.

The Act confers on the Patentee or its authorized agent/licensee the exclusive right for commercial exploitation of his patent in consideration of the disclosure of its invention.

The patent rights are granted only to new inventions, which are capable of industrial application. Patent is the statutory right, which accrues to the inventor on registration of his invention with the Patent office.

A comprehensive review of the Patents Act, 1970 was also made and a bill to amend the Patents Act, 1970 was introduced in the Parliament on 20

December, 1999 and notified on 25-6-2002 to make the patent law TRIPS compatible. Now, it provides for establishment of a mail box system to file patents and accords exclusive marketing rights for five years after being compatible with TRIPS Agreement.

Patenting an intellectual property in India is governed by three parameters:

- Inventive step/Non-obvious
- Novelty
- Utility/Usefulness

A patent is granted for the following:

- A new and utility-bearing article/product, produced by a manufacturer;
- A new process of manufacture to make an article/product, already in existence;
- A machine, apparatus or other article;
- For secondary innovations, such as improvements on existing products or processes.

The Patent (Amendment) Act, 2002 substituted these provisions and defines 'patent' as patent granted under the Act. Also, The Patent Rules, 2003 provides for the application for patents. The Indian Patents Act, 1970 and the Patent Rules, 2003 regulate the grant, the operative period, the revocation and infringement of the patents.

After the commencement of the Patents (Amendment) Act, 2002, the term of patent or the term of every patent, which is not expired and has not ceased to have effect, shall be twenty years from the date of filing of the application for the patent. The explanation added by the Patents (Amendment) Act, 2005 states that the term of patent in case of international applications files under the Patent Co-operation Treaty designating India, shall be twenty years from the international filing date accorded under the Treaty.

4. Geographical Indications: The Geographical Indications Act affords protection to goods that can be identified as originating or manufactured in the territory of a country, or a region or locality in that territory where a given quality, reputation or other characteristic of such goods is essentially attributable to its geographical conditions. In the case where such goods are manufactured goods, one of the activities of production, processing or preparation of the goods concerned takes place in such territory or locality as the case may be. The term is initially for a period of ten years and can be renewed from time to time.

Until recently, India did not have a specific law governing Geographical Indications of goods, which could adequately protect the interests of producers of such goods. Unless a Geographical Indication is protected in the country of its origin, there is no obligation under the Agreement on TRIPS for other countries to extend reciprocal protection.

The TRIPS Agreement contains a general obligation that parties shall provide the legal means for interested parties to prevent the use of any means in the designation or presentation of a good that indicates or suggests that the good in question originates in a geographical area other than the true place of origin in a manner that misleads the public as to the geographical origin of the good.

In view of this, it was considered necessary to have a comprehensive legislation for the registration and for providing adequate protection for Geographical Indications. Thus, the government enacted a pertinent legislation, namely, the Geographical Indications of Goods (Registration and Protection) Act, 1999. This Act seeks to provide for the registration and better protection of geographical indications relating to goods in India. The Act would be administered by the Controller General of Patents, Designs and Trade Marks, who is the Registrar of Geographical Indications. The Geographical Indications Registry would be located at Chennai.

The legislation is administered through the Geographical Indications Registry under the overall charge of the Controller General of Patents, Designs and Trademarks. Appeal against the Registrar's decision would be to the Intellectual Property Appellate Board established under the Trade Marks legislation. This Act, along with the Geographical Indications of Goods (Registration and Protection) Rules, 2002 came into force on September 15, 2003.

Object of the Geographical Indications of Goods (Registration and Protection) Act, 1999 is to provide for the registration and better protection of geographical indications related to goods in India. It is an indication of goods originating from a definite geographical territory. It is used to identify agricultural, natural or manufactured goods; the manufactured goods should be produced or processed or prepared in that territory and have a special quality or reputation.

The primary purpose of this Act is to provide legal protection to Indian Geographical Indications, which in turn boost exports. Registration of Geographical Indication promotes economic prosperity of producers of goods produced in a geographical territory. Examples of geographical indications are Gir Kesar Mango, Bhalia wheat, Kinhal Toys, Nashik Valley wine, Monsoon Malabar Arabica Coffee, Malabar Pepper, Alleppy Green Cardamom and Nilgiris Orthodox Tea. Other examples include Darjeeling Tea, Mysore Silk, Paithani Sarees, Kota Masuria, Kolhapuri Chappals, Bikaneri Bhujia and Agra Petha.

Each of the aforesaid commodities, which have been granted the status of Geographical Indication, possesses distinct features related to their respective territories. For example, Monsoon Malabar coffee has a yellowish tinge due to its exposure to the sea winds for nearly six months in a year. Malabar pepper is grown exclusively in Thalassery and other northern parts of Kerala. Its corns are larger than the typical black pepper corns with a dark brown colour. It is very aromatic and pungent, and the most complex, balanced and elegant of peppers. The Alleppey green cardamom is the traditional grade that is internationally accepted. The size, colour and chemical constituents of this grade of cardamom, with high oil content, sets it apart. The identity of this brand is interwoven with the geographical name Alleppey, a coastal district in Kerala. Nilgiris tea has an exquisite flavour and aroma, accompanied by a creamy mouth feel. These qualities are due to the high elevation of the Nilgiris coupled with its cold, dry and misty weather.

The Act is also significant because the TRIPS Agreement provides that if the Geographical Indication is not protected in its Country of Origin, then it will not be protected in the International arena.

The registration of an authorized user is valid for a period of ten years and, thereafter, it can be renewed for a further period of another ten years. If there is a lapse in renewing the registration, it will be removed from the Register.

The Registration of Geographical Indications is not compulsory, but it affords better legal protection to facilitate an action for infringement.

The Act prohibits licensing, transmission assignment or pledge in respect of any Geographical Indication.

An action for infringement as well as passing off can be brought under the act. Infringement includes unfair competition. A varied number of reliefs, such as Injunction, Discovery of documents delivery up is available.

Geographical Indications of Goods (Registration and Protection) Rules, 2002 provide for the principal place of business in India as the place where the business in the goods bearing a Geographical Indication, is carried on at one place, then that particular place.

Significance of Geographical Indication Registration: Such identification enables the product to gain a reputation and goodwill all over the world, consequently resulting in premium prices in national and international markets.

Geographical Indications of goods are defined as that aspect of industrial property, which adverts the Geographical Indication referring to a country or to a place, situated there as being the country or place or origin of that product. The given product should have a specific geographical origin and posse's qualities or a reputation due to that place of origin. A place name is sometimes used to identify a product. This Geographical Indication not only refers to where the product was made, but more importantly, it identifies the product's special characteristics, which are the result of the products origin. Using the place name, when the product was made elsewhere or when it does not have the usual characteristics, can mislead consumers, and it can lead to unfair competition.

Recognition of a particular commodity as a Geographical Indication also confers the right to protection under the Geographical Indication Act, 1999, thereby preventing unauthorised use of the commodity registered as Geographical Indication by any third party.

Geographical Indication registration encourages community ownership and, therefore, it helps in proper distribution of the economic benefits accrued from commercialisation of the commodity across a wider section of people in that territory.

5. Industrial Designs: Industrial designs refer to creative activity, which results in the ornamental or formal appearance of a product and design right refers to a novel or original design that is accorded to the proprietor of a validly registered design. Industrial designs are an element of intellectual property. Under the TRIPS Agreement, minimum standards of protection of industrial designs have been provided for. As a developing country, India has already amended its national legislation to provide for these minimal standards.

The essential purpose of design law is to promote and protect the design element of industrial production. It is also intended to promote innovative activity in the field of industries. The existing legislation on industrial designs in India is contained in the New Designs Act, 2000 and this Act serves its purpose well in the rapid changes in technology and international developments. India has also achieved a mature status in the field of industrial designs and in view of globalization of the economy, the present legislation is aligned with the changed technical and commercial scenario and made to conform to international trends in design administration.

This replacement Act is also aimed to enact a more detailed classification of design to conform to the international system and to take care of the proliferation of design related activities in various fields.

Industrial design is applied to a wide variety of products of industry or handicraft; from watches, jewellery, fashion and other luxury items to industrial and medical implements; from house ware, furniture and electrical appliances to vehicles and architectural structures, from practical goods and textile designs to leisure items, such as toys and pet accessories.

The Designs Act, 2000, after repealing the Act of 1911 aims at protecting the designs, which serve the purpose of visual appeal.

In 1911, the Designs Act was passed by the then British Government in India, since then extensive amendments have been made in the Designs Act. In the meanwhile, India has made tremendous progress in the field of science and technology. There has been considerable increase in the registration of designs.

To provide more effective protection to registered designs and to promote design activity in order to promote design element in an article of production, it has become necessary to make the legal system of providing protection to industrial designs more efficient.

It is also intended to ensure that the law does not unnecessarily extend protection beyond what is necessary to create the required incentive for design activity, while removing impediments to the free use of available designs. To achieve these objectives and in order to repeal the Designs Act, 1911, which has been extensively amended, the Designs Bill, 1999 was introduced in the Parliament.

Since the enactment of the Designs Act, 1911, considerable progress has been made in the field of science and technology. The legal system of the protection of industrial designs requires to be made more efficient in order to ensure effective protection to registered designs. It is also required to promote design activity in order to promote design element in an article of production.

The Design Act, 2000, lays down 31 classes plus miscellaneous class 99 of goods to which ornamental designs, etc. and which are capable of being registered under this Act generally apply.

The industrial design and product design are covered by the Designs Act, 2000, if a design has been registered under this Act, it cannot be protected by the Copyright Act even though it may be an original artistic work.

The Act provides a right to the owner of the registered industrial design to prevent third parties not having his consent from making, selling or importing articles being or embodying a design, which is a copy or substantially a copy of the protected design, when such acts are undertaken for commercial purposes. The duration of the protection is ten years.

6. Protection of Integrated Circuit layout design: The Semiconductor Integrated Circuits Layout Design Act, 2000 provides protection to semiconductor integrated circuits layout designs in accordance with the provisions of the TRIPS Agreement.

The Act provides for exclusive rights to the registered proprietor of a layout design and also to the registered users. Applications for registration of layout designs should be filed with the Registrar. Appeals against the orders of the Registrar should be filed with the Appellate Board. The Act also provides for criminal prosecution for infringement of layout designs. The administration department for the implementation of the Act is the Department of information Technology, Ministry of Communications and Information Technology, Government of India.

7. Trade Secrets: WTO provisions require member countries to protect trade secrets. The WTO obligation requires that suitable legislations are in place, which enables persons to prevent information lawfully within the control from being disclosed to, acquired by or used by others without their consent in a manner contrary to honest commercial practices. In India, these matters are dealt under Contracts Act, Law of Torts and Special Relief Act.

Ethics of IPR

The ethical issues of IP rights are indeed an obstacle when socially valuable life saving drugs and other things beneficial to the developing countries are given Intellectual Property rights.

It is important here to remember that the poor currently face two problems when it comes to accessing life-saving drugs. First, due to monopoly pricing powers granted to innovators for considerable lengths of time, they cannot afford medicines that are still under patent protection. One can, therefore, speak of an accessibility problem (i.e. medicines are priced beyond the reach of the poor). However, patent protection is not the only problem endangering poor people's health in the context of pharmaceutical innovation. Given that the pharmaceutical industry operates almost exclusively within the profit-making sector, diseases that burden the poor are often not investigated in the first place. These diseases are referred to as 'neglected diseases', since they are often ignored by the international research community. Hence, the second hindrance could be termed as an availability problem (i.e. drugs are not being developed according to the needs of the poor).

16

Copyright Act, 1957

Vir Bala Aggarwal and V.S. Gupta in the 'Handbook of Journalism and Mass Communication' write that Copyright provides the author with protection against unfair appropriation of his or her work. Although its roots go back to the former Copyright Act of 1914, the present Act was passed by the Indian Parliament and received the assent of the President in June 1957.

Copyright is the right, which a person acquires in a work, which is the result of his intellectual work or labour. The primary function of the law of Copyright is to protect from annexation by other people of the fruit of a man's work, labour, skill or test.

The owner has the right to license (permit) to use his work with or without payment. He has the right to transfer, to sell, to counteract, to bequest (depending on the will), to inherit, to assign to any person. Copyright regarding unpublished work will become effective only when the work is actually published.

The first owner has the right to relinquish or disclaim the Copyright. Here is no provision in the government publications. Hence, journalists make full use of such publications in their articles.

Scope

1. It is an Act to amend and consolidate the law related to Copyright. Though, historically, it sprang out of the English law, where the object and the language used by the present Act is different from those of the English statute, the interpretation should be made according to the provisions and the language of the present Act and not according to the English law.
2. Where, however, the Indian Act is silent or does not lay down any specific provision contrary to the English discussions, the principles underlying the latter may be looked at for guidance in applying or interpreting the Indian Act.

Salient Features of the Act

Section 9: There shall be established for the purposes of this Act an office to be called the Copyright Office, which shall be under the immediate control of the Registrar of Copyrights, who shall act under the superintendence and direction of the Central Government.

Section 10: The Central Government shall appoint a Registrar of Copyrights and may appoint one or more Deputy Registrars of Copyrights. A Deputy Registrar of Copyrights shall discharge under the superintendence and direction of the Registrar of Copyrights such functions of the Registrar under this Act as the Registrar may, from time to time, assign to him; and any reference in this Act to the Registrar of Copyrights shall include a reference to a Deputy Registrar of Copyrights when so discharging any such functions.

Section 11: As soon as, may be after the commencement of this Act, the Central Government shall constitute a Board to be called the Copyright Board, which shall consist of a Chairman and not less than two or more than fourteen other members.

The Chairman of the Copyright Board shall be a person who is, or has been, a Judge of a High Court or is qualified for appointment as a Judge of a High Court.

Section 12: This section states the powers and procedure of Copyright Board. The Copyright Board shall, subject to any rules that may be made under this Act, have power to regulate its own procedure, including the fixing of places and times of its sittings.

Section 13: Subject to the provisions of this section and other provisions of this Act, copyright shall subsist throughout India in the following classes of works, that is, original literary, dramatic, musical and artistic works; cinematograph films; and sound recordings.

Section 14: This section states the meaning of copyright. For the purposes of this Act, "copyright" means the exclusive right subject to the provisions of this Act, to do or authorise the doing of any of the following acts in respect of a work or any substantial part thereof, namely:

(a) in the case of a literary, dramatic or musical work, not being a computer programme:
   (i) to reproduce the work in any material form including the storing of it in any medium by electronic means;
   (ii) to issue copies of the work to the public not being copies already in circulation;
   (iii) to perform the work in public, or communicate it to the public;
   (iv) to make any cinematograph film or sound recording in respect of the work;
   (v) to make any translation of the work;

(vi) to make any adaptation of the work;

(viii) to do, in relation to a translation or an adaptation of the work, any of the acts specified in relation to the work in sub-clauses (i) to (vi).

(b) in the case of a computer programme:

(i) to do any of the acts specified in clause (a);

(ii) to sell or give on commercial rental or offer for sale or for commercial rental any copy of the computer programme.

(c) in the case of an artistic work:

(i) to reproduce the work in any material form including depiction in three dimensions of a two dimensional work or in two dimensions of a three dimensional work;

(ii) to communicate the work to the public;

(iii) to issue copies of the work to the public not being copies already in circulation;

(iv) to include the work in any cinematograph film;

(v) to make any adaptation of the work;

(vi) to do in relation to an adaptation of the work any of the acts specified in relation to the work in sub-clauses (i) to (iv);

(d) In the case of cinematograph film:

(i) to make a copy of the film, including a photograph of any image forming part thereof;

(ii) to sell or give on hire, or offer for sale or hire, any copy of the film, regardless of whether such copy has been sold or given on hire on earlier occasions;

(iii) to communicate the film to the public;

(e) In the case of sound recording,

(i) to make any other sound recording embodying it;

(ii) to sell or give on hire, or offer for sale or hire, any copy of the sound recording regardless of whether such copy has been sold or given on hire on earlier occasions;

(iii) to communicate the sound recording to the public.

Section 17: Subject to the provisions of this Act, the author of a work shall be the first owner of the copyright.

Section 18: The owner of the copyright in an existing work or the prospective owner of the copyright in a future work may assign to any person the copyright either wholly or partially and either generally or subject to limitations and either for the whole term of the copyright or any part thereof.

Section 21: This section states the right of author to relinquish copyright. The author of a work may relinquish all or any of the rights comprised in the copyright in the work by giving notice in the prescribed form to the Registrar of Copyrights and thereupon such rights shall cease to exist from the date of the notice.

On receipt of a notice, the Registrar of Copyrights shall cause it to be published in the Official Gazette and in such other manner as he may deem fit.

Section 22: Copyright shall subsist in any literary, dramatic, musical or artistic work (other than a photograph) published within the lifetime of the author until sixty years from the beginning of the calendar year next following the year in which the author dies.

In short, the Copyright lasts for the life of the author plus another sixty years. Earlier it was for fifty years. Copyright for films is twenty years, while copyright for broadcasting is twenty-five years.

Section 45: The author or publisher of, or the owner of or other person interested in the copyright in, any work may make an application in the prescribed form accompanied by the prescribed fee to the Registrar of Copyrights for entering particulars of the work in the Register of Copyrights. On receipt of an application, the Registrar of Copyrights may, after holding such inquiry as he may deem fit, enter the particulars of the work in the Register of Copyrights.

It is to be noted that registration, under this section is only optional, and the only effect of registration is that the Register of Copyrights provides some *prima facie* evidence of the particulars entered therein.

Section 51: Copyright in a work shall be deemed to be infringed when any person, without a licence granted by the owner of the copyright or the Registrar of Copyrights under this Act or in contravention of the conditions of a licence so granted or of any condition imposed by a competent authority under this Act does anything, the exclusive right to do which is by this Act conferred upon the owner of the copyright, or permits for profit any place to be used for the communication of the work to the public where such communication constitutes an infringement of the copyright in the work, unless he was not aware and had no reasonable ground for believing that such communication to the public would be an infringement of copyright; or when any person makes for sale or hire, or sells or lets for hire, or by way of trade displays or offers for sale or hire, or distributes either for the purpose of trade or to such an extent as to affect prejudicially the owner of the copyright, or by way of trade exhibits in public, or imports into India, any infringing copies of the work.

Section 52: This section states the acts that shall not constitute an infringement of copyright. Some of them are as follows:

(a) a fair dealing with a literary, dramatic, musical or artistic work for the purposes of private use, including research; criticism or review, whether of that work or of any other work;

(b) a fair dealing with a literary, dramatic, musical or artistic work for the purpose of reporting current events in a newspaper, magazine or similar periodical, or by broadcast or in a cinematograph film or by means of photographs.

(c) the reproduction of a literary, dramatic, musical or artistic work for the purpose of a judicial proceeding or for the purpose of a report of a judicial proceeding;

(d) the reproduction or publication of a literary, dramatic, musical or artistic work in any work prepared by the Secretariat of a Legislature or, where the Legislature consists of two Houses, by the Secretariat of either House of the Legislature, exclusively for the use of the members of that Legislature;

(e) the reproduction of any literary, dramatic or musical work in a certified copy made or supplied in accordance with any law for the time being in force;

(f) the reading or recitation in public of any reasonable extract from a published literary or dramatic work;

(g) the publication in a collection, mainly composed of non-copyright matter, bona fide intended for the use of educational institutions;

(h) the reproduction of a literary, dramatic, musical or artistic work by a teacher or a pupil in the course of instruction; or as part of the questions to be answered in an examination; or in answers to such questions;

(i) the performance, in the course of the activities of an educational institution, of a literary, dramatic or musical work by the staff and students of the institution, or of a cinematograph film or a sound recording if the audience is limited to such staff and students, the parents and guardians of the students and persons directly connected with the activities of the institution or the communication to such an audience of a cinematograph film or sound recording;

(j) the making of sound recordings in respect of any literary, dramatic or musical work, if sound recordings of that work have been made by or with the licence or consent of the owner of the right in the work; the person making the sound recordings has given a notice of his intention to make the sound recordings, has provided copies of all covers or labels with which the sound recordings are to be sold, and has paid in the prescribed manner to the owner of rights in the work – royalities in respect of all such sound recordings to be made by him, at the rate fixed by the Copyright Board in this behalf;

(k) the causing of a recording to be heard in public by utilising it in an enclosed room or hall meant for the common use of residents in any residential premises (not being a hotel or similar commercial establishment) as part of the amenities provided exclusively or mainly for residents therein; or as part of the activities of a club or similar organisation, which is not established or conducted for profit; as part of the activities of a club, society or other organisation, which is not established or conducted for profit;

(l) the performance of a literary, dramatic or musical work by an amateur club or society, if the performance is given to a non-paying audience, or for the benefit of a religious institution;

(m) the reproduction in a newspaper, magazine or other periodical of an article on current economic, political, social or religious topics, unless the author of such article has expressly reserved to himself the right of such reproduction;

(n) the publication in a newspaper, magazine or other periodical of a report of a lecture delivered in public;

(o) the making of not more than three copies of a book (including a pamphlet, sheet of music, map, chart or plan) by or under the direction of the person in charge of a public library for the use of the library if such book is not available for sale in India;

(p) the reproduction, for the purpose of research or private study or with a view to publication, of an unpublished literary, dramatic or musical work kept in a library, museum or other institution to which the public has access.

Section 55: This section states the Civil remedies for infringement of copyright.

Where copyright in any work has been infringed, the owner of the copyright shall, except as otherwise provided by this Act, be entitled to all such remedies by way of injunction, damages, accounts and otherwise as are or may be conferred by law for the infringement of a right.

Section 62: This section deals with the jurisdiction of court over matters arising under this Chapter.

Every suit or other civil proceeding arising under this Act in respect of the infringement of copyright in any work or the infringement of any other right conferred by this Act shall be instituted in the district court having jurisdiction.

Section 63: This section states the penalty for the offence of infringement of copyright or other rights conferred by this Act. Any person, who knowingly infringes or abets the infringement of the copyright in a work, or any other right conferred by this Act, shall be punishable with imprisonment for a term, which shall not be less than six months, but which may extend to three years and with fine, which shall not be less than fifty thousand rupees, but which may extend to two lakh rupees.

Conclusion

We can conclude with the words of Peeti Misra, who wrote an article, 'The golden rule of Copying vs. the fair use doctrine' in the book 'The Law of Intellectual Property Rights' edited by Shiv Sahai Singh. She says, "As a general rule, if authors and publishers are using a small portion of somebody else's work in a non competitive way and the purpose for their use is to benefit the public, they will be on a pretty safe ground. On the other hand, if they use large portions of someone else's expression for their own purely commercial reasons, the rule usually won't apply. It is usually not difficult to determine whether intended use of another author's protected work constitutes a fair use or not. It is really just a matter of common sense. There is no more commonsensical definition of fair use than the golden rule 'Take from someone else only what you wouldn't mind someone else taking from you'."

Unit 3: Electronic Media Laws

17

Prasar Bharati Act, 1990

The year 1997 was a 'land mark year', which saw far reaching measures to free the broadcast media from the shackles of Government control 50 years after independence.

It was the first instance of a government voluntarily bringing legislation to free the media from its control, which may set in motion a chain of events in the country bringing in revolutionary changes in the field.

For over three decades beginning with the Chanda Committee report in 1966 and continuing through the reports of the Verghese Committee (Akash Bharati) in 1978 and the Joshi Committee in 1985 –expert committees set up by the government made a case for organizational restructuring of broadcasting, so as to give it greater autonomy.

As a result, the Prasar Bharati Act (1990) was formed by the government. It was kept idle for seven years. In July 1997, it was activated after being notified and came into force on September 22, 1997. Then came the amendments to the Act, which was widely seen as ushering in a regime of full autonomy to All India Radio and Doordarshan.

The Prasar Bharati Board has been formed with an executive member and six part-time members, paving the way for granting autonomy to Doordarshan and All India Radio.

Historical Background

Broadcast Media in India, that is, All India Radio and Doordarshan were always government controlled. There was no autonomy given to them.

There was a demand that they should be given autonomy, which would strengthen the democracy and induce transparency.

Keeping this in view, the Morarji Desai government in 1977 made the first attempt to appoint a working group to look into the matter.

This was the first serious effort to legislate a Comprehensive Broadcast

Law. The Draft Akash Bharati Bill, 1978, proposed by the Working Group on Autonomy for Akashvani and Doordarshan was constituted under the chairmanship of Mr. B. G. Verghese. The Draft Bill, intended to be an aid to legislation, provided for a simple statute establishing the National Broadcast Trust, and set out its objectives, scope, powers and basic structure. It was, at that point of time, hoped that the Akash Bharati Act establishing the National Broadcast Trust would come into force from January 1979 and Akashvani and Doordarshan would cease to be the attached offices to the Ministry of Information and Broadcasting. What happened to this initial effort is now a part of history, the Janata party government, which introduced the Bill, with diluted provisions for autonomy, was voted out of office before the legislation could be enacted.

The Prasar Bharati Act, 1990

It was not for another twelve years, that the Parliament in 1990, enacted the Prasar Bharati (Broadcasting Corporation of India) Act, 1990.

A unique feature of this Act was that it enlarged the definition of the term, Broadcasting.

Section 2(c) defines 'Broadcasting' as the dissemination of any form of communication, like signs, signals, writing, pictures, images and sounds of all kinds by transmission of electro-magnetic waves through space or through cables intended to be received by the general public either directly or indirectly through the medium of relay stations and all its grammatical variations and cognate expression shall be construed accordingly.

It is a more comprehensive meaning as it takes care of the transmission of electromagnetic waves through space or through cables.

Salient Features of the Act

Section 3: *Establishment and composition of Corporation*

(1) With effect from such date as the Central Government may, by notification, appoint in this behalf, there shall be established for the purposes of this Act a Corporation, to be known as the Prasar Bharati (Broadcasting Corporation of India).

(2) The Corporation shall be a body corporate by the name aforesaid, having perpetual succession and a common seal with power to acquire, hold and dispose of property, both movable and immovable, and to contract, and shall by the said name sue and be sued.

(3) The headquarters of the Corporation shall be at New Delhi and the Corporation may establish offices, kendras or stations at other places in India and, with the previous approval of the Central Government, outside India.

(4) The general superintendence, direction and management of the affairs

of the Corporation shall vest in the Prasar Bharati Board, which may exercise all such powers and do all such acts and things as may be exercised or done by the Corporation under this Act.

(5) The Board shall consist of:

(a) a Chairman;
(b) one Executive Member;
(c) one Member (Finance);
(d) one Member (Personnel);
(e) six Part-time Members;
(f) Director-General (Akashvani), ex-officio;
(g) Director-General (Doordarshan), ex-officio;
(h) one representative of the Union Ministry of Information and Broadcasting, to be nominated by that Ministry; and
(i) two representatives of the employees of the Corporation, of whom one shall be elected by the engineering staff from amongst themselves and one shall be elected by other employee from amongst themselves.

(6) The Corporation may appoint such committees as may be necessary for the efficient performance, exercise and discharge of its functions, powers and duties:

Provided that all or a majority of the members of each committee shall be Members and a member of any such committee, who is not a Member, shall have only the right to attend meetings of the committee and take part in the proceedings thereof, but shall not have the right to vote.

(7) The Corporation may associate with itself, in such manner and for such purposes as may be provided by regulations, any person whose assistance or advice it may need in complying with any of the provisions of this Act and a person so associated shall have the right to take part in the discussions of the Board relevant to the purposes for which he has been associated, but shall not have the right to vote.

Section 12: *Functions and Powers of Corporation*

(2) The Corporation shall, in the discharge of its functions, be guided by the following objectives, namely:

(a) upholding the unity and integrity of the country and the values enshrined in the Constitution;
(b) safeguarding the citizen's right to be informed freely, truthfully and objectively on all matters of public interest, national or international, and presenting a fair and balanced flow of information including contrasting views without advocating any opinion or ideology of its own;

(c) paying special attention to the fields of education and spread of literacy, agriculture, rural development, environment, health and family welfare and science and technology;

(d) providing adequate coverage to the diverse cultures and languages of the various regions of the country by broadcasting appropriate programmes;

(e) providing adequate coverage to sports and games so as to encourage healthy competition and the spirit of sportsmanship;

(f) providing appropriate programmes keeping in view the special needs of the youth;

(g) informing and stimulating the national consciousness in regard to the status and problems of women and paying special attention to the upliftment of women;

(h) promoting social justice and combating exploitation, inequality and such evils as untouchability and advancing the welfare of the weaker sections of the society;

(i) safeguarding the rights of the working classes and advancing their welfare;

(j) serving the rural and weaker sections of the people and those residing in border regions, backward or remote areas;

(k) providing suitable programmes keeping in view the special needs of the minorities and tribal communities;

(l) taking special steps to protect the interests of children, the blind, the aged, the handicapped and other vulnerable sections of the people;

(m) promoting national integration by broadcasting in a manner that facilitates communication in the languages in India; and facilitating the distribution of regional broadcasting services in every State in the languages of that State;

(n) providing comprehensive broadcast coverage through the choice of appropriate technology and the best utilisation of the broadcast frequencies available and ensuring high quality reception;

(o) promoting research and development activities in order to ensure that radio and television broadcast technology are constantly updated; and

(p) expanding broadcasting facilities by establishing additional channels of transmission at various levels.

Section 13: *Parliamentary Committee*

(1) There shall be constituted a Committee consisting of twenty-two Members of Parliament, of whom fifteen from the House of the People to be elected by the Members thereof and seven from the Council of States to be elected by the Members thereof in accordance with the system of proportional

representation by means of the single transferable vote, to oversee that the Corporation discharges its functions in accordance with the provision of this Act and, in particular, the objectives set out in section 12 and submit a report thereon to Parliament.

(2) The committee shall function in accordance with such rules as may be made by the Speaker of the House of the People.

Section 14: *Establishment of Broadcasting Council, term of office and removal, etc., of members thereof*

(1) There shall be established, by notification, as soon as may be after the appointed day, a Council, to be known as the Broadcasting Council, to receive and consider complaints referred to in section 15 and to advise the Corporation in the discharge of its functions in accordance with the objectives set out in section 12.

(2) The Broadcasting Council shall consist of:

(i) a President and ten other members to be appointed by the President of India from amongst persons of eminence in public life;

(ii) four Members of Parliament, of whom two from the House of the People to be nominated by the Speaker thereof and two from the Council of States to be nominated by the Chairman thereof.

(3) The President of the Broadcasting Council shall be a whole-time member and every other member shall be a part-time member and the President or the part-time member shall hold office as such for a term of three years from the date on which he enters upon his office.

(4) The Broadcasting Council may constitute such number of Regional Councils as it may deem necessary to aid and assist the Council in the discharge of its functions.

Aftermath of the Act

The Prasar Bharati Bill remained a dead letter with the successive governments, never serious about autonomy for the official electronic media. In fact, the demand for autonomy for AIR and DD dates back to mid-sixties, when the first ever expert committee, the Chanda Committee, went into the issue.

Two other committees, The Paswan Committee on National Media Policy and The Nitish Sengupta Committee on AIR and TV, have come up with several suggestions for improvements in the Prasar Bharati Act and bring them in line with present day needs.

The Union Government in 1997 brought about sweeping changes in the revamped Prasar Bharati Act. The changes were brought to rectify the anomalies and flaws in the Act. One such amendment was the scrapping of the 22-member Parliamentary Committee that was supposed to oversee the function of the Corporation.

The Sengupta Committee that was appointed to review the implementation of the Prasar Bharati Act also recommended the scrapping of the Parliamentary Committee.

Another amendment was the scrapping of the Broadcasting Council constituted under Section 14.

Yet another significant feature of the amendments relates to public service broadcasting. It would now be the primary duty of the Corporation to 'organize and conduct public service broadcasting to inform, educate and entertain the public.'

The amendment Act clarifies that the Corporation would ensure comprehensive broadcast coverage through the choice of appropriate technology and the best utilisation of 'broadcast frequencies made available for public service broadcasting', and would also ensure high quality reception.

The Amendment Act mentions that that the Centre would no longer be involved in fixing limits for levy fees and other charges. The amended Act gives full freedom to the Corporation in this respect.

18

Cable TV Network Regulation Act, 1995

Cable Television was first introduced in India mainly in the big hotels of the metro cities during the early 1980s to provide both entertainment and information to the viewers. Being instantly popular, it spread to the residences of industrialists, media-men, politicians and businessmen throughout the country.

B. Manna, in his book, 'Mass Media and related laws in India', writes that after the installation of the facility the cable operator charged 200 to 300 rupees per month, which was convenient for a person of middle income group to pay. So the cable TV operations flourished very quickly. Foreign channels like STAR TV, CNN, BBC, Prime Sports, etc. became extremely popular. Thus, it has spread its wings with the results that there has been a haphazard mushrooming of cable television networks all over the country due to availability of signals of foreign television networks via satellites. The programmes, which are being projected on the satellite channels are predominantly western and are alien to our culture and way of life. On these cable television networks, lot of undesirable programmes and advertisements are also being screened without any fear of being checked. To check this tendency, it has been considered necessary to regulate the operation of cable television networks in the country so as to bring about uniformity in their operation. Thus, seeing the popularity of foreign channels, the Government made the Cable Television Networks (Regulation) Act in 1995 enforcing operators to cater at least three DD channels also in their network.

On 29 September 1994, an Ordinance titled the Cable Television Networks (Regulation) Ordinance, 1994 was promulgated by the President to provide for the regulation of the operation of cable television networks in the country. The Ordinance was re-promulgated by the President on 17 January 1995. To replace the said Ordinance, a Bill was introduced in the Parliament, which was passed by both of the houses.

Statement of Objects and Reasons

There has been haphazard mushrooming of cable television networks all over the country during the last few years as a result of the availability of signals of foreign television networks via satellites. This has been perceived as a "cultural invasion" in many quarters, since the programmes available on these satellite channels are predominantly western and totally alien to our culture and way of life. Since there is no regulation of these cable television networks, lot of undesirable programmes and advertisements are becoming available to the viewers without any kind of censorship.

2. It is also felt that the subscribers of these cable television networks, the programmers and the cable operators themselves are not aware of their rights, responsibilities and obligations in respect of the quality of service, technical as well as content-wise, use of material protected by copyright, exhibition of uncertified films, protection of subscribers from anti-national broadcasts from sources inimical to our national interest, responsiveness to the genuine grievances of the subscribers and perceived willingness to operate within the broad framework of the laws of the land, e.g., the Cinematograph Act, 1952, the Copyright Act, 1957, Indecent Representation of Women (Prohibition) Act, 1986.

3. It is, therefore, considered necessary to regulate the operation of cable television networks in the entire country so as to bring about uniformity in their operation. It will, thus, enable the optimal exploitation of this technology, which has the potential of making available to the subscribers a vast pool of information and entertainment.

Act 7 of 1995

The Bill titled Cable Television Networks (Regulation) Bill, 1995 was passed by both the Houses of Parliament and the same was assented by the President on 25 March 1995. It came on the statute book as " The Cable Television Networks (Regulation) Act, 1995 (7 of 1995)" deemed to have come into force on 29 September 1994.

Salient Features of the Act

The Preamble states that this is an Act to regulate the operation of cable television networks in the country and for matters connected therewith or incidental thereto.

Section 2: This Section deals with the definitions related to the Act. Some of them are:

- "cable operator" means any person, who provides cable service through a cable television network or otherwise controls or is responsible for the management and operation of a cable television network;

- "cable service" means the transmission by cables of programmes including retransmission by cables of any broadcast television signals;
- "cable television network" means any system consisting of a set of closed transmission paths and associated signal generation, control and distribution equipment, designed to provide cable service for reception by multiple subscribers;
- "subscriber" means a person, who receives the signals of cable television network at a place indicated by him to the cable operator, without further transmitting it to any other person.

Section 3: No person shall operate a cable television network unless he is registered as a cable operator under this Act. If a person has been operating a cable television network before the commencement of this Act, he may continue to do so for a period of ninety days from such commencement; and if he has made an application for registration as a cable operator under section 4 within the said period, he may continue until he is registered under that section or the registering authority refuses to grant registration to him under that section.

Section 4: Any person, who is operating or is desirous of operating a cable television network, may apply for registration as a cable operator to the registering authority.

Section 4 A: The Cable Television Networks (Regulation) Amendment Act, 2002 Act 2 of 2003 [31 December 2002] inserted Section 4A after section 4 in the Cable Television Networks (Regulation) Act, 1995 (7 of 1995) (hereinafter referred to as the principal Act).

Transmission of programmes through addressable system, etc.:

(1) Where the Central Government is satisfied that it is necessary in the public interest so to do, it may, by notification in the Official Gazette, make it obligatory for every cable operator to transmit or retransmit programme of any pay channel through an addressable system with effect from such date as may be specified in the notification and different dates may be specified for different States, cities, towns or areas, as the case may be.

(2) If the Central Government is satisfied that it is necessary in the public interest so to do, it may, by notification in the Official Gazette, specify one or more free-to-air channels to be included in the package of channels forming basic service tie and any or more such channels may be specified, in the notification, genre-wise for providing a programme mix of entertainment, information, education and such other programmes.

(3) The Central Government may specify in the notification referred to in sub-section (2), the number of free-to-air channels to be included in the package

of channels forming basic service tier for the purposes different States, cities, towns or areas, as the case may be, of that sub-section and different numbers may be specified for.

(4) If the Central Government is satisfied that it is necessary in the public interest so to do, it may, by notification in the Official Gazette, specify the maximum amount, which a cable operator may demand from the subscriber for receiving the programmes transmitted in the basic service tier provided by such cable operator.

(5) Notwithstanding anything contained in sub-section (4), the Central Government may, for the purposes of that sub-section, specify in the notification referred to in that sub-section different maximum amounts for different States, cities, towns or area, as the case may be.

(6) Notwithstanding anything contained in this section, programmes of basic service tier shall be receivable by any subscriber on the receiver set of a type existing immediately before the commencement of the Cable Television Networks (Regulation) Amendment Act, 2002 without any addressable system attached with such receiver set in any manner.

(7) Every cable operator shall publicise, in the prescribed manner, to the subscribers the subscription rates and the periodic intervals at which such subscriptions are payable for receiving each pay channel provided by such cable operator.

(8) The cable operator shall not require any subscriber to have a receiver set of a particular type to receive signals of cable television network: Provided that the subscriber shall use an addressable system to be attached to his receiver set for receiving programmes transmitted on pay channel.

(9) Every cable operator shall submit a report to the Central Government in the prescribed form and manner containing the information regarding— (i) the number of total subscribers; (ii) subscription rates; (iii) number of subscribers receiving programmes transmitted in basic service tier or particular programme or set of programmes transmitted on pay channel, in respect of cable services provided by such cable operator through a cable television network, and such report shall be submitted periodically at such intervals as may be prescribed and shall also contain the rate of amount, if any, payable by the cable operator to any broadcaster.

Section 6: No person shall transmit or re-transmit through a cable service any advertisement, unless such advertisement is in conformity with the prescribed advertisement code.

Section 7: Every cable operator shall maintain a register in the prescribed form indicating therein in brief the programmes transmitted or re-transmitted through the cable service during a month and such register shall be maintained by the cable operator for a period of one year after the actual transmission or re-transmission of the said programmes.

Section 8: This Section deals with compulsory transmission of Doordarshan channels.

(1) Every cable operator shall, from the commencement of the Cable Television Networks (Regulation) Amendment Act, 2000, re-transmit at least two Doordarshan terrestrial channels and one regional language channel of a State in the prime band, in satellite mode on frequencies other than those carrying terrestrial frequencies.

(2) The Doordarshan channels referred to in sub-section (1) shall be re-transmitted without any deletion or alteration of any programme transmitted on such channels.

Section 9: This Section deals with the use of standard equipment in cable television network.

No cable operator shall, on and from the date of the expiry of a period of three years from the date of the establishment and publication of the Indian Standard by the Bureau of Indian Standards in accordance with the provisions of the Bureau of Indian Standards Act, 1986, use any equipment in his cable television network unless such equipment conforms to the said Indian standard.

Section 10: Every cable operator shall ensure that the cable television network being operated by him does not interfere, in any way, with the functioning of the authorised telecommunication systems.

Section 11: If any authorized officer has reason to believe that the provisions of section 3, 4A, 5, 6 or 8 have been or are being contravened by any cable operator, he may seize the equipment being used by such cable operator for operating the cable television network. But no such equipment shall be retained by the authorised officer for a period exceeding ten days from the date of its seizure, unless the approval of the District Judge, within the local limits of whose jurisdiction such seizure has been made, has been obtained for such retention.

Section 16: This Section provides for the provisions of punishment for contravention of provisions of this Act.

(1) Whoever contravenes any of the provisions of this Act shall be punishable:

(a) for the first offence, with imprisonment for a term, which may extend to two years or with fine, which may extend to one thousand rupees or with both;

(b) for every subsequent offence, with imprisonment for a term, which may extend to five years and with fine, which may extend to five thousand rupees.

(2) Notwithstanding anything contained in the Code of Criminal Procedure, 1973 (2 of 1974), the contravention of section 4A shall be a cognizable offence under this section.

Present Scenario

The Hindu published a report 'Now local TV channels may come under regulatory net' on January 19, 2013 that said that local TV channels, supposedly run by your local cable operator (LCO) could finally come under the regulatory net. The problem arises from the fact that the Cable Television Networks (Regulation) Act, 1995 does not actually define what is the area in which programming generated at the level of a cable operator can be transmitted. As a result, it's easy for the larger operators to transmit the same content over their entire network, and even share it with other operators in other States. In fact, there are multi-system operators (MSO), which merrily transmit multiple "local" channels. Other important points highlighted in the report are:

- The government has *taken note of recent trends*, whereby such local, ground-based channels are actually being transmitted to much wider geographical areas, becoming de facto regional or national channels–without facing any of the regulations that govern registered satellite channels.
- The Information and Broadcasting Ministry has asked the *Telecom Regulatory Authority of India (TRAI) to suggest regulations for the local channels* that have mushroomed over the last few years without any registration or license.
- The intent of allowing cable operators to generate and transmit local programmes is to keep the people informed of relevant local issues. However this intent *is not fulfilled when LCOs and MSOs start networking of the content to cover a larger geographical area.* Given the present state of technological advancement, the tendency to network content at a larger geographical area has gained strength.
- New TRAI regulations *may help create a level playing field* with national and regional broadcasters, who have actually procured permits under the government's uplinking and downlinking guidelines.
- The need for regulations becomes more critical owing to digitalisation. The TRAI has been asked if there is a need to cap the total number of ground-based channels that can be operated by a single MSO or cable operator.

The Ministry of Information and Broadcasting has issued guidelines to define the role of the State and District Monitoring Committees for private television channels. As per the Government of India Order of September, 2005, District and State Level Monitoring Committees were to be set up to enforce Cable Television Networks (Regulation) Act, 1995. The new guidelines have been issued to ensure effective functioning of the Committees. The main provisions of the guidelines are as under:

Scope of the District Level Committee

- To provide a forum where the public may lodge a complaint regarding content aired over cable television and take action on the same as per procedure prescribed herein.
- To review the action taken by Authorized Officers for enforcement of Cable Television Networks (Regulation) Act, 1995.
- To immediately bring to the notice of State and Central Government if any programme is affecting public order or wide spread resentment in any community.
- To keep a watch on content carried by cable television channels at local level and to ensure, through Authorized Officers, that no unauthorized or pirated channels are carried and local news if aired by the cable television operator is restricted to information about local events and is presented in a manner, which is balanced, impartial and not likely to offend or incite any community.
- To monitor the availability of free to air channels and channels notified for mandatory carriage on the cable network.

A complaint Cell headed by a nodal Officer at District level should be established and wide publicity be given regarding the constitution of Monitoring Committee and procedure followed by it, including putting it on website of the State/UT.

In case the complaint concerns content carried locally by Cable TV Network at its own level, the Committee may call for footage/VCD of the programme/advertisement against which the complaint is considered and the common pool of wisdom available within the Committee may form a view about whether a violation has taken place. In case the Committee is of the view that violation has taken place, the Authorized Officer may take action as per the Act.

In case the complaint pertains to national/regional satellite channels, the Committee may forward its recommendations through the State-level Monitoring Committee to the Government of India for dealing with the issue.

In case it is found that a cable network operator is not carrying channels prescribed for mandatory carriage or is carrying them in such a manner that the signal is too poor to be properly visible or audible, the Committee, through Authorized Officer, may direct the cable network to ensure proper carriage of the same and take any other action it may consider necessary under Section 11.

State-level Monitoring Committee

The constitution of both State and District-level Committees to enforce the

Cable TV Networks Rules was envisaged, but the constitution of the State-level Committee was not specified. The constitution of the State-level Committee is hereby specified as follows:

(i) Secretary, Information and Public Relations – Chairman of the State.
(ii) Representative of the DG of State Police – Member
(iii) Secretary, Social Welfare Department – Member of the State
(iv) Secretary, Women and Child Development – Member of the State
(v) Representative of a leading NGO of the State – Member State agency/ department working for women (to be nominated by Chief Secretary)
(vi) Academicians/Psychologists/Sociologists – Member (one each to be nominated by Chief Secretary)
(vii) Director (Information) of the State – Member Secretary

Functions

The functions of the State Level Monitoring Committee will be:

- To see whether District/Local Committees have been formed and are meeting regularly.
- To see whether the authorized officers are effectively performing their duties.
- To give suggestion/guidance to District/Local Level Committee.
- To take decision on the matters referred to it by District/Local level Committee.
- To recommend action and forward complaints against satellite channels (National Channels) to the Ministry of Information and Broadcasting through the Chief Secretary of the State in cases of violation of Government of India's orders on the Programme and Advertising Codes.

It had been noticed that the enforcement of the said Act in many parts of the country was not satisfactory either due to lack of clear understanding of the role of the District Monitoring Committees or a suitable mechanism to enforce the provisions of the Act. Also, increasing number of petitions are being received by the Ministry of Information and Broadcasting, Government of India, from viewers regarding malpractices by Cable Operators and undesirable content being shown at the local level by the cable operators.

19

The Cinematography Act, 1952

Films can be publicly exhibited in India only after they have been certified by the Central Board of Film Certification (CBFC). The Board set up under the Cinematography Act 1952, consists of a Chairman and a minimum of 12 and maximum of 25 non official members, all appointed by the government.

The Board functions with Headquarters at Mumbai and nine regional offices at Bangalore, Kolkata, Chennai, Hyderabad, Guwahati, Thiruvananthapuram, New Delhi and Cuttack.

The regional offices are assisted in the examination of films by members of advisory panels, which include eminent educationists, art-critics, journalists, social workers, psychologists, etc.

The Board examines films for certification in accordance with the provisions contained in the Cinematography Act 1952, the Cinematography (Certification) Rules 1983 and the guidelines issued by the Central government.

Historical Background

Rulers of independent India stuck to pre-censorship with vengeance. The ruling government that ruled India between 15 August 1947 and 25 January 1950 instituted a centralized system by amending the Indian Cinematograph Act 1918. A Central Board of Film Censors was set up under the Cinematograph (Certification) Rules, 1951.

By then, a set of Fundamental Rights was enshrined under Article 19 in the Indian constitution that became effective from 26 January 1950.

At the top of the list was the 'Right to Freedom of Speech and Expression'. While Article 19(1)(a) declared, 'All citizens will have the right to freedom of speech and expression', Article 19(2) spelt out,

> 'Nothing in sub-clause (a) of Clause (1) shall affect the operation of any existing law in so far as it relates to, or prevents the state from making any law relating to libel, slander, defamation, contempt of

> court or any matter, which offends against decency or morality or which undermines the security of, or tends to overthrow the state.'

The state felt alarmed that any form of prior restraint on the freedom of expression, including pre-censorship, would prima-facie be construed as infringement of Article 19 (1)(a).

To correct the perceived flaw, an amended Article 19(2) replaced, retrospectively, the original Article in 1951. The amended Article 19(2) read,

> 'Nothing in sub clause (a) of clause (1) shall affect the operation of any existing law, or prevent the State from making any law, in so far as such law imposes reasonable restrictions on the exercise of the right conferred by the said sub clause in the interests of the sovereignty and integrity of India, the security of the State, friendly relations with foreign States, public order, decency or morality or in relation to contempt of court, defamation or incitement to an offence.'

After this amendment, the judiciary was compelled to examine the term 'reasonable restrictions' and shortly thereafter, The Cinematography Act 1952 ushered in a complete redefinition of the system for content control in cinema.

Salient Features of the Act

Section 2: *Definitions—*

(b) "Board" means the Board of Film Certification constituted by the Central Government under section 3;

(bb) "certificate" means the certificate granted by the Board under section 5A;

(c) "cinematograph" includes any apparatus for the representation of moving pictures or series of pictures.

Section 3: *Board of Film Censors* (1) For the purpose of sanctioning films for public exhibition, the Central Government may, by notification in the official Gazette, constitute a Board to be called the [Board of Film Certification, which shall consist of a Chairman and not less than twelve and not more than twenty five] other members appointed by the Central Government.

Section 4: *Examination of films* (1) Any person desiring to exhibit any film shall in the prescribed manner make an application to the Board for a certificate in respect thereof, and the Board may, after examining or having the film examined in the prescribed manner:

(i) sanction the film for unrestricted public exhibition;
(ii) sanction the film for public exhibition restricted to adults; or
(iia) sanction the film for public exhibition restricted to members of any

profession or any class of persons, having regard to the nature, content and theme of the film; or

(iii) direct the applicant to carry out such excisions or modifications in the film as it thinks necessary before sanctioning the film for public exhibition under any of the foregoing clauses; or

(iv) refuse to sanction the film for public exhibition.

(2) No action under clause (i), clause (ii), clause (iia), clause (iii) or clause (iv)] of sub-section (1) shall be taken by the Board except after giving an opportunity to the applicant for representing his views in the matter.

Section 5: *Advisory Panels:* (1) For the purpose of enabling the Board to efficiently discharge its functions under this Act, the Central Government may establish at such regional centres as it thinks fit, advisory panels each of which shall consist of such number of persons, being persons qualified in the opinion of the Central Government to judge the effect of films on the public, as the Central Government may think fit to appoint thereto.

(2) At each regional centre, there shall be as many regional officers as the Central Government may think fit to appoint, and rules made in this behalf may provide for the association of regional officers in the examination of films.

(3) The Board may consult in such manner as may be prescribed any advisory panel in respect of any film for which an application for a certificate has been made.

(4) It shall be the duty of every such advisory panel whether acting as a body or in committees as may be provided in the rules made in this behalf to examine the film and to make such recommendations to the Board, as it thinks fit.

5A: *Certification of Films* (1) If, after examining a film or having it examined in the prescribed manner, the Board considers that –

(a) the film is suitable for unrestricted public exhibition, or as the case may be, for unrestricted public exhibition with an endorsement of the nature mentioned in the proviso to clause (i) of sub-section (1) of section 4, it shall grant to the person applying for a certificate in respect of the film a "U" certificate or, as the case may be, a "UA" certificate, or

(b) the film is not suitable for unrestricted public exhibition, but is suitable for public exhibition restricted to adults or, as the case may be, is suitable for public exhibition restricted to members of any profession or any class of persons, it shall grant to the person applying for a certificate in respect of the film an "A" certificate or, as the case may be, a "S" certificate.

(2) A certificate granted or an order refusing to grant a certificate in respect of any film shall be published in the Gazette of India.

(3) Subject to the other provisions contained in this Act, a certificate granted by the Board under this section shall be valid throughout India for a period of ten years.

5B: *Principles for Guidance in Certifying Films* (1) A film shall not be certified for public exhibition if, in the opinion of the authority competent to grant the certificate, the film or any part of it is against the interests of the sovereignty and integrity of India, the security of the State, friendly relations with foreign States, public order, decency or morality, or involves defamation or contempt of court or is likely to incite the commission of any offence.

(2) Subject to the provisions contained in sub-section (1), the Central Government may issue such directions as it may think fit setting out the principles, which shall guide the authority competent to grant certificates under this Act in sanctioning films for public exhibition.

5C: *Appeals:* (1) Any person applying for a certificate in respect of a film, who is aggrieved by any order of the Board –

(a) refusing to grant a certificate; or
(b) granting only an "A" certificate; or
(c) granting only a "S" certificate; or
(d) granting only a "UA" certificate; or
(e) directing the applicant to carry out any excisions or modifications, may, within thirty days from the date of such order, prefer an appeal to the Tribunal:

Provided that the Tribunal may, if it is satisfied that the appellant was prevented by sufficient cause from filing the appeal within the aforesaid period of thirty days, allow such appeal to be admitted within a further period of thirty days.

5D: *Constitution of Appellate Tribunal* (1) For the purpose of hearing appeals against any order of the Board under section 5C, the Central Government shall, by notification in the Official Gazette, constitute an Appellate Tribunal.

(3) Such Tribunal shall consist of a Chairman and not more than four other members appointed by the Central Government.

(4) A person shall not be qualified for appointment as the Chairman of the Tribunal unless he is a retired Judge of a High Court, or is a person, who is qualified to be a Judge of High Court.

(5) The Central Government may appoint such persons, who, in its opinion, are qualified to judge the effect of films on the public, to be members of the Tribunal.

(10) Subject to the provisions of this Act, the Tribunal may regulate its own procedure.

(11) The Tribunal may, after making such inquiry into the matter as it considers necessary, and after giving the appellant and the Board an opportunity of being heard in the matter, make such order in relation to a film as it thinks fit and the Board shall dispose of the matter in conformity with such order.

5E: *Suspension and Revocation of Certificate* (1) Notwithstanding anything contained in sub-section (2) of section 6, the Central Government may, by notification in the Official Gazette, suspend a certificate granted under this Part, for such period as it thinks fit or may revoke such certificate if it is satisfied that:

(i) the film in respect of which the certificate was granted, was being exhibited in a form other than the one in which it was certified; or

(ii) the film or any part thereof is being exhibited in contravention of the provisions of this Part or the rules made thereunder.

(2) Where a notification under sub-section (1) has been published, the Central Government may require the applicant for certificate or any other person to whom the rights in the film have passed, or both, to deliver up the certificate and all duplicate certificates, if any, granted in respect of the film to the Board or to any person or authority specified in the said notification.

(3) No action under this section shall be taken except after giving an opportunity to the person concerned for representing his views in the matter.

(4) During the period in which a certificate remains suspended under this section, the film shall be deemed to be an uncertified film.

Section 7: *Penalties for contraventions of this Part:* (1) If any person–

(a) exhibits or permits to be exhibited in any place –

(i) any film other than a film, which has been certified by the Board as suitable for unrestricted public exhibition or for public exhibition restricted to adults or to members of any profession or any class of persons and which, when exhibited, displays the prescribed mark of the Board and has not been altered or tampered with in any way since such mark was affixed thereto,

(ii) any film, which has been certified by the Board as suitable for public exhibition restricted to adults, to any person, who is not an adult,

(iia) any film, which has been certified by the Board as suitable for public exhibition restricted to any profession or class of persons, to a person, who is not a member of such profession or who is not a member of such class, or

(b) without lawful authority (the burden of proving which shall be on him), alters or tampers with in any way any film after it has been certified,

He shall be punishable with imprisonment for a term, which may extend to three years, or with fine, which may extend to one lakh rupees, or with both, and in the case of a continuing offence with a further fine, which may extend to twenty thousand rupees for each day during which the offence continues:

(2) If any person is convicted of an offence punishable under this section committed by him in respect of any film, the convicting court may further direct that the film shall be forfeited to the Government.

(3) The exhibition of a film, in respect of which an "A" certificate or a "S" certificate or a "UA" certificate] has been granted, to children below the age of three years accompanying their parents or guardians shall not be deemed to be an offence within the meaning of this section.

7A: *Power of seizure:* (1) Where a film in respect of which no certificate has been granted under this Act is exhibited, or a film certified as suitable for public exhibition restricted to adults is exhibited to any person, who is not an adult or a film is exhibited in contravention of any of the other provisions contained in this Act or of any order made by the Central Government or the Board in the exercise of any of the powers conferred on it, any police officer may enter any place in which he has reason to believe that the film has been or is being or is likely to be exhibited, search it and seize the film.

(2) All searches under this Act shall be carried out in accordance with the provision of the Code of Criminal Procedure, 1973, relating to searches.

Conclusion

Part III of the Act deals with regulations of exhibition by means of Cinematographs and Part IV deals with repeals.

20

Information Technology Act, 2000

The Indian Penal Code, 1860 was found insufficient to cater to the needs of new crimes emerging from internet expansion. Even some of the traditional crimes, such as conspiracy, solicitation, securities, fraud, espionage, etc. are now being committed through Internet, which necessitates a new law to curb them. It was in this background that the Information Technology Act, 2000 was enacted in India for the prevention and control of cyber crimes.

Prior to the enactment of this Act, the law applicable to cyber offences was the Indian Penal Code, which was enacted long back in 1860 when no one even thought of computer technology or cyber criminality.

With the coming into force of Information Technology Act, 2000, it became necessary to introduce certain consequential changes in certain provisions of the Penal Code as also in the Indian Evidence Act, 1872, in order to meet the new requirements of the cyber space crimes.

With a view to widening the scope of applicability of the provisions of the IPC so as to include within its ambit, offences involving electronic records, a new Section 29-A has been inserted after Section 29 of the Indian Penal Code, which reads as follows:

> "**29-A Electronic Record:** The words electronic record shall have the meaning assigned to them in clause (1) of sub-section (1) of Section 2 of the Information Technology Act, 2000."

Section 2(1) (t) of the Information Technology Act, 2000 defines "electronic record", which means "data record or data generated image or sound stored, received or sent in an electronic form or micro-film or computer generated micro-fiche."

As a result of this amendment in the Indian Penal Code, all the offences related to "documents" shall also include offences related to "electronic records", which are committed through cyber space or Internet.

The Information Technology Act is based on UNCITRAL Model Law on e-commerce, 1996 in furtherance of the U.N. General Assembly resolution urging the member states to enact or revise their cyber laws to create a uniform environment for regulating e-commerce at the international level.

The object is to "provide legal recognition for transactions carried out by electronic data interchange and other means of electronic communications commonly referred to as e-commerce, which involves the use of alternatives to paper based methods of communication and storage of information to facilitate electronic filing of documents." The Act seeks to prevent offences, which result out of e-commerce and e-governance.

The Information Technology Act, 2000, came into force with effect from 17 October 2000. It has been amended in 2008 and the Amended Act is effective from February 5, 2009. The Rules under the Amended Act have also been framed, which became effective from October 27, 2009.

Salient Features of the IT Act, 2000

The salient features of the Information Technology Act, 2000 may briefly be stated as follows:

1. The Act provides legal recognition to e-commerce, which facilitates commercial e-transactions.
2. It recognises records kept in electronic form like any other documentary record. In this way, it brings electronic transactions at par with paper transactions in documentary form.
3. The Act also provides legal recognition to digital signatures, which need to be duly authenticated by the certifying authorities.
4. Cyber Law Appellate tribunal has been set up to hear appeal against adjudicating authorities.
5. The provisions of the IT Act have no application to negotiable instruments, power of attorney, trust, will and any contract for sale or conveyance of immovable property.
6. The Act applies to any cyber offence or contravention committed outside India by a person irrespective of his/her nationality.
7. As provided under Section 90 of the Act, the State Government may, by notification in 'Official Gazette' make rules to carry out the provisions of the Act.
8. Consequent to the passing of this Act, the SEBI had announced that trading of securities on the internet will be valid in India, but initially there was no specific provision for protection of confidentiality and net trading. This lacuna has been removed by the IT (Amendment) Act, 2008.

Penalties and Adjudication

The various offences and the punishment provided for them are contained in Chapters IX and XI of the Act. These offences are briefly stated as follows:

1. *Penalty for damage to computer, computer system, etc. (Section 43)*: The section lays down that any person, who accesses or secures access to a computer, computer system or computer network without permission of the owner or any person in charge of such computer, computer system or computer network, shall be liable to pay damages by way of compensation not exceeding one crore rupees to the person, who is so affected.

The term "access" as defined in Section 2(1)(a) of the IT Act means gaining entry into, instructing or communicating with the logical, arithmetical, or memory function resources of a computer, computer system or computer network resources of a computer, computer system or computer network."

2. *Penalty for failure to furnish information return, etc. (Section 44)*: If any person, who is required under this Act or any rules or regulations made thereunder to:

(a) furnish any document, return or report to the Controller or The Certifying Authority fails to furnish the same, he shall be liable to a penalty not exceeding one lakh and fifty thousand rupees for each such failure;
(b) file any return or furnish any information, books or other documents within the time specified therefore in the regulations fails to file return or furnish the same within the time specified therefore in the regulations, he shall be liable to a penalty not exceeding five thousand rupees for every day during which such failure continues;
(c) maintain books of account or records, fails to maintain the same, he shall be liable to a penalty not exceeding ten thousand rupees for every day during which the failure continues.

3. *Power to adjudicate (Section 46):* (1) For the purpose of adjudging under this Chapter whether any person has committed a contravention of any of the provisions of this Act or of any rule, regulation, direction or order made thereunder, the Central Government shall, subject to the provisions of sub-section (3), appoint any officer not below the rank of a Director to the Government of India or an equivalent officer of a State Government to be an adjudicating officer for holding an inquiry in the manner prescribed by the Central Government.

(2) The adjudicating officer shall, after giving the person referred to in sub-section (1) a reasonable opportunity for making representation in the matter and if, on such inquiry, he is satisfied that the person has committed the contravention, he may impose such penalty or award such compensation as he thinks fit in accordance with the provisions of that section.

(3) No person shall be appointed as an adjudicating officer unless he possesses such experience in the field of Information Technology and legal or judicial experience as may be prescribed by the Central Government.

(4) Where more than one adjudicating officers are appointed, the Central Government shall specify by order the matters and places with respect to which such officers shall exercise their jurisdiction.

(5) Every adjudicating officer shall have the powers of a civil court, which are conferred on the Cyber Appellate Tribunal under sub-section (2) of section 58, and –

(a) all proceedings before it shall be deemed to be judicial proceedings within the meaning of sections 193 and 228 of the Indian Penal Code;
(b) shall be deemed to be a civil court for the purposes of sections 345 and 346 of the Code of Criminal Procedure, 1973.

4. *Factors to be taken into account by the adjudicating officer (Section 47)*: While adjudging the quantum of compensation under this Chapter, the adjudicating officer shall have due regard to the following factors, namely:

(a) the amount of gain of unfair advantage, wherever quantifiable, made as a result of the default;
(b) the amount of loss caused to any person as a result of the default;
(c) the repetitive nature of the default.

5. *Tampering with computer source documents (Section 65)*: Whoever knowingly or intentionally conceals, destroys or alters or intentionally or knowingly causes another to conceal, destroy or alter any computer source code used for a computer, computer programme, computer system or computer network, when the computer source code is required to be kept or maintained by law for the time being in force, shall be punishable with imprisonment up to three years, or with fine, which may extend up to two lakh rupees, or with both.

6. *Hacking (Section 66)*: (1) Whoever with the intent to cause or knowing that he is likely to cause wrongful loss or damage to the public or any person destroys or deletes or alters any information residing in a computer resource or diminishes its value or utility or affects it injuriously by any means, commits hack;

(2) Whoever commits hacking shall be punished with imprisonment up to three years, or with fine, which may extend upto two lakh rupees, or with both.

7. *Publishing of information, which is obscene in electronic form (Section 67)*: Whoever publishes or transmits or causes to be published in the electronic form, any material, which is lascivious or appeals to the prurient

interest or if its effect is such as to tend to deprave and corrupt persons, who are likely, having regard to all relevant circumstances, to read, see or hear the matter contained or embodied in it, shall be punished on first conviction with imprisonment of either description for a term, which may extend to five years and with fine, which may extend to one lakh rupees and in the event of a second or subsequent conviction with imprisonment of either description for a term, which may extend to ten years and also with fine, which may extend to two lakh rupees

8. *Power of Controller to give directions (Section 68)*: (1) The Controller may, by order, direct a Certifying Authority or any employee of such Authority to take such measures or cease carrying on such activities as specified in the order if those are necessary to ensure compliance with the provisions of this Act, rules or any regulations made thereunder.

(2) Any person, who fails to comply with any order under sub-section (1) shall be guilty of an offence and shall be liable on conviction to imprisonment for a term not exceeding three years or to a fine not exceeding two lakh rupees or to both.

9. *Directions of Controller to a subscriber to extend facilities to decrypt information (Section 69)*: (1) If the Controller is satisfied that it is necessary or expedient so to do in the interest of the sovereignty or integrity of India, the security of the State, friendly relations with foreign Stales or public order or for preventing incitement to the commission of any cognizable offence, for reasons to be recorded in writing, by order, direct any agency of the Government to intercept any information transmitted through any computer resource.

(2) The subscriber or any person in-charge of the computer resource shall, when called upon by any agency, which has been directed under sub-section (1), extend all facilities and technical assistance to decrypt the information.

(3) The subscriber or any person, who fails to assist the agency referred to in sub-section (2) shall be punished with an imprisonment for a term, which may extend to seven years.

10. *Protected system (Section 70)*: (1) The appropriate Government may, by notification in the Official Gazette, declare that any computer, computer system or computer network to be a protected system.

(2) The appropriate Government may, by order in writing, authorise the persons, who are authorised to access protected systems notified under sub-section (1).

(3) Any person, who secures access or attempts to secure access to a protected system in contravention of the provisions of this section shall be punished with imprisonment of either description for a term, which may extend to ten years and shall also be liable to fine.

11. *Penalty for misrepresentation (Section 71)*: Whoever makes any misrepresentation to, or suppresses any material fact from, the Controller or the Certifying Authority for obtaining any licence or Digital Signature Certificate, as the case may be, shall be punished with imprisonment for a term, which may extend to two years, or with fine, which may extend to one lakh rupees, or with both.

12. *Penalty for breach of confidentiality and privacy (Section 72)*: Save as otherwise provided in this Act or any other law for the time being in force, any person who, in pursuance of any of the powers conferred under this Act, rules or regulations made thereunder, has secured access to any electronic record, book, register, correspondence, information, document or other material without the consent of the person concerned discloses such electronic record, book, register, correspondence, information, document or other material to any other person shall be punished with imprisonment for a term, which may extend to two years, or with fine, which may extend to one lakh rupees, or with both.

13. *Penalty for publishing Digital Signature Certificate false in certain particulars (Section 73)*:

(1) No person shall publish a Digital Signature Certificate or otherwise make it available to any other person with the knowledge that:

(a) the Certifying Authority listed in the certificate has not issued it; or
(b) the subscriber listed in the certificate has not accepted it; or
(c) the certificate has been revoked or suspended, unless such publication is for the purpose of verifying a digital signature created prior to such suspension or revocation.

(2) Any person, who contravenes the provisions of sub-section (1) shall be punished with imprisonment for a term, which may extend to two years, or with fine, which may extend to one lakh rupees, or with both.

14. *Publication for fraudulent purpose (Section 74)*: Whoever knowingly creates, publishes or otherwise makes available a Digital Signature Certificate for any fraudulent or unlawful purpose shall be punished with imprisonment for a term, which may extend to two years, or with fine, which may extend to one lakh rupees, or with both.

15. *Act to apply for offence or contravention committed outside India (Section 75)*: (1) Subject to the provisions of sub-section (2), the provisions of this Act shall apply also to any offence or contravention committed outside India by any person, irrespective of his nationality.

(2) For the purposes of sub-section (1), this Act shall apply to an offence or contravention committed outside India by any person if the act or conduct constituting the offence or contravention involves a computer, computer system or computer network located in India.

16. *Power to investigate offences (Section 78)*: Notwithstanding anything contained in the Code of Criminal Procedure, 1973, a police officer not below the rank of Deputy Superintendent of Police shall investigate any offence under this Act.

Conclusion

Chapter XII dealing with Section 79 provides that network service providers are not liable in certain cases, whereas the last Chapter XIII deals with miscellaneous provisions of which some important ones are as follows:

- Section 84: Protection of action taken in good faith.
- Section 85: Offences by companies.
- Section 87: Power of Central Government to make rules.
- Section 88: Constitution of Advisory Committee.
- Section 89: Power of Controller to make regulations.
- Section 90: Power of State Government to make rules.

21

Convergence Laws

In the year 2000, the Government of India introduced a proposed Communication Convergence Bill (the "Convergence Bill"). As its name indicates, the objective of the Convergence Bill is to establish a new "converged" regulatory framework to promote and develop the communications sector (including broadcasting, telecommunications and "multimedia") in an environment of increasing convergence of technologies, services and service providers.

The Convergence Bill proposes to repeal and replace existing sector laws, including:

(a) The Indian Telegraph Act, 1885;
(b) The Indian Wireless Telegraphy Act, 1933;
(c) The Cable Television Networks Regulation Act, 1995;
(d) The Telecom Regulatory Authority of India Act, 1997.

Main Objectives

(a) To facilitate development of a national communications infrastructure, in order to provide a wide choice of services to consumers.
(b) To establish a regulatory framework that addresses the convergence of technologies, and defines the powers and roles of a single regulatory and licensing authority for broadcasting, telecommunications and multimedia.
(c) To establish a basis for codes and standards for broadcasting content.

The Convergence Bill proposes to achieve these objectives by establishing a new regulatory body to be known as the Communications Commission of India ("CCI"). CCI would replace TRAI, and would become the sole regulator of the broadcasting, telecommunications and multimedia sectors.

The Convergence Bill has been pending in India's Parliament for a number of years. It is unclear when the Government will move forward with its implementation.

Pavan Duggal, Advocate, Supreme Court of India and a Cyber Law Consultant gives a crisp view of the status of Convergence Laws in India. A few points are highlighted as follows:

- The new proposed Convergence Law aims to promote, facilitate and develop in an orderly manner the carriage and content of communications including broadcasting, telecommunications and multimedia. It further aims to establish an autonomous commission to regulate carriage of all forms of communication.
- The new proposed law mandates that no one shall use any part of the spectrum without assignment from the Central Government or the statutory body under the new law, namely, the Communications Commission of India.
- Similarly, owning or providing any network infrastructure facility or providing any network services or any network application services or any value added network application services or any content application services without a proper license or registration under the proposed law has been made illegal. It has been mandatory to have a license before possessing any wireless equipment.
- The new proposed law seeks to establish the Communications Commission of India (CCI in short) as the super-regulator in India in the context of convergence of telecommunications, broadcasting, data communication, multimedia and other related technologies and services. The objectives of the proposed CCI range from developing communications sector in a competitive environment and in consumer interests to making the communication services available at affordable costs to all. It further aims to increase access to information for greater empowerment of citizens and hopes to make strides in the direction of establishing a modern and effective communication infrastructure taking into account the convergence of Information technology, media, telecommunications and consumer electronics.
- The Communications Commission of India (CCI) seeks to establish an open licensing policy and ensure a level playing field for all operators and to promote equitable, non-discriminatory interconnection across various networks. Towards that end in view, the CCI has been given immense powers. The new law deals with the important issue of licensing or registration of the specified categories of services. The CCI has been empowered to grant licenses in its discretion for five different categories:

  a) To provide or own network infrastructure facilities. This category has been defined by the explanation to include earth stations, cable infrastructure, wireless equipments, towers, posts, ducts and pits used in conjunction with other communication infrastructure, and distribution facilities including facilities for broadcasting distribution;

b) To provide networking services. This category has been defined to include band-width services, fixed links and mobile links;

c) To provide network application services. This category has been defined to include public switched telephony, public cellular telephony, global mobile personal communication by satellite, internet protocol telephony, radio paging services, public mobile radio trunking services, public switched data services and broadcasting (radio or television service excluding continued)

d) To provide content application services. This category has been defined to include satellite broadcasting, subscription broadcasting, terrestrial free to air television broadcasting and terrestrial radio broadcasting;

e) To provide value added network application services, such as internet services and unified messaging services. This category has been defined to specifically exclude information technology enabled services. Thus, IT enabled services, such as call centres, electronic-commerce, tele-banking, tele-education, tele-trading, tele-medicine, videotex and video conferencing shall not be licensed under the new legislation.

- The new proposed law seeks to establish a distinction between civil wrongs and penal offences. The new proposed law also deals with the important issue of right of way for laying cables and erection of posts. Various offences have been detailed under the proposed new law, which have been made cognizable and can be tried by a Court of Sessions.
- The new law has also given immense powers to Central Government and the CCI to make rules and regulations, respectively to carry out the purposes of proposed law.
- Finally, the proposed law seeks to repeal five different existing legislations of our country, namely The Indian Telegraph Act, 1885, The Indian Wireless Telegraph Act, 1931, The Telegraph Wires (Unlawful Possession) Act, 1950, The Telecom Regulatory Authority of India Act, 1987 and The Cable Television Networks (Regulation) Act, 1995.
- The newly proposed Communication Convergence Bill, 2001 has got noble objectives in terms of providing for the establishment of a structured mechanism to promote, facilitate and develop in an orderly manner, the carriage and contents of communications in the scenario of increasing convergence of technologies.

Demerits

There are many demerits in proposed law, some of these are—

- It does not define the word 'convergence'.
- It does not seek to make a marked departure from the previous drafts.
- It provides for immense control of the Government.
- It makes it abundantly clear that the CCI is a commission, which is everything, but not autonomous. The Government has retained all powers to appoint the Chairperson and the members of the CCI on the recommendations of a search committee, which shall be constituted by the Central Government.
- It has left very vague the parameters of appointing the members of the CCI. The proposed law states that the members shall be appointed from amongst persons of eminence in the field of literature, performing arts, media, culture, education, films, persons prominent in social and consumer activities, telecommunications, broadcasting technology, IT, finance and administration or law. Who shall be "persons of eminence" in the said fields has been left upon the subjective discretion of the Central Government, thereby bringing immense control of the Government over the CCI.
- It is also silent on the factors, which the commission (CCI) has to follow as in order to ensure fairness and impartiality.
- No parameters or standards have been laid down under the Communication Convergence Bill.

Unit 4: Media Councils and Commissions

22

Press Commissions

The government of India appointed two Press Commissions to make a comprehensive enquiry into the state of press in India and examine issues associated with its working-working conditions of journalists, freedom of the press, machinery for ensuring high standard of journalism, pattern and economics of ownership and ways and means to promote growth of language press and the regional press.

First Press Commission

The First Press Commission was appointed on 23 September 1952 as a commission of inquiry for the purpose of making an inquiry into the state of press in India, its past, present and future lines of development.

The Chairman of the Commission was Justice G.S. Rajadhyaksha; the other ten members included Dr. C.P. Ramaswamy Aiyar, Dr. Zakir Hussain, Dr. V.K.R.V. Rao, P.H. Patwardhan, J. Natarajan and Chalapathi Rau.

Its brief was to examine in particular the following vital areas of the Indian Press:

1. The control, management and ownership; and financial structure of newspapers, periodicals, news agencies and feature syndicates;
2. The effect of holding companies, the distribution of advertisements, and other external influences on healthy journalism;
3. The method of recruitment and training of journalists;
4. The working of monopolies and chains and their effect on the presentation of accurate news and fair views;
5. Machinery for ensuring high standards of journalism, liaison between Government and the press; the functioning of the Press Advisory Committees and organisations of editors and working journalists;
6. Newsprint supplies, and printing and composing machinery;
7. Freedom of press and repeal or amendment of laws not in consonance with it.

Cooperation from press and other agencies were minimal. The Commission had to send several reminders to journalists' associations, newspaper owners and editors in order to collect preliminary evidence. Out of 362 associations addressed for information, only 81 responded; only 26 out of 86 associations of working journalists; only one of the four associations of editors and only eight out of 101 Chambers of Commerce, bothered to return the questionnaire.

The response to the general questionnaire sent out was no better: the response rate was less than five per cent; barely 318 out of 11780 copies of the questionnaire mailed. Only 111 out of 7335 editors of newspapers and periodicals, 41 out of 88 working journalists, ten out of 300 advertising agencies, and 77 out of 1350 members of the public returned the copies duly filled in.

The commission also conducted a sample survey of readers, and collected oral evidence on camera of over 4000 witnesses in the metropolitan cities.

The Commission's Report was submitted in 1954 in two parts. Part I contained the massive report and recommendations; Part II was a detailed study of the history and development of journalism in India, researched and written up by J. Natarajan, who was also a member of the Commission.

It is the point of view of the public that dominates the Report and it is within this framework that the Commission deals with the overriding social aspect, the true nature of the freedom of press, the need for restraint and regulation, the healthy growth of the Press, the place of small newspapers, the working of news agencies or the meaning of editorial freedom. Even the recommendations on collective bargaining and service conditions had to be viewed within the framework of public interest.

The report found out that out of 330 dailies published at the time, five owners controlled 29 newspapers and 31.2 per cent of circulation, and while a mere 15 owners controlled 54 newspapers and over 50 per cent of the circulation.

The Commission warned against this tendency towards concentration of ownership, and towards monopolies. It provided a list of unfair and restrictive practices in the press and, in general, the lack of financial soundness and the excessive dependence on advertising in the industry.

Some of the recommendations and observations of the First Press Commission are as under:

(i) A Press Council be established whose objects should be:
   - (1) To safeguard the freedom of the press and help the press to maintain its independence;
   - (2) To censure objectionable types of journalistic conduct and by all other possible means to build up a code in accordance with the highest professional standards;

(3) To keep under review any development likely to restrict the supply and dissemination of news of public interest and importance;
(4) To encourage the growth of a sense of responsibility and of public service among those engaged in the profession of journalism;
(5) To study the developments in the press, which may tend towards concentration or monopoly, and if necessary, to suggest remedies therefore;
(6) To publish reports, at least once a year, recording its work and reviewing the performance of the press, its development and factors affecting them; and
(7) To improve methods of requirement, education and training for the profession by the creation of suitable agencies for the purpose, such as a press institute.

(ii) Decline in editor's status: There has been a general decline in the status and independence of the editor and this decline is noticeable, particularly, in the case of daily newspaper. In the past, it was quite usual for the majority of the readers to be both aware and conscious of the role played by the editor in the formulation of the views set out in a paper, and it was quite usual to refer to the paper not merely by its name, but by the name of the editor… The position has changed today and we feel that the bulk of the newspaper readers today may be unaware of who is the editor of their newspaper and indifferent to the name that appears on small print on the last page.

(iii) The news agencies should not merely keep themselves from bias and follow strictly the principles of integrity, objectivity and comprehensiveness in the coverage of news, but it should also appear to the newspaper, and to the public, that the news agencies are maintaining such a course.

(iv) While condemning the practice of giving astrological predictions, the commission said: The spread of the habit of consultation of, and reliance upon astrological predictions, particularly of the nature and in the manner they are published at present is certain to produce an unsettling effect on the minds of readers. We would describe the practice of publishing such prediction as undesirable.

(v) The commission found that the emoluments received by the journalists were on the whole unsatisfactory and recommended the appointment of a wage board for working journalist.

(vi) The commission recommended the appointment of the Registrar of Newspapers for India (RNI).

(vii) As a result of this recommendation, the office of RNI was created from 1 July 1956. The RNI verifies and regulates the availability of newspapers, registers them, containing detailed information on newspapers. The office also issues entitlement certificates to the newspapers/periodicals for the import of newsprint and import of printing machinery and allied materials required by the newspapers.

The Commission's recommendations were aimed at the development of public service-oriented press. A major recommendation was the appointment of a Press Registrar to maintain accurate data on the press, and its working, and a Press Council to act as a watchdog on the press (through self-regulation), to help raise standards of journalism and to build up a Code of Ethics to guide journalists. It also strongly recommended the development of the Indian language press, especially the growth of small newspapers in the smaller towns. To assist in this development, it recommended to the Government the setting up of a State Trading Corporation for newsprint, a reasonable scale of tariff for news services, a price-page schedule, readjustment of advertisement allotments and rates, and elimination of unfair and restrictive practices, including crossword and other prize competitions.

Also recommended were the principle of collective bargaining and trade unionism, and the fixation of minimum wages for working journalists.

The Report argued against concentration of ownership and the rise of monopolistic trends, recommending 'diffusion of ownership and control among a large number of persons, so that the chances of any dominant interests among the group of owners could be eliminated or cancelled mutually'.

It further recommended that 'diffusion be brought about by the gradual distribution of shares to the employees and, to a small extent, to the public, both in existing undertaking and in those to be started in future'.

The press Registrar and the press council were given the responsibility of investigating into monopolies that went against public interest. The Report deprecated the pressures brought to bear on newspapers by advertisers, both corporate and Government. It condemned practices, such as the publication of 'supplements' where 'a large amount of space is devoted to puffs', of reviews of the balance sheets and annual reports of only those companies that regularly advertised, of the influence of advertisers on news columns and editorials, and of the Government practice of withholding advertisements from 'Communist' and 'communal' publications.

The Report upheld the authority and status of the editor, and recommended that he be given administrative control over his staff, and that appointments of editorial staff be made with his consultation, as 'the future of the press depends on the independence of the editor'. It also recommended that the press eschew 'yellow journalism' and be independent, accurate and fair in the presentation of news. Besides, it recommended the streamlining of procedures of recruitment and training of journalists, and of the laws that related to the practice of journalism.

The Second Press Commission

The second commission was set up in May 1978; the Report was submitted in 1982. Its brief was to 'enquire into the growth and status of the Indian press since the last press Commission reported and suggest how it should develop in future'. To being with, Justice P.K. Goswami chaired the Commission, but he and his colleagues resigned when a new Government came to power at the Centre, in January 1980. The new Chairman was Justice K.K. Matthew and the members included Girilal Jain, Rajendra Mathur, Ranbir Singh, Amrita Pritam, P.V. Gadgil, Prof. H.K. Paranjape and others.

The terms of reference were revised, through many of the areas covered were very similar. They included the following areas:

1. The role of the press in a developing and democratic society;
2. The adequacy of the present constitutional guarantees on the freedom of speech and expression;
3. Constitutional and legal safeguards to protect the citizen's right to privacy;
4. Safeguarding the independence of the press against economic and political pressures, and from proprietors and management;
5. Responsibilities of the press, especially with regard to developmental policies;
6. The press as an industry, a social institution and a forum for discussion of public affairs;
7. Ownership pattern, chain newspaper, management practices, financial structure, and the economics of the press;
8. Advertising – Government and private, educational and commercial;
9. Government, Press Relations and role of official agencies;
10. Growth of small and medium newspapers and of the Indian language press; the periodical press and specialist journals;
11. News coverage and news values; news agencies and feature agencies; flow of news from and to India; the new international information order;
12. Training of journalists; research in journalism and mass communication; newspaper development.

The method of collecting data were the same as those followed by the First Press Commission: the use of questionnaires (32 in all on various areas enumerated in the terms of Reference), evidence from over 800 witnesses, recording of memoranda from 230 individuals and institutions, and 245 commissioned studies on various aspects of the Indian press. The Report critically analyses each of the above areas in 12 chapters, focusing on developments since 1952. Comparisons with developments in the press of other countries are frequently made. Based on this detailed analysis and criticism, the Commission drew up recommendations on each area of study.

The Commission, which submitted its report in 1982, said: "The role of the press in a developing and democratic society should neither be that of an adversary nor an ally of government. To be a mindless adversary or an unquestioning ally would be to abdicate judgement. A free press in our view should be a constructive critic."

The Commission said; "The press as a medium of communication is a modern phenomenon. It has immense power to advance or thwart the progress of civilization. Its freedom can be used to create a brave new world or to bring about universal catastrophe."

The Commission made concrete suggestion to curb the influence of foreign money on the press and suggested enactment of necessary changes in the laws for the purpose. It recommended the following five steps:

1. There should be specific legal provision under which no newspaper undertaking should have any foreign ownership either in the form of shares or in the form of loans,
2. Advertisements as well as printing contracts from foreign sources should be on terms no different from those applicable to similar work done for others,
3. Advertisement rates must be published each year and on every revision, and there should be no discrimination in their application to foreign advertisers,
4. Once a year, every newspaper should publish its profit and loss account with separate information about foreign and Indian sources,
5. Every newspaper undertaking must submit with its annual account, the following information to the Press Council.
   (a) Details of revenue obtained from advertisements and printing contracts in respect of foreign sources country-wise, including advertisements and printing contracts received through an Indian agency, and
   (b) Names of the top 100 shareholders with their nationality and address and the number and proportion of shares held.

Recommendations

The commission saw the role of the press in a developing and democratic society as being 'neither that of an adversary nor an ally of the Government'. It declared: 'To be a mindless adversary or an unquestioning ally would be to abdicate judgement. A free press should be a constructive critic'. Hence, the need for development Journalism, for news values that are 'in the interest of social health and national development', and for Investigative Journalism, which is oriented to social and economic issues.

A major concern of the Commission was 'objectionable communal writing'. It recommended that 'on the outbreak of a communal disturbance, newspapers should refrain from sensational presentation of the news and from giving community-wise figures of those killed and injured. However, when the situation gets stabilized, there should be no hesitation in investigating the causes of the rioting and its consequences, with identification of the communities concerned'. It recommended 'a stricter enforcement of the provisions in the Indian Penal Code with regard to communal incitement'. The Report, thus, argued for a 'positive role of the press – of bringing together the diverse elements in the nation's life by emphasizing those aspects, which tend towards unifying the communities', and 'strengthening of the moral fabric of society and discouraging the trend towards conspicuous and excessive consumption'. 'Public interest' should be the main criterion in Journalism, for 'the press has a social responsibility and accountability to the public'.

The Commission recommended that the press council should continue, but should be given powers to deny facilities of accreditation for a specific period if held guilty thrice, of violating journalistic ethics. However, 'it would not be desirable to draw up a Code of Ethics for newspapers; such a code could be built up case by case over a period of time.' A further recommendation was the amendment of the Press Council Act to enable the council to review the quality and adequacy of training facilities for journalists and for monitoring the performance of newspapers. A third recommendation was the inclusion of 'respect for privacy' in the Press Council Act of 1978, rather than any legislation incorporating a general right to privacy.

It further recommended that the editor take the responsibility for all matter published in his newspaper, including advertisements. The editor's authority should extend not only to the contents of advertisements, but also to the proportion of space devoted to them. Complaints of violation of the codes of ethics governing advertising should be examined by the Press Council. The commission wanted journalists to resist external pressures and 'to be on guard against the temptation to enjoy favours, whether from Government authorities, employers, advertisers or others'.

A significant recommendation of the Report was the establishment of a newspaper Development Commission, a body to promote the development of the press 'in directions, which will facilitate the growth in particular of Indian language newspapers of whatever circulation category, and of local interest and other publications of small and medium size in terms of circulation'. The Commission would promote research and development in the entire newspaper industry, liaise with various Government Departments concerned with the needs of the industry, and promote and coordinate training in journalism. It would be funded by an initial grant from the Government, a small cess on news on all newsprint consumption and a tax on advertisement revenue of newspapers.

The Commission proposed that the news agencies in the country explore hitherto untapped areas of news to give reporting a new purpose and unity. The agencies suffer from an urban bias and are preoccupied with political developments as in the national and state capitals. The news agencies are hardly in a position to report the social or economic changes taking place or intended changes not taking place – in the countryside. Because of the obsession of the newspapers with the political news, the news agencies spend much of their energy in reporting political events.

There is scope for pooling and countrywide dissemination of more significant stories of success or failure in rural development. This could form the nucleus of a rural news service, which would enable readers, including farmers, administrators and legislators in one part of the country to profit from the experiences in other parts.

The members of the Commission expressed the fear that suggestion for the introduction of price-page schedule and fixing the ratio of news and advertisement amounted to abridgement of the freedom of the press.

23

The Press Council/Media Council

The Press Council of India

Press Council is a mechanism for the Press to regulate itself. The *raison d'etre* of this unique institution is rooted in the concept that in a democratic society, the press needs at once to be free and responsible.

If the press is to function effectively as the watchdog of public interest, it must have a secure freedom of expression, unfettered and unhindered by any authority, organised bodies or individuals. But, this claim to press freedom has legitimacy only if it is exercised with a due sense of responsibility. The press must, therefore, scrupulously adhere to accepted norms of journalistic ethics and maintain high standards of professional conduct.

Where the norms are breached and the freedom is defiled by unprofessional conduct, a way must exist to check and control it. But, control by Government or official authorities may prove destructive of this freedom. Therefore, the best way is to let the peers of the profession, assisted by a few discerning laymen to regulate it through a properly structured representative impartial machinery. Hence, the Press Council.

Vir Bala Aggarwal and V.S. Gupta in the 'Handbook of Journalism and Mass Communication' elaborately write about the history as well as the composition, objectives and functions of the Press Council of India.

The Third International conference on Press Council was held in New Delhi. The conference decided to establish a world Association of Press Council. India and Sweden abstained from voting although they did not approve the motion. Sweden abstained from voting on the grounds that the members of the team had not been given the mandate to vote. India abstained for different reasons. The Press Council of India felt that an informational body would be preferable to a formal body. Proposals to form an International Code of Ethics were dropped, instead countries had been asked to form their own codes.

The institution of the Press Council emerged for the first time in Sweden in 1916 known as the Court of Honour. The idea gained quick acceptance in other Scandinavian countries, and later in other parts of Europe, Canada, Asia, Australia and New Zealand. Today, the Press Councils or similar other media bodies are in place in more than four dozen nations.

Now it has been established in more than 40 countries. In all the countries, except Italy and Holland, Press Councils have been set up voluntarily. The functions of the Press Councils differ from country to country. The British Press Council came into existence in 1953. It has served as a model for many countries.

The basic concept of self-regulation, which is the basis of founding Press Councils and similar media bodies world over, was articulated by Mahatma Gandhi, who was an eminent journalist in his own right, thus: "The sole aim of journalist should be service. The newspaper press is a great power, but just as unchained torrent of water submerges the whole country side and devastates crops, even so an uncontrolled pen serves, but to destroy. If the control is from without, it proves more poisonous than want of control. It can be profitable only when exercised from within."

Pandit Jawaharlal Nehru, while defending Press freedom, warning of the danger its irresponsible exercise entails, stressed: "If there is no responsibility and no obligation attached to it, freedom gradually withers away. This is true of a nation's freedom and it applies as much to the Press as to any other group, organisation or individual."

The First Press Commission (1954) came across in some sections of the Press, instances of yellow journalism of one type or another, scurrilous writing – often directed against communities or groups, sensationalism, bias in presentation of news and lack of responsibility in comment, indecency and vulgarity and personal attacks on individuals. The Commission, however, pointed out that the well-established newspapers had, on the whole, maintained a high standard of journalism. They had avoided "cheap sensationalism and unwarranted intrusion into private lives." But it remarked that "whatever the law relating to the Press may be, there would still be a large quantum of objectionable journalism, which, though not falling within the purview of the law, would still require to be checked." It was of the view that the best way of maintaining professional standards of journalism would be to bring into existence a body of people principally connected with the industry, whose responsibility it would be to arbitrate on doubtful points and to censure any one guilty of infraction of the code of journalistic ethics.

The Commission recommended the setting up of a Press Council. Among the objectives visualised for the Council were: "to safeguard the freedom of the press", "to ensure on the part of the Press the maintenance of High standards of public taste and to foster due sense of both the rights and responsibilities of citizenship" and "to encourage the growth of sense of responsibility and public service among all those engaged in the profession of journalism." The Commission recommended the establishment of the Council on a statutory basis on the ground that the Council should have legal authority to make inquiries as otherwise each member, as well as the Council as a whole, would be subject to the threat of legal action from those whom it sought to punish by exposure.

The Commission said that the Council should consist of men, who would command general confidence and respect of the profession and should have 25 members excluding the Chairman. The Chairman was to be a person, who was or had been a Judge of the High Court and was to be nominated by the Chief Justice of India.

The Press Council of India was first constituted on 4 July 1966 as an autonomous, statutory, quasi-judicial body, with Shri Justice J.R. Mudholkar, then a Judge of the Supreme Court, as Chairman. The Press Council Act, 1965, listed the following functions of the Council in furtherance of its objects:

- to help newspapers to maintain their independence;
- to build up a code of conduct for newspapers and journalists in accordance with high professional standards;
- to ensure on the part of newspapers and journalists the maintenance of high standards of public taste and foster a due sense of both the rights and responsibilities of citizenship;
- to encourage the growth of a sense of responsibility and public service among all those engaged in the profession of journalism;
- to keep under review any development likely to restrict the supply and dissemination of news of public interest and importance;
- to keep under review such cases of assistance received by any newspaper or news agency in India from foreign sources, as are referred to it by the Central Government.

Provided that nothing in this clause shall preclude the Central Government from dealing with any case of assistance received by a newspaper or news agency in India from foreign sources in any other manner it thinks fit;

- to promote the establishment of such common service for the supply and dissemination of news to newspapers as may, from time to time, appear to it to be desirable;
- to provide facilities for the proper education and training of persons in the profession of journalism;
- to promote a proper functional relationship among all classes of persons engaged in the production or publication of newspapers;
- to study developments, which may tend towards monopoly or concentration of ownership of newspapers, including a study of the

ownership or financial structure of newspapers, and if necessary, to suggest remedies thereof;
- to promote technical or other research; and
- to do such other acts as may be incidental or conducive to the discharge of the above functions.

The Act of 1965 provided that the Council shall consist of a Chairman and 25 other members. Of the 25 members, three were to represent the two houses of Parliament, 13 were to be from amongst the working journalists, of which not less than six were to be editors, who did not own or carry on the business of management of newspapers and the rest were to be the persons having special knowledge or practical experience in respect of education and science, law, literature and culture. By an amendment of the Act in 1970, the membership of the Council was raised by one to provide a seat for persons managing the news agencies.

The Chairman under the Act of 1965, was to be nominated by the Chief Justice of India. Of the three Members of Parliament, two representing Lok Sabha were to be nominated by the Speaker of the Lok Sabha and one representing Rajya Sabha, was to be nominated by the Chairman of the Rajya Sabha. The remaining 22 members were to be selected by a three-men Selection Committee comprising the Chief Justice of India, Chairman of the Press Council and a nominee of the President of India. The Chairman and the members were to hold office for a period of three years provided that no member could hold office for a period exceeding six years in the aggregate.

When in the early years of the Council's existence, a grievance was aired about the selection of a category of members, Parliament embarked on a search for a meticulous formula, which would ensure uncompromising impartiality and fairness in the selection of Chairman and other members. This led to the amendment of the 1965 Act, entrusting this work to a Committee comprising the incumbent of the three highest offices, which are considered as an embodiment of these attributes, namely, Chairman of Rajya Sabha, Speaker of Lok Sabha and Chief Justice of India. But, the pursuit for still less subjective scheme continued. Even a statistical formula was evolved for equitable presentation of the various representative organisations of the profession.

As has been referred to earlier, the composition of the nominating committee was changed by an amendment of the said Act in 1970, according to which the Chairman and the members from the press were to be nominated by a Nominating Committee consisting of the Chairman of the Rajya Sabha, the Chief Justice of India and the Speaker of the Lok Sabha.

The amending Act of 1970 introduced several other provisions in the Act. The manner of selection of persons of special knowledge or practical experience was specified. It provided that of the three persons to be nominated from among such people, one each shall be nominated by the University Grants Commission, the Bar Council of India and the Sahitya Academy. It also provided for raising the membership of the Council to give one seat to the persons managing the news agencies. Out of the six seats for proprietors and managers of newspapers, two each were earmarked for big, medium and small newspapers. No working journalist, who owned or carried on the business of management of newspapers, could now be nominated in the category of working journalists. Also, it was specified that not more than one person interested in any newspaper or group of newspapers under the same control, could be nominated from the categories of editors, other working journalists, proprietors and managers.

The Nominating Committee was empowered to review any nomination on a representation made to it by any notified association or by any person aggrieved by it or otherwise. The amended Act also barred re-nomination of a retiring member for more than one term. Where any association failed to submit a panel of names when invited to do so, the Nominating Committee could ask for panels from other associations or persons of the category concerned or nominate members after consultation with other such individuals or interests concerned as it thought fit.

Under the original Act, the Chairman was nominated by the Chief Justice of India. But, after this amendment, nomination of the Chairman was also left to the Nominating Committee.

The Council set up under the Act of 1965 functioned till December 1975. During the internal emergency, the Press Council was abolished on the expiry of the term on 31 December 1975. The Press council Act was expelled. It was stated that the council was being abolished because it was not able to carry on its functions effectively to achieve the objects for which the council was established. The Annual Report of the Ministry of Information and Broadcasting for 1975-76 said: The Press Council during the nine years of its existence had failed to curb the tendentious, provocative and unrestrained writings in the Press. It was unable to frame a code of conduct for editors and complaints of minor character mostly engaged its attention. Accordingly, the Press Council of India was abolished w.e.f. 1 January 1976.

Press Council of 1979

A fresh legislation providing for the establishment of a Press Council was enacted in 1978. The Act came into force on 1 March 1979. The objectives of the revised Press Council are:

1. To preserve the freedom of Press.
2. To improve standards of newspapers and news agencies in the country.

One of the main functions of Council is to enquire into complaints received by it and building up a code of conduct for newspapers, news agencies and journalists in accordance with high professional standards.

Composition of the Press Council

It should already be clear that the Press Council was brought about by an Act of the Parliament and derives its authority from that Act.

The present Council is a body corporate having perpetual succession. It consists of a Chairman and 28 other members. Of the 28 members, 13 represent the working journalists, of whom six are to be editors of newspapers and the remaining seven are to be working journalists other than editors. Six members are to be from among persons, who own or carry on the business of management of newspapers. One is to be from among the persons, who manage news agencies. Three are to be persons having special knowledge or practical experience in respect of education and science, law and literature and culture. The remaining five are to be Members of Parliament: three from Lok Sabha, and two from Rajya Sabha.

The new Act provides for selection of the Chairman by a Committee consisting of the Chairman of the Rajya Sabha, the Speaker of Lok Sabha and a person elected by the members of the Council from among themselves. The twenty representatives of the Press are nominated by the associations of aforesaid categories of newspapers and news agencies notified for the purpose by the Council in each category. One member each is nominated by the University Grants Commission, the Bar Council of India and the Sahitya Academy. Of the five Members of Parliament, three are nominated by the Speaker of the Lok Sabha and two by the Chairman of the Rajya Sabha.

Term: The term of the Chairman and the members of the Council is three years. After every three years, new members are appointed to the council. A retiring member is eligible for re-nomination for not more than one term. The present Chairman is Hon'ble Mr. Justice Markandey Katju (Judge, Supreme Court of India (Retd.)

An extremely healthy feature of the Indian Press Council is the scheme and procedure of the nomination of its Chairman and other members, following a long search based on the experience of several years of functioning of the Council. Despite being a statutory body, the Government and its authorities have been completely kept out of the nomination process except for publishing the notification in the official gazette of the names of the members nominated. Nor has it been left to any individual to decide, however eminent or highly placed he may be.

A totally non-subjective procedure, which leaves no scope for interference or influence by the Government or any other agency, was evolved with remarkable ingenuity. The scheme is in force since the enactment of the Press

Council Act of 1978 under which the revived Press Council was set up in 1979.

For the purpose of performing its functions or holding an enquiry under the Act, the council has been clothed its powers exercisable throughout India as are vested in a civil court while trying a suit under the Code of Civil Procedure, 1908. Thus, the Council can summon and enforce the attendance of persons and examine them under oath. It can require discovery and production of documents, receive evidence on affidavits, requisition public records or copies thereof from any court or office, issue commissions for the examination of persons or documents and finally for any other matter, which may be prescribed. The Act, however, recognizes immunity of a journalist from disclosing his source of information.

In his book, 'The Journalists' Handbook', M.V. Kamath says: The Council, it is important to remember, is NOT a court of law. It is a court of honour. Its verdicts are not judicial pronouncements. Therefore, there is no question of punishment imposed on an offending journalist or newspaper. By that same token, the Council cannot award damages to the aggrieved party. As Mudholkar puts it: The only weapon in its armoury is moral authority. The sole strength of the Council lies in its appeal to conscience.

Who can lodge a complaint against newspaper or journalist to the Council? Anybody. The Council does not even have to wait for someone to make a complaint if it thinks that a case against a newspaper can be made on its own. The complainants, incidentally, need not necessarily have a personal interest in the matter complained against. A complaint can merely be filed where the complainant has "reasons to believe that a newspaper has offended against the standards of journalistic ethics or public taste or that an editor or a working journalist has committed any professional misconduct or a breach of journalistic ethics."

Objectives and Functions of the Council

The objectives, some of which are given below, of the Council shall be to preserve the freedom of the press and to maintain and improve the standards of newspapers and news agencies in India:

(a) To help newspapers and news agencies to maintain their independence;
(b) To build up a code of conduct for newspapers, news agencies and journalists in accordance with high professional standards;
(c) To ensure on the part of newspapers, news agencies and journalists, the maintenance of high standards of public taste and foster a due sense of both the rights and responsibilities of citizenship;
(d) To encourage the growth of the sense of responsibility and public service among all those engaged in the profession of journalism;

(e) To keep under review any development likely to restrict the supply and dissemination of news of public interest and importance;
(f) To keep under review cases of assistance received by any newspaper or news agency in India from any foreign source including such cases as by any individual, association of persons or any other organization;
(g) To undertake studies of foreign newspapers, including those brought out by any embassy or other representative in India of a foreign State, their circulation and impact;
(h) To promote a proper functional relationship among all classes of persons engaged in the production or publication of newspapers or in news agencies;
(i) To concern itself with development such as a concentration of, or other aspects of, ownership of, newspapers and news agencies, which may affect the independence of the Press; and
(j) To undertake such studies as may be entrusted to the Council and to express its opinion in regard to any matter referred to it by the Central Government.

The Former Chairman, Press Council of India, Justice P.B. Sawant, in his paper 'Press Council: the Conscience Keeper' has said that during the last thirty years, the Council received 8939 complaints. Out of them, 2693 were by the Press against the police, the publicity department and revenue authorities, individual politicians or bureaucrats. The rest 6246 were against the Press. The complaints against the government and governmental authorities were mainly of false and malicious charges, false arrests and detentions in police custody, threats to life and property, non-cognizance of and inaction by police on complaints filed by the journalists, the collusion of the police with the anti-social elements criticized by the Press, and connivance at their violence, and threats to life, liberty and property of the journalists and owners of the newspapers, vindictive suspension and cancellation of advertisement bills, cancellation or suspension of accreditation press, withholding of or reduction in news-print quota, stoppage of electricity and water supply, attempt to demolish the premises where the newspapers were published or raids on newspaper offices, seizure of the copies of the newspapers and their destruction, etc. The complaints against the press have been mainly for publication of unverified and abusive language, printing of obscene pictures, communal and casteist writing and attempts to inflame communal passions, refusal to publish replies, encroachment on privacy, distorted and prejudiced reporting, suppression of facts, sensational and misleading headings completely at variance with the contents of the report, malicious reporting and writings, non-publication of the other side of the views expressed, mixing comments with fratricidal conflicts, plagiarism, *et al.*

Powers of the Council

Since the Council has no punitive powers to punish violations of the professional ethics by the press or the encroachment on the freedom of the press by the authorities, the Council has come to be looked upon as a toothless tiger. The critics, however, forget that the Council has been designed essentially as an internal regulatory mechanism of and by the press.

The exercise of powers by the Council will not only destroy the character of the Council as an internal mechanism of the Press, but will also embroil it in a large number of Court cases defeating the very objectives for which the Council was established.

This representative body has the power to warn, admonish, and censure any editor or journalist, who flouts the standards of journalistic ethics or public taste. It has the powers of a civil court and can, therefore, summon witnesses, inspect documents and receive evidence. Cases relating to the laws of libel, obscenity and contempt as also the invasion of privacy can be taken up by it for adjudication. It handles about 500 complaints against newspapers and journalists every year.

The Indian Press Council has, besides, 'not only to help newspapers and news agencies to maintain independence, but also to build up principles for maintenance of high standards of the journalistic profession with a stress on public taste, and fostering a due sense of rights and responsibilities of citizenship. It is for the press Council to keep under review all developments likely to restrict the supply and dissemination of news of public interest, including the question of concentration of ownership of newspapers and news agencies that may affect the freedom of the press.'

In June 1980, the Council decided to recommend to the Central Government the need to amend the press Council Act, 1978 so as to empower it to take penal action against defaulting newspapers 'which are indicted or censured', for infringement of journalistic ethics. The action suggested for newspapers were cessation of Central and State Government advertisements; and against journalists and editors, the withdrawal of accreditation facilities. The Second Press Commission recommended the arming of the press Council with power to improve penalties, but the Editors' Guild has not approved the move.

Role of the Council

M.V. Kamath, in his book, 'The Journalist's Handbook', wonderfully describes the role of the Council. He questions that if the Press Council has really no punitive power to enforce its rulings, what role can it play in keeping the press on the straight and narrow path? Answering the question himself, he writes that one answer is that the opinions expressed by the Council on the validity of complaints fulfil two useful functions: First, they would show that the abuses do not pass without anybody noticing or daring to raise a protest and second, the opinions would be a reminder to the press itself that both for its self-respect and its own interest, certain things, which have appeared wrong to a fair-minded body should not be done.

Kamath further quotes Justice Grover, who believes that 'the moral force of the Council's adjudication is not inconsiderable.'

But, we often ask of the consequences if a newspaper defies the ruling of the Council. In his first annual report, the Council's chairman, Justice Grover made the point that one form of 'bite' could be to suspend a newspaper or journalist from publication or professional practice, respectively. The still sharper 'bite' could be to send an editor to jail for the commission of offences. But there was no assurance that an editor, who had been jailed, would become a reformed character after his release from prison.

Justice Grover noted: "In the prevailing climate when moral values stand eroded, some sanctions, which will affect the erring newspapers financially, may turn out to be more effective than the punitive measures emanating from the ancient idea of 'tooth for a tooth'. The Council can only try and persuade the Government to initiate amendatory legislation in its behalf."

Recommendations of the Council

The Council in a resolution passed on 16 June 1980 in a meeting in Shimla where it decided to recommend to the Central Government that the Press Council Act, 1978 needed amendment empowering the Council to recommend to the Central and State Governments and to public sector undertakings, etc. to discontinue issuance of advertisements or to disallow any growth rate in the allocation of newsprint or to recommend to the Post and Telegraph Department of the Central Government to suspend the concessational postage registration for a specified period of defaulting newspapers, which are indicted or censured repeatedly.

The Council was also of the view that journalists and editors, who, in the opinion of the Council, violated the accepted principles of journalistic ethics should also be denied the facilities of accreditation for a specified period.

The Council also felt the need to introduce a suitable provision to make it obligatory on the concerned authorities to carry out the directions of the Council on its behalf.

The Council believed that such minimal powers were necessary to improve the health of the press in general.

Procedure for lodging a complaint and the process thereafter:

It is open to any person to lodge a complaint to the Council against a newspaper for breach of recognized ethical standards of journalistic propriety and taste. Herein, it is not necessary that the complainant be directly involved.

His complaint can be for the cause of the public at large. The motive behind his complaint can be in public interest.

M.V. Kamath, in his book, 'The journalist's Handbook', writes that the complaint again does not necessarily have to deal with breach of ethical standards: the alleged breach may be even in the non-publication of a news item or statement. Professional misconduct by freelance writer can also be a reason for complaint. In any event, the complainant will have to state precisely the manner in which the journalistic ethics have been breached.

There is a time limit though for lodging the complaint. The limit for lodging the complaint is two months from the time of the alleged breach of ethics the matters relating to the publication or non-publication of any matter in respect of dailies and weeklies or in regard of any matter transmitted by the news agencies. But the complaint has to be lodged within four months of commitment of the misconduct if the same is against any professional misconduct by an editor or a working journalist.

There is a requirement that the complainant should first write to the editor of the newspaper concerned drawing his attention to his alleged offence. The intention is to provide the editor with a fair chance to take such remedial steps as he thinks fit. The Council considers this rule necessary because there can be instances when the complainant has been wrongly informed or has misinterpreted facts; or that it may be a case of 'inadvertent error', which the editor would be ready to admit and rectify.

It is only when the complainant is not satisfied with the result of his correspondence with the editor that he could then take his complaint to the Council, backing it with the correspondence he has in hand. A lack of response from the editor, too, would be a fit case to be referred to the Council. As it is obvious that the Council will deal with any matter that is *sub judice* in the court of law so, it is required, that while filing a complaint before the Council, the complainant will have to declare that he has placed all the relevant facts before the Council and that no proceedings are ending in any court of law in respect of any matter alleged in the complaint to the best of his knowledge and belief. A declaration that he shall notify the Council 'forthwith, if during the pendency of the inquiry before the Council any matter alleged in the complaint becomes a subject matter of any proceedings in a court of law' is also necessary.

Reforming the Press Council

Frontline in Volume 28, Issue 24 (November 19-December 02, 2011) published an article 'Reforming the Press Council' written by A.G. Noorani. The important points are as follows:

- The new Chairman of the Press Council of India, Markandey Katju, wants to make it *an instrument of mediation in addition to adjudication.*

- There are two ways to remove these defects in the media. One is the democratic way (discussions, consultations, persuasion, negotiation, mediation and others); and the other way is by using harsh measures against the media (imposition of heavy fines on defaulters, stopping government advertisements to them, suspending their licences, and so on). If the media prove incorrigible, harsh measures may be required. But that should be done only as a last resort and in extreme situations. Ordinarily, the democratic method is the preferred one.
- But the archaic Press Council Act, 1978, is most unsuited to serve as a platform for such an imaginative enterprise. It was atrophied at its very birth by imposing (Section 5 (3)) a strange composition of the Press Council, which ensures its own irrelevance and cynicism by the press.
- Justice Katju rightly holds that the *electronic media should also be brought within the remit of the Press Council.* Indeed, failure to do so would violate the constitutional guarantee of equality (Article 14). Equals must be treated alike. Cinematograph films are different in that, unlike the print and electronic media, they are subject to pre-censorship. A ramshackle system of supposedly quasi-judicial institutions is set up by the Cinematograph Act, 1952. Meanwhile, the electronic media roams at large like a rogue elephant.
- However, if television is to be brought within the purview of the Act of 1978, as it must be, *the statute will have to undergo a drastic overhaul beginning with its title.*
- *The composition of the PCI must be changed fundamentally.* This would provide an excellent opportunity for reform, in which Justice Katju's PCI can perform the role as an instrument of mediation. But nowadays the media are more assertive. No reform will be acceptable or will work unless it is based on the largest measure of consensus in the print as well as the electronic media.
- The PCI *should no longer be headed by a former judge of the Supreme Court,* but by a person elected by the media itself. Appointment of a judge by the government adds an "outside" element to what is a "Court of Honour" comprising the media, mandated to discipline its own erring members. The task will be more effectively performed if the PCI represents both the wings of the media, print and electronic, and is headed by one of their own.

Madabhushi Sridhar, Professor and Coordinator of Center for Media Law and Public Policy, NALSAR University of Law, Hyderabad has written an article, 'What the Press Council could have been' on November 27, 2012 in 'thehoot.org' on the purposes the Press Council should serve, but does not. Some important points are:

- The present Press Council Act need to be fine-tuned, restructured and reformed to make it a comprehensive institution to achieve media accountability besides performing the prescribed functions.
- There is also a strong necessity to consider a change in the law to review whether the chairmanship of Press Council should be entrusted to an eminent professional journalist.
- The Press Council of India has two challenges before it. The first challenge is securing independence of the press; and secondly, making the press accountable.
- Press Council of India chairmen have repeatedly demanded reforms to give it more powers, teeth to enforce its directions and orders to make it almost like a court of law imposing punishments and penalties.
- Though it is a court for some purposes, it has no power of contempt to secure enforcement of its orders, which is a reasonable demand. At least, the Press Council should be in a position to deny certain government facilities to the media if it defies the orders of Press Council.
- However, the very concept of making a former Judge of Supreme Court the chairman of Press Council of India appears to be not conducive to the nature, character and functioning of the Council in relation to the dynamics of Press.
- There is absolutely no connection or relation between journalistic functioning and adjudication. Those, who understood the character of press, gave tremendous leadership. But most of the times, it remained a body of hearing complaints and passing orders of censure or admonition plus offering some advices, good words and morals, etc.
- Very little was done to achieve the statutorily prescribed functions such as, (a) foster a due sense of both the rights and responsibilities of citizenship, (b) provide facilities for the proper education and training of persons in the profession of journalism, (c) promote a proper functional relationship among all classes of persons engaged in the production or publication of newspapers and (d) study developments, which may tend towards monopoly or concentration of ownership of newspapers, including a study of the ownership or financial structure of newspapers, and if necessary, to suggest remedies thereof. A person without specialized expertise of

professional aspects of journalism may not be comfortable in leading the Council to achieve these stipulated statutory functions.

- Justice Goda Raghuram of the Andhra Pradesh High Court reviewed the working of Press Councils and their structures generally and stated in his address on the occasion of National Press Day (2011): "Operational deficit with many Press Councils is that they tend to consider themselves as complaints councils and insist on mediating and not on adjudicating against the Media, if they can avoid. On a holistic perspective, the role of Council is not just to satisfy a few individuals or groups, who have been hurt by the media; not just to avoid law suits; and not just to discourage the State or limiting the freedom of the Media to make money. A Press Council is meant to improve the news Media." (emphasis is added).
- Justice Raghuram suggested that "a vibrant council, on the other hand, should not avoid seeking publicity, taking positions, establishing case law and taking initiatives even when no complaint is lodged. It should also assume functions like reporting on the state and evolution of the media and periodic audit of the Media in terms of its essential functions. A Press Council should take interest in the training of journalists to improve professionalism and take up research on how the media actually functions, what influence it exercises and what citizens need from them… The Press Council should also encourage evolution of other Media Accountability systems, like documents, people and processes." Justice Raghuram detailed several measures for achieving accountability. For instance, corporatization of Media Houses has a serious impact on the profession, which transformed into news business. This tendency need to be researched properly, which might lead to effective alternatives to shape the ownership policy.
- The Press Council has no role to play in shaping journalistic education and institutional organization unlike the other professional councils, such as the Bar Council and Medical Council. The Press Council is a multimember, representative body imposed from top rather than emerging from the bottom.
- A Press Council is an essential concept, but it has to be comprehensively structured and provided with enough funds and infrastructure with proper demarcation of increased functions.

Criticism of the Council

The Hindu and the India Today published the articles 'Press Council has failed: Justice Verma' on November 5, 2011 and 'PCI ineffective body', says ex-Chief Justice of India on November 6, 2011 respectively. The following criticism can be highlighted:

> "Everyone knows the Press Council has failed in its mandate, and how ineffective it has been. So why not wind it up or scrap it?" Justice Verma said in an interview to *Outlook* magazine. "[PCI] is run on public money, so why not save some money?"

Justice Verma mentioned the following points in his criticism of the Council:

- The council is an "ineffective" body, which should be shut down if it fails to meet its mandate.
- The right to freedom of speech and freedom was supreme and self-regulation was the best way to check transgressions by media houses and journalists. There should be no intervention in this regard. We have the experience of Emergency when freedom of the press was muzzled.
- Channels listen to what we say on the content and depiction of news. It will take some time before broadcast journalism becomes perfect, but this is the way to go about this issue.
- The PCI Chairman (Justice Katju) should first put print media regulation in order and then comment on television news.
- Over the years, however, the PCI's record in fulfilling its mandate has been dismal – it lacks teeth since it has little power to impose a fine, leave alone putting a violator from either side behind bars.
- The NBA, set up only three years ago, has been more successful than the PCI. "Participatory self-regulation" is much more desirable than any regulations from above.

The Economic and Political Weekly, in its issue of January 3, 2009 published an article with the headline, 'The Press Council: An Expensive Irrelevance' wherein they wrote, "There are proposals to amend the Press Council Act 1978 to give the Press Council of India more powers, including the power to withhold advertisements. These are dangerous proposals. Contrary to conventional wisdom, the PCI does not need more powers. It needs a speedy burial by a statute."

From the above mentioned reports, we find that the Press Council of India has been criticized on several grounds. These grounds can be summarized as follows:

1. It has failed in its mandate and has not been effective.
2. It is better to wind it up as tax payer's money can be saved in this way.

3. The council, a quasi-judicial body, was set up for "preserving the freedom of the press" and "maintaining and improving standards of the press", while acting as "watchdog" of the press; so it should not extend itself to regulating electronic media.
4. It is expected to adjudicate on complaints against and by the press, respectively, for violation of ethics and violation of journalistic freedom. But over the years, however, the PCI's record in fulfilling its mandate has been dismal – it lacks teeth since it has little power to impose a fine, leave alone putting a violator from either side behind bars.

Amendments to the Press Council Act to introduce a new Media Council: The Press Council of India, a quasi-judicial body that oversees the functioning of print media, wants to adjudicate over the electronic media as well. It is in consultation with the Information and Broadcasting Ministry (I&B) over its long-standing demand to be converted into the Media Monitoring Commission of India, arguing that principles of good journalism, ethics, morality and freedom of speech apply to both print and electronic media in equal measure and hence, the two should be held to the same standards of accountability.

This proposal was first put forth by former chairman, Justice Sawant in 2000, but the government then had turned it down. The council, however, stuck to it over the years. The proposal is now under active discussion with the I&B Ministry.

In its proposal to the government, the council has also said that the print media was by and large more responsible compared to television channels, and the code of conduct defined under Section 13(2) of the Press Council Act, 1978, must apply to broadcasters too.

The PCI Chief Justice (retired) Katju said that he had proposed that the Press Council should be expanded to include 20 representatives of the electronic media industry and the body be named as Media Council. But he wondered what objection people had to this suggestion demanded for amendments.

'Self regulation' as practised by the electronic media is a 'ploy' to escape accountability, Press Council of India (PCI) chairperson Markandey Katju claimed and favoured bringing them under the ambit of the media watchdog. 'Everybody is accountable to people, but media people say we should not be accountable. We will practice self regulation. Self regulation is no regulation. It is an oxymoron. It is a deliberate ploy so that there is no regulation,' he said.

He said that the media often did not highlight the real issues like poverty and malnutrition that the country is facing and that the media created a hype around certain events like the Anna Hazare anti corruption protests, which often did not reach any conclusion. He added that paid news and other evils were widespread, yet it was being ignored.

Katju said that he was the person, who had strongly taken up the cause of freedom of expression on several occasions. He said that he is criticised when he says that freedom is coupled with responsibility. He further clarified that he wanted regulation and not control.

The proposed media council should have 48 members as against 28 members in the Press Council of India. Of the 48 members, 40 members should be representatives of the media (20 from print and 20 from broadcast). Katju said that the electronic media would also have their representatives in the proposed Media Council and their voices would also be heard.

The council should be given the power to punish the media that violates the media's code of conduct and the punishment could be in the form of suspending licence in the case of repeated violations, he said. He added that the council needs the teeth "not to bite, but to deter the offenders".

At a meeting with some senior editors on October 10, 2011, Katju had said that there were two ways to remove "defects" that have crept into the media. One is a democratic way, that is, by discussions, consultations and persuasion, which is the method he prefers. The other way is by using harsh measures against the media, e.g., by imposing heavy fines on the defaulters, stopping government advertisements for them, suspending their licence, etc.

If lawyers, judges, doctors and chartered accountants could be held accountable, he asked, "Why not the media? The media says that there should be no restriction on us. Are you not accountable? Everyone should be accountable in a democracy. are they above the law? Are they Gods?" He said that the electronic media should be under the PCI purview as "every social activity has to be regulated. There cannot be any freedom, which is absolute. Every freedom has to be subjected to reasonable restriction in the public interest.

"In a democracy, everybody should be regulated, be it media or any other organisation. The media freedom should be coupled with reasonable restrictions, which is common to all the professions. The media must enjoy the freedom to report, but at the same time, it should restrain itself from losing accountability. As the Chairman of PCI, I support the reasonable regulation on media, but not the control of media," Katju said.

"But there should be some regulation with some powers to punish, if you do something anti-national and anti-social." Rejecting the concept of self-regulation, Katju said that there had to be some external regulation, which should not be by the government, but by a statutory body, like the PCI.

Holding that media mainly focus on profit margins, Katju said, "The owners are asking the managers to keep up the TRP ratings. TRP ratings are kept high by showing things like astrology, half naked women and ghost stories."

Emphasising the role of media at a time when India is passing through a transition period from feudal agricultural society to that of modern industrial society, he said that the media should be pro-people at this juncture as they are undergoing a very painful period. "At this point of time, the role of idea, accompanied by the role of media becomes significant," the PCI Chairman opined.

Regretting that 90 per cent of people in India believe in Astrology, he appealed the members of the public to use common sense, develop scientific temper and to be rational.

At the same time, he also flayed the television channels and publications, which air/write on Dooms Day. "The Dooms Day is nothing, but nonsense," he said and added that such programmes should not be allowed to aired/telecast.

To give more teeth to the media watchdog, the government also said that it will amend the Press Council of India Act to empower it to suspend accreditation of a journalist or editor and registration of a publication besides stopping advertisements if they abuse their independence.

"The government is considering amendment in the Press Council of India Act," Information and Broadcasting Minister, Manish Tewari said in the Rajya Sabha, while replying to a resolution made by a member on March 15, 2013.

He said that the amendment, which was in the draft stage, would empower the Press Council of India (PCI) to direct authorities in states to suspend distribution of a publication and government advertisements to it for a period up to six months. Tewari also said that the proposed amendments included granting powers to the PCI to "suspend accreditation of journalist or editor for a period up to three months" and in case of non-compliance, it may direct suspension of registration for a period of up to a fortnight. He added that the amendments in the Act were to make it more adaptable to the changing times.

Stating that media was like any other business, the Minister said, "It may sound lousy, but media is a business like any other business in the world and, unfortunately, in this business the revenue models are flawed."

Justice Katju defends his demand with the statement, "Because at the end of the day, they are also in the same profession and need to follow the same principles of good journalism as their print counterparts."

24

Working Journalists and Other Newspaper Employees (Conditions of Service) and Miscellaneous Provisions Act, 1955

Introduction

This is an Act to regulate certain conditions of service of working journalists and other persons employed in newspaper establishments.

The First Press Commission found that the emoluments received by journalists were on the whole unsatisfactory. It could not undertake a detailed investigation for fixing scales of pay for different categories of employees but it recognized the necessity of fixing a minimum wage for the journalist employees and made recommendations relating to the minimum wages to be paid to them.

In 1955 this Act was enacted and the Industrial Disputes Act, 1947 was made applicable to working journalists also.

Salient Features of the Act

Section 2: *Definitions*: In this Act, unless the context otherwise requires:

(a)"Board" means–

(i) in relation to working journalists, the Wage Board constituted under section 9; and

(ii) in relation to non-journalists newspaper employees, the Wage Board constituted under section 13-C;

(b) "newspaper" means any printed periodical work containing public news or comments on public news and includes such other class of printed periodical work as may, from time to time, be notified in this behalf by the Central Government in the Official Gazette;

(c) "newspaper employee" means any working journalist, and includes any other person employed to do any work in or in relation to any newspaper establishment;

(d) "newspaper establishment" means an establishment under the control of any person or body of persons, whether incorporated or not, for the production or publication of one or more newspaper or for conducting any news agency or syndicate;

(dd) "non-journalist newspaper employee" means a person employed to do any work in, or in relation to, any newspaper establishment, but does not include any such person who—

(i) is a working journalist, or

(ii) is employed mainly in a managerial or administrative capacity, or

(iii) being employed in a supervisory capacity, performs either by the nature of the duties attached to his office or by reason of the powers vested in him, functions mainly of a managerial nature;

(e) "prescribed" means prescribed by rules made under this Act;

(ee) Tribunal means-

(i) in relation to working journalists, the Tribunal constituted under sec. 13-AA; and

(ii) in relation to non-journalists newspaper employees, the Tribunal constituted under sec. 13-DD

(eee) "wages" means all remuneration capable of being expressed in terms of money, which would, if the terms of employment, expressed or implied, were fulfilled, be payable to a newspaper employee in respect of his employment or of work done in such employment, and includes—

(i) such allowances (including dearness allowance) as the newspaper employee is for the time being entitled to;

(ii) the value of any house accommodation, or of supply of light, water, medical attendance or other amenity or of any service or of any concessional supply of food grains or other articles;

(iii) any traveling concession, but does not include—

(a) any bonus;

(b) any contribution paid or payable by the employer to any person fund or provident fund or for the benefit of the newspaper employee under any law for the time being in force;

(c) any gratuity payable on the termination of his service.

(f) "working journalist" means a person whose principal avocation is that of a journalist and who is employed as such, either whole-time or part-time, in, or in relation to, one or more newspaper establishment and includes an editor, a leader, writer, news-editor, sub-editor, feature-writer, copy-tester, reporter, correspondent, cartoonist, news-photographer and proof-reader, but does not include any such person who—

(i) is employed mainly in a managerial or administrative capacity; or
(ii) being employed in a supervisory capacity, performs, either by the nature of the duties attached to his office or by reason of the powers vested in him, function mainly of a managerial nature.

Section 5: *Payment of Gratuity*: Where any working journalist has been in continuous service, whether before or after the commencement of this Act, for not less than three years in any newspaper establishment, and his services are terminated by the employer in relation to that newspaper establishment for any reason whatsoever, otherwise than as a punishment inflicted by way of disciplinary action; or he retires from service on reaching the age of superannuation; or any working journalist has been in continuous service whether before or after the commencement of this Act, for not less than ten years in any newspaper establishment, and he voluntarily resigns on or after the 1st day of July, 1961, from service in that newspaper establishment on any ground whatsoever other than on the ground of conscience; or any working journalist has been in a continuous service, whether before or after the commencement of this Act, for not less than three years in any newspaper establishment, and he voluntarily resigns on or after the 1st day of July, 1961, from service in that establishment on the ground of conscience; or any working journalist dies while he is in service in any newspaper establishment; the working journalist or, in the case of his death, his nominee or nominees or if there is no nomination in force at the time of the death of the working journalist his family, as the case may be shall, without prejudice to any benefits or rights accruing under the Industrial Disputes Act, 1947 (14 of 1947), be paid, on such termination, retirement, resignation or death, by the employer in relation to that establishment, gratuity which shall be equivalent to fifteen days' average pay for every competed year of service or any part thereof in excess of six months.

Section 6: *Hours of Work*: No working journalist shall be required or allowed to work in any newspaper establishment for more than one hundred and forty-four hours during any period of four consecutive weeks, exclusive of the time for meals. Every working journalist shall be allowed during any period of seven consecutive days rest for a period of not less than twenty-four consecutive hours, the period between 10 p.m. and 6 p.m. being included therein.

Section 7: *Leave*: Every working journalist shall be entitled to earned leave on full wages for not less than one-eleventh of the period spent on duty; and leave on medical certificate on one-half of the wages for not less than one-eighteenth of the period of service.

Section 8: *Fixation or revision of rates of wages:* The Central Government may fix rates of wages in respect of working journalist; revise, from time to time, at such intervals as it may think fit.

Section 9: *Procedure for fixing and revising rates of wages*: For the purpose of fixing or revising rates of wages in respect of working journalists under this Act, the Central Government shall, as and when necessary, constitute a Wage Board which shall consist of—

(i) two persons representing employers in relation to newspaper
(ii) establishments;
(iii) two persons representing working journalists;
(iv) three independent persons, one of whom shall be a person who is or has been a Judge of High Court or the Supreme Court and who shall be appointed by that Government as the Chairman thereof.

Section 13-AA: *Constitution of Tribunal for fixing or revising rates of wages in respect of working journalists*: Notwithstanding anything contained in this Act, where the Central Government is of opinion that the Board constituted under Section 9 for the purpose of fixing or revising rates of wages in respect of working journalist under this Act had not been able to function (for any reason whatsoever) effectively, and in the circumstances, it is necessary so to do, it may, be notification in the official Gazette, Gazette, constitute a Tribunal, which shall consist of a person who is or has been, a Judge of a High Court or the Supreme Court for the purpose of fixing or revising rates of wages in respect of working journalists under this Act.

Section 13-B. *Fixation or revision of rates of wages of non-journalist newspaper employees*: The Central Government may fix rates of wages in respect of non-journalist newspaper employees; and revise, from time to time, at such intervals as it may think fit, the rates of wages fixed under this section.

Section 13-C: *Wage Board for revising rates of wages in respect of non-journalist newspaper employees:* For the purpose of fixing or revising rates of wages in respect of non-journalist newspaper employees under this Act, the Central Government shall, as and when necessary, constitute a Wage Board which shall consist of—

(i) two persons representing employers in relation to newspaper establishment;
(ii) two persons representing non-journalist newspaper employees; and
(iii) three independent persons, one of whom shall be a person who is or has been, a Judge of a High Court or the Supreme Court and who shall be appointed by that Government as the Chairman thereof.

Section 13-DD: *Constitution of Tribunal for fixing or revising rates of wages in respect of non-journalist newspaper employees:* Notwithstanding anything contained in this Act, where the Central Government is of opinion that the Board constituted under Sec.13-C for the purpose of fixing or revising rates of wages in respect of non-journalist newspaper employees under this Act has not been able to function (for any reason whatsoever) effectively, and in the circumstances, it is necessary to do it may, by notification in the official Gazette, constitute a tribunal which shall consist of a person who is, or has been, a Judge of a High Court or the Supreme Court, for the purpose of fixing or revising rates of wages in respect of non-journalist newspaper employees under this Act.

Punishment: It should be noted that the provisions of this Act shall apply to every newspaper establishment employing twenty or more persons; and is any employer contravenes the provisions of this Act, he shall be punishable with fine which may extend to two hundred rupees. If the offence is committed for second time, the fine may extend to five hundred rupees.

Express Newspapers (Private) vs The Union of India and Others: These petitions on behalf of certain newspaper establishments challenged, in the Supreme Court, the constitutional validity of the Working journalists (Conditions of Service) and Miscellaneous Provisions Act, 1955, and the legality of the decision of the Wage Board, constituted thereunder, purporting to act under s. 9 of the Act. The impugned Act, which was passed in order to implement the recommendations of the Press Commission and had for its object the regulation of the conditions of service of working journalists and other persons employed in newspaper establishments, provided, *inter alia*, for the payment of gratuity to a working journalist who had been in continuous service, whether before or after the commencement of the Act, for not less than three years, even when he voluntarily resigned from service, regulated hours of work and leave, provided for the payment of retrenchment compensation with retrospective effect in certain cases and by s. 9(1) laid down the principles that the Wage Board was to follow in fixing the rates of wages of working journalists. Under those principles the Wage Board was to have regard to the cost of living, the prevalent rates of wages for comparable employments, the circumstances relating to the newspaper industry in different regions of the country and to any other circumstances which it might consider relevant. The petitioners contended on various grounds that the provisions of the impugned Act violated their fundamental rights under Arts. 19(1)(a), 19(1)(g), 14 and 32 of the Constitution and that the decision of the Wage Board fixing the rates and scales of wages, which was arrived at without any consideration whatsoever as to the capacity of the newspaper industry to pay the same, imposed too heavy a financial burden on the industry and spelled its total ruin, was vitiated by a wrong approach and non-application of the proper criteria and transgressed the principles of natural justice and was, therefore, illegal and void: Held, that the constitutional validity of the impugned

Act, with the sole exception of s. 5(1)(a)(iii) of the Act which infringed Art. 19(1)(g) of the Constitution, was beyond question and as that section, severable as it was from the rest of the Act, must alone be declared ultra vires.

Gratuity, however, was a reward for good, efficient and faithful service rendered for a considerable period and there could be no justification for awarding the same when an employee voluntarily resigned, except in certain exceptional circumstances. The award of gratuity, therefore, to an employee who voluntarily resigned from service after a period of only three years, under s. 5(1)(a)(iii) of the Act, must be held to be unreasonable and wholly unjustified.

Although this Court would not normally enter into questions of fact, in this case the Wage Board had wholly ignored an essential condition for the exercise of its function and imposed a very heavy financial burden on the newspaper industry. Although the Classification of the newspaper industry on the basis of gross revenue, fixation of scales of wages, provisions as to the, hours of work, leave, retrospective operation in specified cases, and grouping of newspapers into chains or multiple units could not be said to be improper or unjustified, they made the burden heavier still.

The Board made no enquiry whatsoever as to the ability of the industry to pay either as a whole or region-wise and did not call for or hear representations from them before finalising its decision. Its decision was, therefore, ultra vires the Act and contrary to the principles of natural justice.

IJU'S Demands to Amend the Working Journalist Act

1. An amendment to make the non-implementation of wage awards a cognizable offence to ensure that no newspaper management gets away into not to implementing it.
2. Amendment to increase the age of superannuation from 58 to 60 years.
3. To amend the provisions of gratuity in working journalists act to provide for grant of gratuity after 5 year service.
4. To make it mandatory for the employers to issue appointment letters to all mofussial and part-time correspondents, by whatever name called, according to a fixed forma as suggested by Bachawat Wage Board.

Unit 5: Media Codes and Ethics

25

Advertising Standards Council of India (ASCI)

ASCI is a self regulatory voluntary organization of the Advertising Industry. It's mission is to maintain and enhance the public's confidence in Advertising.

The Advertising Standards Council of India (ASCI), established in 1985, is committed to the cause of Self-Regulation in Advertising, ensuring the protection of the interests of consumers. ASCI was formed with the support of all four sectors connected with Advertising, viz. Advertisers, Advertising Agencies, Media (including Broadcasters and the Press) and others like PR Agencies, Market Research Companies etc.

The Consumer Complaints Council is ASCI's heart and soul. It is the dedicated work put in by this group of highly respected people that has given tremendous impetus to the work of ASCI and the movement of self- regulation in the advertising.

ASCI is a voluntary Self-Regulation council, registered as a not-for-profit Company under section 25 of the Indian Company's Act. The sponsors of the ASCI, who are its principal members, are firms of considerable repute within Industry in India, and comprise Advertisers, Media, Ad. Agencies and other Professional/Ancillary services connected with advertising practice. The ASCI is not a Government body, nor does it formulate rules for the public or the relevant industries.

The Code for Self-Regulation in Advertising Purpose

The purpose of the Code is to control the content of advertisements, not to hamper the sale of products which may be found offensive, for whatever reason, by some people. Provided, therefore, that advertisements for such products are not themselves offensive, there will normally be no ground for objection to them in terms of this Code.

Declaration of Fundamental Principles

This Code for Self-Regulation has been drawn up by people in professions and industries in or connected with advertising, in consultation with representatives of people affected by advertising, and has been accepted by individuals, corporate bodies and associations engaged in or otherwise concerned with the practice of advertising, with the following as basic guidelines, with a view to achieve the acceptance of fair advertising practices in the best interest of the ultimate consumer:

(i) To ensure the truthfulness and honesty of representations and claims made by advertisements and to safeguard against misleading advertisements.
(ii) To ensure that advertisements are not offensive to generally accepted standards of public decency.
(iii) To safeguard against the indiscriminate use of advertising for the promotion of products which are regarded as hazardous to society or to individuals to a degree or of a type which is unacceptable to society at large.
(iv) To ensure that advertisements observe fairness in competition so that the consumer's need to be informed on choices in the market-place and the canons of generally accepted competitive behaviour in business are both served.

The Code's rules form the basis for judgement whenever there may be conflicting views about the acceptability of an advertisement, whether it is challenged from within or from outside the advertising business. Both the general public and an advertiser's competitors have an equal right to expect the content of advertisements to be presented fairly, intelligibly and responsibly. The Code applies to advertisers, advertising agencies and media.

Responsibility for the Observance of this Code

The responsibility for the observance of this Code for Self-Regulation in Advertising lies with all who commission, create, place or publish any advertisement or assist in the creation or publishing of any advertisement. All advertisers, advertising agencies and media are expected not to commission, create, place or publish any advertisement which is in contravention of this Code. This is a self-imposed discipline required under this Code for Self-Regulation in Advertising from all involved in the commissioning, creation, placement or publishing of advertisements. This Code applies to advertisements read, heard or viewed in India even if they originate or are published abroad so long as they are directed to consumers in India or are exposed to significant number of consumers in India.

The Code and the Law

The Code's rule are not the only ones to affect advertising.

There are many provisions, both in the common law and in the statutes, which can determine the form or the content of an advertisement. The Code is not in competition with law. Its rules, and the machinery through which they are enforced, are designed to complement legal controls, not to usurp or replace them.

Definitions

For the purpose of this Code:

- an advertisement is defined as a paid-for communication, addressed to the Public or a section of it, the purpose of which is to influence the opinions or behaviour of those to whom it is addressed. Any communication which in the normal course would be recognised as an advertisement by the general public would be included in this definition even if it is carried free-of-charge for any reason.
- a product is anything which forms the subject of an advertisement, and includes goods, services and facilities.
- a consumer is any person or corporate body who is likely to be reached by an advertisement whether as an ultimate consumer, in the way of trade or otherwise.
- an advertiser is anybody, including an individual or partnership or corporate body or association, on whose brief the advertisement is designed and on whose account the advertisement is released.
- an advertising agency includes all individuals, partnerships, corporate bodies or associations, who or which work for planning, research, creation or placement of advertisements or the creation of material for advertisements for advertisers or for other advertising agencies.
- media owners include individuals in effective control of the management of media or their agents; media are any means used for the propagation of advertisements and include press, cinema, radio, television, hoardings, hand bills, direct mail, posters, internet, etc.
- minors are defined as persons who are below the age of 18 years.
- any written or graphic matter on packaging, whether unitary or bulk, or contained in it, is subject to this Code in the same manner as any advertisement in any other medium.
- to publish is to carry the advertisement in any media whether it be by printing, exhibiting, broadcasting, displaying, distributing, etc.

Standards of Conduct

Advertising is an important and legitimate means for the seller to awaken interest in his products. The success of advertising depends on public confidence. Hence no practice should be permitted which tends to impair this confidence. The standards laid down here should be taken as minimum standards of acceptability which would be liable to be reviewed from time to time in relation to the prevailing norm of consumers' susceptibilities.

Chapter *I*

To ensure the Truthfulness and Honesty of Representations and Claims made by Advertisements and to Safeguard against misleading Advertisements:

1. Advertisements must be truthful. All descriptions, claims and comparisons which relate to matters of objectively ascertainable fact should be capable of substantiation. Advertisers and advertising agencies are required to produce such substantiation as and when called upon to do so by The Advertising Standards Council of India.
2. Where advertising claims are expressly stated to be based on or supported by independent research or assessment, the source and date of this should be indicated in the advertisement.
3. Advertisements shall not, without permission from the person, firm or institution under reference, contain any reference to such person, firm or institution which confers an unjustified advantage on the product advertised or tends to bring the person, firm or institution into ridicule or disrepute. If and when required to do so by the Advertising Standards Council of India, the advertiser and the advertising agency shall produce explicit permission from the person, firm or institution to which reference is made in the advertisement.
4. Advertisements shall neither distort facts nor mislead the consumer by means of implications or omissions. Advertisements shall not contain statements or visual presentation which directly or by implication or by omission or by ambiguity or by exaggeration are likely to mislead the consumer about the product advertised or the advertiser or about any other product or advertiser.
5. Advertisements shall not be so framed as to abuse the trust of consumers or exploit their lack of experience or knowledge. No advertisement shall be permitted to contain any claim so exaggerated as to lead to grave or widespread disappointment in the minds of consumers.
6. Obvious untruths or exaggerations intended to amuse or to catch the eye of the consumer are permissible provided that they are clearly to be seen as humorous or hyperbolic and not likely to be understood as making literal or misleading claims for the advertised product.
7. In mass manufacturing and distribution of goods and services it is possible that there may be an occasional, unintentional lapse in the fulfilment of an advertised promise or claim. Such occasional, unintentional lapses may not invalidate the advertisement in terms of this Code.

In judging such issues, due regard shall be given to the following:

(a) Whether the claim or promise is capable of fulfillment by a typical specimen of the product advertised.
(b) Whether the proportion of product failures is within generally acceptable limits.
(c) Whether the advertiser has taken prompt action to make good the deficiency to the consumer.

Chapter II

Advertisement should contain nothing indecent, vulgar, especially in depiction of women, or nothing repulsive which is likely, in the light of generally prevailing standards of decency and propriety, to cause grave or widespread offence"

Chapter III

To safeguard against the indiscriminate use of Advertising in situations or of the Promotion of Products which are regarded as Hazardous or Harmful to society or to individuals, particularly minors, to a degree or of a type which is Unacceptable to Society at Large.

1. No advertisement shall be permitted which:

(a) Tends to incite people to crime or to promote disorder and violence or intolerance.
(b) Derides any race, caste, colour, creed, gender or nationality"
(c) Presents criminality as desirable or directly or indirectly encourages people-particularly minors-to emulate it or conveys the modus operandi of any crime.(d) Adversely affects friendly relations with a foreign State.

2. Advertisements addressed to minors shall not contain anything, whether in illustration or otherwise, which might result in their physical, mental or moral harm or which exploits their vulnerability. For example, Advertisements:

(a) Should not encourage minors to enter strange places or to converse with strangers in an effort to collect coupons, wrappers, labels or the like.
(b) Should not feature dangerous or hazardous acts which are likely to encourage minors to emulate such acts in a manner which could cause harm or injury.
(c) Should not show minors using or playing with matches or any inflammable or explosive substance; or playing with or using sharp knives, guns or mechanical or electrical appliances, the careless use of which could lead to their suffering cuts, burns, shocks or other injury.

(d) Should not feature minors for tobacco or alcohol-based products.
(e) Should not feature personalities from the field of sports, music and cinema for products which, by law, either require a health warning in their advertising or cannot be purchased by minors.

3. Advertisements shall not, without justifiable reason, show or refer to dangerous practices or manifest a disregard for safety or encourage negligence.

4. Advertisements should contain nothing which is in breach of the law nor omit anything which the law requires.

5. Advertisements shall not propagate products, the use of which is banned under the law.

6. Advertisements for products whose advertising is prohibited or restricted by law or by this Code must not circumvent such restrictions by purporting to be advertisements for other products the advertising of which is not prohibited or restricted by law or by this Code. In judging whether or not any particular advertisement is an indirect advertisement for a product whose Advertising is restricted or prohibited, due attention shall be paid to the following:

(a) Whether the unrestricted product which is purportedly sought to be promoted through the advertisement under complaint is produced and distributed in reasonable quantities having regard to the scale of the advertising in question, the media used and the markets targeted.
(b) Whether there exist in the advertisement under complaint any direct or indirect clues or cues which could suggest to consumers that it is a direct or indirect advertisement for the product whose Advertising is restricted or prohibited by law or by this Code.
(c) Where Advertising is necessary, the mere use of a brand name or company name that may also be applied to a product whose Advertising is restricted or prohibited, is not reason to find the advertisement objectionable provided the advertisement is not objectionable in terms of (a) and (b) above.

Chapter IV

To ensure that Advertisements observe fairness in competition such that the Consumer's need to be informed on choice in the Market-Place and the Canons of generally accepted competitive behaviour in Business are both served.

1. Advertisements containing comparisons with other manufacturers or suppliers or with other products including those where a competitor is named, are permissible in the interests of vigorous competition and public enlightenment, provided:

(a) It is clear what aspects of the advertiser's product are being compared with what aspects of the competitor's product.

(b) The subject matter of comparison is not chosen in such a way as to confer an artificial advantage upon the advertiser or so as to suggest that a better bargain is offered than is truly the case.
(c) The comparisons are factual, accurate and capable of substantiation.
(d) There is no likelihood of the consumer being misled as a result of the comparison, whether about the product advertised or that with which it is compared.
(e) The advertisement does not unfairly denigrate, attack or discredit other products, advertisers or advertisements directly or by implication.

2. Advertisements shall not make unjustifiable use of the name or initials of any other firm, company or institution, nor take unfair advantage of the goodwill attached to the trade mark or symbol of another firm or its product or the goodwill acquired by its advertising campaign.

3. Advertisements shall not be similar to any other advertiser's earlier run advertisements in general layout, copy, slogans, visual presentations, music or sound effects, so as to suggest plagiarism.

4. As regards matters covered by sections 2 and 3 above, complaints of plagiarism of advertisements released earlier abroad will lie outside the scope of this Code except in the under-mentioned circumstances:

(a) The complaint is lodged within 12 months of the first general circulation of the advertisements/campaign complained against.
(b) The complainant provides substantiation regarding the claim of prior invention/usage abroad.

Conclusion

The Advertising Standards Council of India (ASCI), established in 1985, is committed to the cause of Self- Regulation in Advertising, ensuring the protection of the interests of consumers. ASCI seeks to ensure that advertisements conform to its Code for Self Regulation, which requires advertisements to be legal, decent, honest and truthful and not hazardous or harmful while observing fairness in competition.

And apart from the general Code of Self Regulation in Advertising, ASCI also has special Self-Regulation Guidelines on Advertising of Foods & Beverages (F&B), special Guidelines for Advertising of Educational Institutions and Programmes and Self-Regulation Guidelines on Advertisements for Automotive vehicles.

ASCI also mentions the minimum lettering size and duration requirement of "Supers" communicating disclaimers, qualifications etc. in an advertisement.

In the end it sets the guidelines for qualification of brand extension product or service.

26

Parliamentary Privileges

Article 105, 193, 194 and 361A of Constitution

Article 105: Powers, privileges, etc of the Houses of Parliament and of the members and committees thereof—

(1) Subject to the provisions of this constitution and the rules and standing orders regulating the procedure of Parliament, there shall be freedom of speech in Parliament.

(2) No Member of Parliament shall be liable to any proceedings in any court in respect of anything said or any vote given by him in Parliament or any committee thereof, and no person shall be so liable in respect of the publication by or under the authority of either House of Parliament of any report, paper, votes or proceedings.

(3) In other respects, the powers, privileges and immunities of each House of Parliament, and of the members and the committees of each House, shall be such as may from time to time be defined by Parliament by law, and, until so defined shall be those of that House and of its members and committees immediately before the coming into force of Section 15 of the Constitution (Forty fourth Amendment) Act 1978.

(4) The provisions of clauses (1), (2) and (3) shall apply in relation to persons who by virtue of this constitution have the right to speak in, and otherwise to take part in the proceedings of, a House of Parliament or any committee thereof as they apply in relation to members of Parliament.

Article 193: Penalty for sitting and voting before making oath or affirmation under Article 188 or when not qualified or when disqualified. If a person sits or votes as a member of the Legislative Assembly or the Legislative Council of a State before he has complied with the requirements of Article 188, or when he knows that he is not qualified or that he is disqualified for membership thereof, or that he is prohibited from so doing by the provisions of any law made by Parliament or the legislature of the State, he shall be liable in respect of each day on which he so sits or votes to a penalty of five hundred rupees to be recovered as a debt due to the State Powers, Privileges and Immunities of State Legislatures and their Members.

Article 194: Powers, privileges, etc, of the House of Legislatures and of the members and committees thereof—

(1) Subject to the provisions of this Constitution and to the rules and standing orders regulating the procedure of the Legislature, there shall be freedom of speech in the Legislature of every State.

(2) No member of the Legislature of a State shall be liable to any proceedings in any court in respect of anything said or any vote given by him in the Legislature or any committee thereof, and no person shall be so liable in respect of the publication by or under the authority of a House of such a Legislature of any report, paper, votes or proceedings.

(3) In other respects, the powers, privileges and immunities of a House of the Legislature of a State, and of the members and the committees of a House of such Legislature, shall be such as may from time to time be defined by the Legislature by law, and, until so defined, shall be those of that House and of its members and committees immediately before the coming into force of Section 26 of the Constitution forty fourth Amendment Act, 1978.

(4) The provisions of clauses (1), (2) and (3) shall apply in relation to persons who by virtue of this Constitution have the right to speak in, and otherwise to take part in the proceedings of a House of the Legislature of a State or any committee thereof as they apply in relation to members of that Legislature.

Article 361(A): Protection of publication of proceedings of Parliament and State Legislatures—

(1) No person shall be liable to any proceedings, civil or criminal, in any court in respect of the publication in a newspaper of a substantially true report of any proceedings of either House of Parliament or the Legislative Assembly, or, as the case may be, either House of the Legislature, of a State, unless the publication is proved to have been made with malice:

> Provided that nothing in this clause shall apply to the publication of any report of the proceedings of a secret sitting of either House of Parliament or the Legislative Assembly, or, as the case may be, either House of the Legislature, of a State.

(2) Clause (1) shall apply in relation to reports or matters broadcast by means of wireless telegraphy as part of any programme or service provided by means of a broadcasting station as it applies in relation to reports or matters published in a newspaper.

Explanation: In this article, "newspaper" includes a news agency report containing material for publication in a newspaper.

27

Guidelines for Parliamentary Coverage

(Geeta Mukherjee Committee's Report)

Coverage of Parliament in All India Radio and Doordarshan Broadcast

In a democratic country like India, coverage of parliament proceedings in news and reviews has a special importance. It deserves proper care and attention. Parliament represents the people and the government is accountable to it. Its legislative functions are most important and concern the entire nation. Similarly, statements of government policies and discussions thereon are of great interest to the people. The deliberations in the two Houses project the views of political parties, groups and individual Member of Parliaments which are also of interest to the people. Adjournment motions, Callings, Attention notices, Interpretations, etc. should be taken into account for reporting. Therefore, important happenings in ethics of the two Houses should find a place in the news bulletins or reviews.

However, in order to make the coverage of the proceedings of the Parliament meaningful and non repetitive, it is necessary to have a clearly defined approach to the selection of material and its treatment in the news bulletins and in the reviews. Obviously announcements of important decisions on policy statements by Ministers and speeches by Members belonging to the ruling party and the opposition parties should find a place in the news bulletins on the basis of their news values. The review should avoid needless repetition and aim at giving an overview of the entire day's proceedings. They should also not be a mere chronological account but reflect the colour and the atmosphere of the day's proceedings, providing background, wherever necessary, of the subject discussed.

It is possible that in the news bulletins and in the Parliament reviews in English/Hindi from Delhi, some of the speakers and their observation may not get adequate notice especially if the subject happens to be of limited regional interest. This can be remedied by making the news bulletins in the regional languages beamed to specific regions providing adequate coverage of this part of the Parliament proceedings. To achieve this, the duration of regional language bulletin from Delhi may have to be increased.

The various stations of AIR also have their own regional language bulletins. Topics which are of specific interest to the region should find adequate coverage in these regional bulletins. In view of the importance of parliamentary coverage it may be necessary for AIR to set up a separate desk. The desk under the charge of a senior newsman conversant with the working of Parliament should coordinate the material put out in the news bulletins and in the reviews and also decide which items are more suitable for inclusion in regional bulletins from Delhi or the regional stations.

The policy of parliamentary coverage should be extended to the coverage of proceedings in State Assemblies by the regional stations of AIR. The coverage should be both objective and balanced. Important policy statements and announcements of the CM and other ministers should be given due importance.

Guidelines for Coverage of Parliamentary Proceedings by Air and Doordarshan

In May 1993, the Government of India appointed a Committee headed by Ms. Geeta Mukherjee, MP, to go into the process of coverage of Parliamentary proceedings by AIR and DD. The other members of the Committee were Ms. Veena Verma, Mr. David Ladger, Mr. Arvind Trivedi and Mr. Nandi Yellaiah, all of whom were Members of Parliament.

The following guidelines are based on the recommendations of the Committee:

1. AIR and DD will provide comprehensive coverage to Parliamentary proceedings, ensuring a balance between different points of view without violating Parliamentary privileges.
2. There should be a faithful summing up of views both in support of the government and against it. A balanced picture should be presented and the view point of the government's critics should find adequate representation. It should be ensured that there is no partiality in reporting the proceedings.
3. Important issues raised in both Houses should be covered properly and the focus should not be lost sight of. It should be ensured that all important points are covered in both English and Hindi.
4. A high standard of accuracy in covering the Parliamentary proceedings is required. Professional responsibility should be the hallmark of reporting.

5. Items should be included depending upon their news values and on the basis of professional judgement whether a particular issue merits being noticed or not. Announcements, statements and discussions should be judged by their news values and public interest. This will also apply to questions, answers and supplementaries and other proceedings of Parliament.
6. A remark which has been expunged or not taken on record should not be reported. Whenever in doubt, the official record of the proceedings should be consulted. It should be ensured that the discussions, conducted whether in Hindi or English, are faithfully reported. In case of serious allegations against the government or the opposition party, extra care should be taken to ensure balanced reporting.
7. There should be balance between the coverage of the Lok Sabha and that of Rajya Sabha.
8. The news bulletins should take note of important contributions by members and should not read like a string of names.
9. **Questions:** While including the replies given to Parliamentary Questions in the news, inclusion of names of questioner or his/her party affiliation in the news bulletin is not necessary. In the case of short notice questions, however, name(s) of the questioner(s) may be given.
10. **Zero Hour:** Extra care should be taken while reporting proceedings during the Zero Hour. The inclusion of an item raised during the Zero Hour in the news bulletin will depend upon the importance of the subject, mood of the House, time spent over it, the support received by it and the frequency with which the matter has been raised. Whenever a matter raised during the Zero Hour is reported, the name(s) of the member(s) who raised it, should be reported.
11. **Parliamentary Debates:** In all cases of Parliamentary Debate, the name of the member who initiates the debate should be given. The view point of other members who speak should be summed up. Mentioning names of participants in order in which they speak is not necessary.
12. **Motion:** Whenever news of an Adjournment Motion or Calling Attention Motion or Privilege Motion or Special Mention or half an hour discussion is included in the news bulletin, the name of the mover of the motion should be given. If there are more than one sponsors, the name of the first mover be given. Discussions on subjects of wide public interest should be noticed adequately.
13. **No Confidence Motion:** The name of the movers of such motions along with their party affiliation should be given. Names of the

Ministers intervening on behalf of the government should also be mentioned. The name of the Leader of the Opposition and the names of the former Prime Ministers, if they participate in the debate, should also be mentioned without giving their party affiliation. The view of the major political parties represented in the Lok Sabha should be mentioned without giving names of the Members representing the political party.

14. **Papers laid on the table:** Stories pertaining to reports which have news value may be included.
15. **Legislative business:** On coverage of a government Bill, the practice should be to give the name of the concerned Minister only along with important points made by him. But there should be a faithful summing up of the views both in support of the Bill and against it. In case where the Bill is opposed at the introduction stage and there is scope for inclusion of the same in the news story, the names and arguments of the members who opposed the introduction of the Bill should be given invariably along with the Minister's reply to such questions.
16. **President's address:** The news story should do full justice to the Address in view of its importance.
17. **Incidents:** When incidents in Parliament are reported because of their news values, no attempt should be made to dramatize them or devote disproportionate time to them. In incidents of walkout, dharna, movement of the MPs towards the well of the House, if the names of Members of parties are reported, care should be taken that the news stories are completely accurate and can be defended.

Sansad Samachar and Today in Parliament

18. **Selection of script writers:** Experienced persons should be engaged for writing the scripts of Sansad Samachar, Today in Parliament and Parliament News. Only those persons should be selected as script writers who have experience of covering at least two or three sessions of Parliament.
19. **Training of script writers:** Services of senior and experienced journalists should be utilized for training persons included in the panel of script writers. The possibility of arranging an orientation course for script writers similar to the one arranged for the new MPs should be examined.

Norms for Coverage of Today in Parliament and Sansad Samachar

20. All important points raised in Parliament should be covered in the scripts in both English and Hindi. Important issues raised in both

Houses should be covered properly and the focus should not be lost sight of. It should be ensured that the discussions conducted, whether in Hindi or English, are faithfully reported. There should be no partiality in reporting the proceedings.

21. Names of MPs and their party affiliation should be reported correctly. It should be ensured that the names of the MPs are pronounced correctly.
22. Supplementaries should be included. All points raised during the Zero Hour by Members, according to the record, should be noticed. Special mentions in the Rajya Sabha and points raised under Rule 377 in the Lok Sabha should be covered properly.
23. Efforts should be made to cover the proceedings till an hour before the broadcast/telecast of Parliamentary news/*Samachar*. In the case either of the Houses sitting late, another script for covering the portion of the debate left out should be broadcast/telecast the next morning.
24. The script should be vetted by a Senior News Editor of AIR/DD.
25. The persons deployed for reading Parliament News/Sansad Samachar should be of some standard in quality as those who read the news and, as far as possible, should be from the panel of News Readers.

Coverage of Parliamentary Proceedings over Doordarshan

26. While covering the Question Hour/important debates, the camera should not focus only on the Speaker, but scan the House also.
27. During the coverage of the Question Hour, Members who raise their hands for specific questions should also be focussed upon. This is necessary as people should know that the Members were keen to raise questions/issues but were not able to do so because of shortage of time.
28. Photographs of initiators of important topics and discussions like Calling Attention Motions under rules 193, 184 in the Lok Sabha and half an hour short duration discussions in the Rajya Sabha should be shown. This would not cover special Mentions, Zero Hour and points raised under rule 377.

28

Air Code for Election Coverage

Guidelines for Covereage of Elections by Akashvani and Doordarshan

General

1. All personnel in *Akashvani* and DD engaged in coverage of elections must familiarize themselves with the provisions of Representation of People Act and the Rules issued thereunder. Strict adherence to the legal provisions must be ensured.

2.1. *Akashvani* and DD should, in close coordination with the Election Commission and Chief Electoral officers, arrange programmes and broadcasts with a view to:

(a) Explaining to voters their rights and duties in connection with the election;
(b) Urging every voter to exercise his democratic right to vote;
(c) Helping to create a climate of opinion in which free, fair and peaceful elections are possible;
(d) Assuring the weaker sections of society and minorities of the steps taken for their protection during and after the elections;
(e) Informing the voters about procedural matters and arrangements that are being made for the conduct of the elections;
(f) Explaining the arrangements made to ensure that there is no intimidation of voters or coercion during and after the election and complete secrecy of voting is maintained.

2.2. For this purpose, *Akashvani* and DD should arrange broadcasts, in general programmes as well as special audience programmes, by Chief Election Commissioner, Chief Electoral officers and prominent non-political personalities.

2.3. The text of these broadcasts might be released to the local press through the Information Department of the State government and the Regional Information Officer of the Press Information Bureau and also utilized as part of the comparing material in special audience programmes.

Coverage of News and General Information

1. AIR and DD should treat all election news factually, objectively and impartially.

2. *Talks and broadcasts*

(i) Ministers, Members of Rajya Sabha, Members of Lok Sabha, Members in Legislative Assemblies and Councils in the states, political leaders, election candidates or their agents, and persons who are closely identified with political parties, even though they may not be holding any office in a party organisation, should not be invited by AIR and DD to broadcast on any subject that is related to elections.

(ii) 'Spotlight', 'Current Affairs', 'Mid Week Review', 'Newsreel' and the corresponding programmes in Hindi and other languages will continue to deal with the topical issues and problems.

3. *News*: The following maybe noticed by AIR and DD for news coverage:

(a) *Election manifestoes*:

  (i) Election manifestoes of political parties recognized as All India parties by the Election Commission should be given fair, impartial and adequate coverage in the Central news bulletins. The manifesto of each party should be noticed only once in the major English, Hindi and other Indian language news bulletins.

  (ii) Election manifestoes of parties recognized at the state level will be noticed in similar manner in the regional news bulletins and the central bulletins concerned.

  (iii) Election manifestoes, if any, of regional units of All India parties will be covered only in the regional bulletins of the area concerned.

  (iv) Manifestoes will be covered when they are released to the Press and only a brief summary with amendments, if any, will be given when formally and finally adopted.

(b) *Party alliance*: Alliance between various parties for election purposes, when announced officially should be covered in the central news bulletins. Regional news bulletins may also carry such announcements when covered in the central news bulletins. Adjustments made at the state level may be noticed only on news value.

(c) *List of candidates*:

  (i) Both English and language news bulletins broadcast from Delhi should notice final lists of candidates whether in part or as a whole, when officially released by the Central Committees of the various political parties. Only the total number of candidates filed by the party should be announced. The news of prominent and well known personalities contesting the election may be noticed in central and regional news bulletins. The name of the constituency may also be mentioned if it has some special significance. Notice may also be taken, if any prominent person decides not to contest the election.

(ii) After the withdrawal stage, whenever the name of anyone candidate is mentioned, names of other candidates contesting from the same constituency should be given.

(d) *Speeches and announcements*:

(i) Speeches made by Central and State Ministers or prominent leaders of political parties may be noticed on the basis of their news value, with the provision that portions which are in the nature of party propaganda or electioneering, should be kept out.

(ii) Policy announcements or decisions of government even when these are made at election meetings will continue to be noticed. AIR and DD will continue to provide coverage of government activities, programmes and achievements. Sober criticism of government policies and their implementation may also be covered.

(iii) Attacks or criticism of personal nature should scrupulously be avoided.

(iv) Constructive activities and programmes unrelated to election will continue to be noticed by AIR and DD on their news and information value.

(e) *Coverage of polling*: Central and regional news bulletins will try to present a picture of the polling scene, giving the various interesting features. The percentage of polling should be reported, but after due verification. The pre-election scene in a state or the country as a whole, may also be covered by AIR and DD, but without expressing views or comments, one way or the other.

(f) *Election incidents*: Any serious election incident, if it is of sufficient news value, should be reported, but the facts and seriousness of such incidents should be checked with district authorities.

29

Doordarshan Commercial Code

Doordarshan provides a code that was passed by the Parliament in 1987. It illustrates 33 do's and don't's for private companies and advertising agencies for commercial broadcasting.

The codes are also designed to counter act the misuse of advertising and to further develop the sense of responsibility on the part of advertisers and consumers.

The Codes are exhaustively laid out. It clarifies a number of issues in considerable detail. There are general codes, codes for children, codes in relation to the advertising of medicines and treatments; 15 different Acts and Rules are mentioned and recommended to be familiar with the legislations affecting advertising.

The central government has also asked the state governments to constitute monitoring committees at the district levels to monitor private satellite television channels and local cable channels to detect and look into violation of advertising code.

Code for Commercial Advertising on Doordarshan

Definitions: In this Code, unless the context otherwise requires:

(i) "Government" means, Government of India.

(ii) "Director General" means, the Director General, Doordarshan or any officer duly authorised by him on his behalf and includes the Director, Doordarshan Kendra.

(iii) "Advertiser" means any individual or organisation including a commercial concern which has offered any advertisement to telecast over television.

(iv) "Advertising Agency" means any organisation which is accredited to, or registered with Doordarshan as such.

(v) "Advertisement" includes any item of publicity for goods or services inserted in the programme telecast by Doordarshan with a view to increase sales.

(vi) "Spot Advertisement" means any direct advertisement mentioning products/services, their merits and other related details.

(vii) "Advertising Association" means an Association or Society or any other body of whose constituent members are advertising Agencies registered or accredited to Doordarshan.

Scope: (a) The Director General, Doordarshan shall be the sole judge of the suitability or otherwise of an advertisement for telecast and his decision in this regard shall be final.

(b) Doordarshan time shall be sold to the Advertisers/Advertising Agencies at the sole discretion of the Director General, Doordarshan according to the prescribed rates.

(c) The advertisement should be clearly distinguishable from the programme by using suitable wipes/blank, in order to avoid the message of the programme getting mixed up with the content and images of the advertisement.

I. Introduction

Advertising is an important and legitimate means for the seller to awaken interest in his goods and services. The success of advertising depends on public confidence. Hence no practice should be permitted which tends to impair this confidence. The standards laid down here should be taken as minimum standards of acceptability which would be liable to be reviewed from time to time in relation to the prevailing norms of viewer's susceptibilities.

The following standards of conduct are laid down in order to develop and promote healthy advertising practices in Doordarshan. Responsibility for the observance of these rules rests equally upon the Advertiser and the Advertising Agency.

All those engaged in advertising are strongly recommended to familiarise themselves with the legislation affecting advertising in this country, particularly the following Acts and the Rules framed under them:

(1) Drugs and Cosmetics Act, 1940.
(2) Drugs Control Act, 1950.
(3) Drugs and Magic Remedies (Objectionable Advertisements) Act, 1954.
(4) Copyright Act, 1957.
(5) Trade and Merchandise Marks Act, 1958.
(6) Prevention of Food Adulteration Act, 1954.
(7) Pharmacy Act, 1948.
(8) Prize Competition Act, 1955.
(9) Emblems and Names (Prevention of Improper Use) Act, 1950.

(10) Consumer Protection Act, 1986.
(11) Indecent Representation of Women (Prohibition) Act, 1986.
(12) AIR/Doordarshan Code.
(13) Code of Ethics for advertising in India issued by the Advertising Standard Council of India.
(14) Code of 'Standards in relation to the advertising of medicine and treatments'.
(15) Standards of practice for Advertising Agencies (The list is illustrative and not exhaustive).

II. The Code

General Rules of Conduct in Advertising

1. Advertising shall be so designed as to conform to the laws of the country and should not offend morality, decency and religious susceptibilities of the people.

2. No Advertisement shall be permitted which:

(i) derides any race, caste, colour, creed and nationality;
(ii) is against any of the directive principles, or any other provision of the Constitution of India;
(iii) tends to incite people to crime, cause disorder or violence, or breach of law of glorifies violence or obscenity in any way;
(iv) presents criminality as desirable;
(v) adversely affects friendly relations with foreign States;
(vi) exploits the national emblem, or any part of the Constitution or the person or personality of a national leader or State Dignitary;
(vii) relates to or promotes cigarettes and tobacco products, liquor, wines and other intoxicants;
(viii) in its depiction of women violates the constitutional guarantees to all citizens such as equality of status and opportunity and dignity of the individual. In particular, no advertisement shall be permitted which projects a derogatory image of women. Women must not be portrayed in a manner that emphasises passive, submissive qualities and encourages them to play a subordinate, secondary role in the family and society. The portrayal of men and women should not encourage mutual disrespect. Advertiser shall ensure that the portrayal of the female form is tasteful and aesthetic, and is within the well established norms of good taste and decency.

3. No advertisement message shall in any way be presented as News.

4. No advertisement shall be permitted the objects whereof are wholly or mainly of a religious or political nature; advertisements must not be directed towards any religious or political end or have any relation to any industrial dispute.

5. Advertisement for services concerned with the following shall not be accepted.

(i) Unlicenced employment services;
(ii) Sooth-sayers etc., and those with claims of hypnotism;
(iii) Betting tips and guide books etc., relating to horse-racing or other games of chance.

6. Doordarshan accepts the advertisements of educational institutions/ colleges. However, it must be ensured that the institutions/colleges are genuine so as to ensure that students do not get misled.

Doordarshan will also accept advertisements relating to holiday resorts and hotels.

Doordarshan also accepts the advertisements relating to real estate including sale of flats/land, flats for rent both commercial and residential. However, to ensure that viewers do not get misled by false claims, it has been decided that all such advertisements must carry a statutory message at the end in the form of super imposition or caption as follows:

"viewers are advised to check the genuineness of the claims made".

Doordarshan has also allowed the telecast of:

(i) Foreign products and foreign banks including financial services;
(ii) Jewellery and precious stones;
(iii) Mutual funds approved by SEBI;
(iv) Hair dyes;
(v) Matrimonial agencies;

7. The items advertised shall not suffer from any defect or deficiency as mentioned in Consumer Protection Act 1986.

8. No advertisement shall contain references which are likely to lead the public to infer that the product advertised or any of its ingredients has some special or miraculous or super-natural property or quality, which is difficult of being proved, e.g. cure for baldness, skin whitener, etc.

9. No advertisement shall contain the words 'Guarantee' or 'Guaranteed', etc. unless the full terms of the guarantee are available for inspection by the Director General, Doordarshan, and are clearly set out in the advertisement and are made available to the purchaser in writing at the point of sale or with the goods. In all cases terms must include details of the remedial action available to the purchaser. No advertisement shall contain a direct or implied reference to any guarantee which purports to take away or diminish the legal rights of a purchaser.

10. Scientific or statistical excerpts from technical literature etc., may be used only with a proper sense of responsibility to the ordinary viewer. Irrelevant data and scientific jargon shall not be used to make claims appear to have a

scientific basis they do not possess. Statistics of limited validity should not be presented in a way as to make it appear that they are universally true.

11. Advertisers or their agents must be prepared to produce evidence to substantiate any claims or illustrations. The Director General reserves the right to ask for such proofs and get them examined to his full satisfaction. In case of goods covered by mandatory quality control orders, the advertiser shall produce quality certificate from the institutions recognised by the Government for this purpose.

12. Advertisements shall not contain disparaging or derogatory references to another product or service.

13. Imitation likely to mislead viewers shall be avoided.

14. Visual and verbal representation of actual and comparative prices and costs shall be accurate and shall not mislead on account of undue emphasis or distortion.

15. Testimonials must be genuine and used in a manner not to mislead the viewers. Advertisers or advertising Agencies must be prepared to produce evidence in support of their claims.

16. The picture and the audible matter of the advertisement shall not be excessively 'loud'. This is to ensure that between the programme and the advertisement there is a smooth change-over avoiding jerkiness or shock to the viewers.

17. Information to consumer in matters of weight, quality or prices of products where given shall be accurate.

18. Advertisements indicating price comparisons or reductions must comply with relevant laws.

19. No advertisement shall be accepted which violates AIR and TV Broadcast Code which is reproduced below:

General AIR/TV Code

- Criticism of friendly countries;
- attack on religions or communities;
- anything obscene or defamatory;
- incitement to violence or anything against maintenance of law and order;
- anything amounting to contempt of court;
- aspersions against the integrity of the President and Judiciary;
- anything affecting the integrity of the Nation; and
- criticism by name of any person.

20. Any such effects which might startle the viewing public must not be incorporated in advertisements. For example, and without limiting the scope, the use of the following sound effects will not be permitted:

- Rapid gunfire or rifle shots Sirens
- Bombardments
- Screams
- Raucous laughter and the like.

21. Any pretence in advertising copy must be avoided and such copy shall not be accepted by Doordarshan Kendras. The 'simulation' of appearance or voice of a personality in connection with advertisements for commercial products is also prohibited unless bonafide evidence is available that such personality has given permission for the simulation and it is clearly understood that stations telecasting such announcements are indemnified by the advertiser or advertising agency against any possible legal action.

Advertising and Children

22. No advertisement for a product or service shall be accepted if it suggests in any way that unless the children themselves buy or encourage other people to buy the products or services, they will be failing in their duty or lacking in loyalty to any person or organisation.

23. No advertisement shall be accepted which leads children to believe that if they do not own or use the product advertised they will be inferior in some way to other children or that they are liable to be condemned or ridiculed for not owning or using it.

24. Any advertisement which endangers the safety of the children or creates in them any interest in unhealthy practices, shall not be accepted, e.g. playing in the middle of the road, leaning dangerously out of a window, playing which match boxes and other goods which can cause accidents.

25. Children shall not be shown begging or in undignified or indecent manner.

26. No advertisement likely to bring advertising into contempt or disrepute shall be permitted. Advertising shall not take advantage of the superstition or ignorance of the general public.

27. No advertisements of talismans, charms and character reading from photographs or such other matter as well as those which trade on the superstition of general public shall be permitted.

28. Advertising shall be truthful, avoid distorting facts and misleading the public by means of implications and omissions. For instance, it shall not mislead the consumer by false statements, as to:

(i) the character of the merchandise, i.e. its utility, materials, ingredients, origin etc.
(ii) the price of the merchandise, its value, its suitability or terms of purchase.
(iii) the services accompanying purchase, including delivery, exchange, return, repair, upkeep etc.

(iv) personal recommendations of the article or service. The quality or the value of competing goods or the trustworthiness of statements made by others.

29. Testimonials of any kind from experts etc. other than Government recognised standardisation agencies shall not be permitted.

30. No advertisement shall be permitted to contain any claims exaggerated as to lead inevitably to disappointment in the minds of the public.

31. Methods of advertising designed to create confusion in the mind of the consumer as between goods by one maker and another maker are unfair and shall not be used. Such methods may consist in:

(i) the imitation of the trademark or name of competition or the packaging or labelling of goods; or

(ii) the imitation of advertising devices, copy, layout or slogans.

32. Indecent, vulgar, suggestive, repulsive or offensive themes or treatment shall be avoided in all advertisements. This also applies to such advertisements which in themselves are not objectionable as defined above, but which advertise objectionable books, photographs or other matter and thereby lead to their sale and circulation.

33. No advertisement in respect of medicines and treatments shall be accepted which is in contravention of the Code relating to Standards for advertising of medicines and treatments.

III. Procedure for the Enforcement of the Code

1. Complaints or reports on contraventions of the Code, received by Doordarshan may in the first instance be referred by Director General to the Advertisers' Association(s) concerned with request for suitable action.

2. If complaints under the Code cannot be satisfactorily resolved at association(s)'s level they shall be reported to the Director General who will then consider suitable action.

3. For any complaint under the Code received by Doordarshan concerning a party outside the purview of the various member association(s), the Director General will draw attention of such party to the complaint and where necessary, take suitable action on his own.

Conclusion

The Code has two Annexures attached. They are:

1. Code of Standards in Relation to the Advertising of Medicines and Treatments.
2. Standards of Practice for Advertising Agencies (As approved by the Advertising Agencies Association of India, Bombay.)

30

Press Council of India's Norms of Journalistic Conduct

Norms of Journalistic Conduct (Edition 2005)

The Code has the following content:

- Preface
- Part A: Principles and Ethics
- Part B: Guidelines on specific issues
- Part C: Laws relating to the Press
- Part D: Press Council's Powers, Practices and Procedures

We will take a detailed look at the Code of ethics mentioned in Part A.

Principles and Ethics

The fundamental objective of journalism is to serve the people with news, views, comments and information on matters of public interest in a fair, accurate, unbiased, sober and decent manner. To this end, the Press is expected to conduct itself in keeping with certain norms of professionalism, universally recognised. The norms enunciated below and other specific guidelines appended thereafter, when applied with due discernment and adaptation to the varying circumstance of each case, will help the journalist to self-regulate his or her conduct.

1. Accuracy and Fairness

i) The Press shall eschew publication of inaccurate, baseless, graceless, misleading or distorted material. All sides of the core issue or subject should be reported. Unjustified rumours and surmises should not be set forth as facts.

2. Pre-publication Verification

i) On receipt of a report or article of public interest and benefit containing imputations or comments against a citizen, the editor should check with due care and attention its factual accuracy apart from other authentic sources—with the person or the organisation concerned to elicit his/her or its version, comments or reaction and publish the same alongside with due correction in the report where necessary. In the event of lack or absence of response, a footnote to that effect may be appended to the report.

ii) Publication of news such as those pertaining to cancellation of examinations or withdrawal of candidates from election should be avoided without proper verification and cross checking.

iii) A document, which forms a basis of a news report, should be preserved at least for six months.

3. Caution against defamatory writings

(i) Newspaper should not publish anything which is manifestly defamatory or libellous against any individual/organisation unless after due care and verification, there is sufficient reason/evidence to believe that it is true and its publication will be for public good.

(ii) Truth is no defence for publishing derogatory, scurrilous and defamatory material against a private citizen where no public interest is involved.

(iii) No personal remarks which may be considered or construed to be derogatory in nature against a dead person should be published except in rare cases of public interest, as the dead person cannot possibly contradict or deny those remarks.

(iv) The Press has a duty, discretion and right to serve the public interest by drawing reader's attention to citizens of doubtful antecedents and of questionable character but as responsible journalists they should observe due restraint and caution in hazarding their own opinion or conclusion in branding these persons as 'cheats' or 'killers' etc. The cardinal principle being that the guilt of a person should be established by proof of facts alleged and not by proof of the bad character of the accused. In the zest to expose, the Press should not exceed the limits of ethical caution and fair comment.

(v) The Press shall not rely on objectionable past behaviour of a citizen to provide the background for adverse comments with reference to fresh action of that person. If public good requires such reference, the Press should make pre-publication inquiries from the authorities concerned about the follow up action, if any, in regard to earlier adverse actions.

(vi) Where the impugned publication is manifestly injurious to the reputation of the complainant, the onus shall be on the respondent to show that it was true or to establish that it constituted fair comment made in good faith and for public good.

(vii) Newspapers cannot claim privilege or licence to malign a person or body claiming special protection or immunity on the plea of having published the item as a satire under special columns such as 'gossip', 'parody', etc.

(viii) Publication of defamatory news by one paper does not give licence to others to publish news/ information reproducing or repeating the same.

(ix) Insertion of out -of -context, uncalled for and irrelevant statements likely to malign a person or an organisation must be eschewed.

(x) Freedom of Press does not give licence to a newspaper to malign a political leader or mar his future political prospects by publishing fake and defamatory writings.

(xi) Locus Standi: In cases involving personal allegations /criticism, only the concerned person enjoying the locus standi can move the plaint or claim right to reply.
However a representative organisation of persons attached to an organisation or a sect / group has the locus standi to move complaints against a publication directly criticising the conduct of a leader.

(xii) Public Interest and Public Bodies: As a custodian of public interest, the Press has a right to highlight cases of corruption and irregularities in public bodies but such material should be based on irrefutable evidence and published after due inquiries and verification from the concerned source and after obtaining the version of the person/ authority being commented upon. Newspapers should refrain from barbed, stinging and pungent language and ironical /satirical style of comment.

4. Parameters of the right of the Press to comment on the acts and conduct of public officials

(i) So far as the government, local authority and other organs/institutions exercising governmental power are concerned, they cannot bring charge of defamation for reports critical of their acts and conduct relevant to the discharge of their official duties unless the official establishes that the publication was made with reckless disregard for the truth. However, judiciary, which is protected by the power to punish for contempt of court, and the Parliament and Legislatures, protected as their privileges are by Articles 105 and 194 respectively of the Constitution of India, represent exception to this rule.

(ii) The central and local bodies are not entitled to bring a civil or criminal action for defamation in respect of article/report criticising their functioning.

(iii) Publication of news or comments/information on public officials conducting investigations should not have a tendency to help the commission of offences or to impede the prevention or detection of offences or prosecution of the guilty. The investigative agency is also under a corresponding obligation not to leak out or disclose such information or indulge in misinformation.

(iv) The Official Secrets Act, 1923 or any other similar enactment or provision having the force of law equally bind the press or media though there is no law empowering the state or its officials to prohibit, or to impose a prior restraint upon the Press/media.

(v) Those who hold public office and by their own conduct give scope for criticising them, cannot be heard to complain against such criticism.

5. *Criticism of Public Figures/Music Reviews:* An actor or singer who appears on a public stage submits his performance to the judgement of public and as such the critics' comments having proximate nexus with the merits of artists performance can not be held to be defamatory. However, the critics should refrain from writing anything, which could, be construed as remotely casting cloud on the artist's personal credibility.

6. *Right to Privacy*: (i) The Press shall not intrude or invade the privacy of an individual, unless outweighed by genuine overriding public interest, not being a prurient or morbid curiosity. So, however, that once a matter becomes a matter of public record, the right to privacy no longer subsists and it becomes a legitimate subject for comment by the Press and the media, among others.

Explanation: Things concerning a person's home, family, religion, health, sexuality, personal life and private affairs are covered by the concept of PRIVACY excepting where any of these impinges upon the public or public interest.

(ii) Caution against Identification: While reporting crime involving rape, abduction or kidnap of women/females or sexual assault on children, or raising doubts and questions touching the chastity, personal character and privacy of women, the names, photographs of the victims or other particulars leading to their identity shall not be published.

(iii) Minor children and infants who are the offspring of sexual abuse or 'forcible marriage' or illicit sexual union shall not be identified or photographed.

7. *Privacy of Public figures*: (i) Right to Privacy is an inviolable human right. However, the degree of privacy differs from person to person and from

situation to situation. The public person who functions under public gaze as an emissary/representative of the public cannot expect to be afforded the same degree of privacy as a private person. His acts and conduct as are of public interest ('public interest' being distinct and separate from 'of interest to public') even if conducted in private may be brought to public knowledge through the medium of the press. The press has however, a corresponding duty to ensure that the information about such acts and conduct of public interest of the public person is obtained through fair means, is properly verified and then reported accurately. For obtaining information in respect of acts done or conducted away from public gaze, the press is not expected to use surveillance devices. For obtaining information about private talks and discussion while the press is expected not to badger the public persons, the public persons are also expected to bring more openness in their functioning and co-operate with the press in its duty of informing the public about the acts of their representatives.

(ii) The interviews/articles or arguments pertaining to public persons which border on events that are in public knowledge, if reported correctly, cannot be termed as intrusion into private life. There is a very thin line between public and private life and public persons should not to be too skinned to criticism

(iii) Newspapers are allowed latitude in criticising persons who are in seats of power because their conduct discloses public interest provided their criticism is not motivated to gratify private spite of opponent/rival of public figure.

8. *Recording interviews and phone conversation*: (i) The Press shall not tape-record anyone's conversation without that person's knowledge or consent, except where the recording is necessary to protect the journalist in a legal action, or for other compelling good reason.

(ii) The Press shall, prior to publication, delete offensive epithets used by a person whose statements are being reported.

(iii) Intrusion through photography into moments of personal grief shall be avoided. However, photography of victims of accidents or natural calamity may be in larger public interest.

9. *Conjecture, comment and fact*: (i) Newspaper should not pass on or elevate conjecture, speculation or comment as a statement of fact. All these categories should be distinctly identified.

(ii) Cartoons and caricatures depicting good humour are to be placed in a special category of news that enjoy more liberal attitude.

10. *Newspapers to eschew suggestive guilt*: (i) Newspapers should eschew suggestive guilt by association. They should not name or identify the family or relatives or associates of a person convicted or accused of a crime, when

they are totally innocent and a reference to them is not relevant to the matter being reported.

(ii) It is contrary to the norms of journalism for a paper to identify itself with and project or promote the case of any one party in the case of any controversy/dispute.

11. *Reporting-Proceedings of Legislature*: The newspapers have a duty to report faithfully the proceedings of either House of Parliament, Legislative Assembly and in this regard the newspapers shall not be liable for any proceedings civil or criminal in any court unless it is proved that reporting have been made with malice. However, the newspapers should not publish any report based on proceedings of a sitting of either House of Parliament or Legislative Assembly or as the case may be either House of the Legislature of a State, which is not open to the media.

12. *(a) Caution in criticising judicial acts:*

(i) Excepting where the court sits 'in-camera' or directs otherwise, it is open to a newspaper to report pending judicial proceedings, in a fair, accurate and reasonable manner. But it shall not publish anything:

- which, in its direct and immediate effect, creates a substantial risk of obstructing, impeding or prejudicing seriously the due administration of justice; or
- is in the nature of a running commentary or debate, or records the paper's own findings conjectures, reflection or comments on issues, *sub judice* and which may amount to abrogation to the newspaper the functions of the court; or
- regarding the personal character of the accused standing trial on a charge of committing a crime.

(ii) Newspaper shall not as a matter of caution, publish or comment on evidence collected as a result of investigative journalism, when, after the accused is arrested and charged, the court becomes seized of the case: Nor should they reveal, comment upon or evaluate a confession allegedly made by the accused.

(iii) While newspapers may, in the public interest, make reasonable criticism of a judicial act or the judgement of a court for public good; they shall not cast scurrilous aspersions on, or impute improper motives, or personal bias to the judge. Nor shall they scandalise the court or the judiciary as a whole, or make personal allegations of lack of ability or integrity against a judge.

(iv) Newspaper shall, as a matter of caution, avoid unfair and unwarranted criticism which, by innuendo, attributes to a judge extraneous consideration for performing an act in due course of his/her judicial functions, even if such criticism does not strictly amount to criminal Contempt of Court.

(b) Reporting News pertaining to Court Proceedings: Before publishing a news item about court proceedings, it will be appropriate for the correspondent and editor to ascertain its genuineness and, correctness and authenticity from the records so that the concerned person can be held guilty and accountable for furnishing incorrect facts or wrong information about the court proceedings.

13. *Corrections*: When any factual error or mistake is detected or confirmed, the newspaper should *suo-motu* publish the correction promptly with due prominence and with apology or expression of regrets in a case of serious lapse.

14. *Right of Reply*: (i) The newspaper should promptly and with due prominence, publish either in full or with due editing, free of cost, at the instance of the person affected or feeling aggrieved/or concerned by the impugned publication, a contradiction/reply/ clarification or rejoinder sent to the editor in the form of a letter or note. If the editor doubts the truth or factual accuracy of the contradiction/reply/clarification or rejoinder, he shall be at liberty to add separately at the end, a brief editorial comment doubting its veracity, but only when this doubt is reasonably founded on unimpeachable documentary or other evidential material in his/her possession. This is a concession which has to be availed of sparingly with due discretion and caution in appropriate cases.

(ii) However, where the reply/contradiction or rejoinder is being published in compliance with the directions of the Press Council, it is permissible to append a brief editorial note to that effect.

(iii) Right of rejoinder cannot be claimed through the medium of Press Conference, as publication/coverage of a news of a conference is within the discretionary powers of an editor.

(iv) Freedom of the Press involves the readers' right to know all sides of an issue of public interest. An editor, therefore, shall not refuse to publish the reply or rejoinder merely on the ground that in his opinion the story published in the newspaper was true. That is an issue to be left to the judgement of the readers. It also does not behove an editor to show contempt towards a reader.

15. *Letters to editor*: (i) An editor who decides to open his columns for letters on a controversial subject, is not obliged to publish all the letters received in regard to that subject. He is entitled to select and publish only some of them either in entirety or the gist thereof. However, in exercising this discretion, he must make an honest endeavour to ensure that what is published is not one-sided but represents a fair balance between the views for and against with respect to the principal issue in controversy.

(ii) In the event of rejoinder upon rejoinder being sent by two parties on a controversial subject, the editor has the discretion to decide at which stage to close the continuing column.

16. *Editors' Discretion*: (i) In the matter of writing an editorial, the editor enjoys a good deal of latitude and discretion. It is for him to choose the subject and it is also for him to use such language as he considers appropriate, provided that in writing the editorial he doesn't transgress the law and violate the norms of journalism and editorial comments published in the newspaper should be couched in sober and dignified language.

(ii) Selection of the material for publication as reports/articles/letter is within the discretion of an editor, therefore it is his duty to see that on a controversial issue of public interest, all views are given equal prominence so that the people can form their independent opinion in the matter.

(iii) The editor should not publish the news report/article if his mind is in doubt about the truth of the news report/article. If the veracity of any part of the news report/article is in doubt, that portion should be omitted and rest be published provided the editor is satisfied that the remainder is substantially true and its publication will be for public benefit.

17. *Obscenity and vulgarity to be eschewed*: (i) Newspapers/journalists shall not publish anything which is obscene, vulgar or offensive to public good taste.

(ii) Newspapers shall not display advertisements which are vulgar or which, through depiction of a woman in nude or lewd posture, provoke lecherous attention of males as if she herself was a commercial commodity for sale.

(iii) Whether a picture is obscene or not, is to be judged in relation to three tests; namely

(a) Is it vulgar and indecent?

(b) Is it a piece of mere pornography?

(c) Is its publication meant merely to make money by titillating the sex feelings of adolescents and among whom it is intended to circulate? In other words, does it constitute an unwholesome exploitation for commercial gain.

Other relevant considerations are whether the picture is relevant to the subject matter of the magazine. That is to say, whether its publication serves any preponderating social or public purpose, in relation to art, painting, medicine, research or reform of sex.

(iv) The globalisation and liberalisation does not give licence to the media to misuse freedom of the press and to lower the values of the society. The media performs a distinct role and public purpose which require it to rise above commercial consideration guiding other industries and businesses. So far as that role is concerned, one of the duties of the media is to preserve and promote our cultural heritage and social values.

(v) Columns such as 'Very Personal' in a newspaper replying to personal queries of the readers must not become grossly offensive presentations, which either outrage public decency or corrupt public moral.

18. (a) *Glorification/encouragement of social evils to be eschewed*: Newspapers shall not allow their columns to be misused for writings which have a tendency to encourage or glorify social evils like 'Sati Pratha' or ostentatious celebrations.

(b) *Reporting on natural calamities*: Facts and data relating to spread of epidemics or natural calamities shall be checked up thoroughly from authentic sources and then published with due restraint in a manner bereft of sensationalism, exaggeration, surmises or unverified facts.

19. *Violence not to be glorified*: (i) *Photo Coverage on Terrorist Attack, Communal Clashes and Accidents*: While reporting news with regard to terrorist attacks or communal riots, the media should refrain from publishing/telecasting pictures of mangled corpses or any other photographic coverage which may create terror, or revulsion or ignite communal passion among people.

(ii) Newspapers/journalists shall avoid presenting acts of violence, armed robberies and terrorist activities in a manner that glorifies the perpetrators on their acts, declarations or death in the eyes of the public. Publication of interviews of anti-social elements by the newspapers glorifying the criminals and their activities with the resultant effects are to be avoided.

20. *Covering communal disputes/clashes* (i) News, views or comments relating to communal or religious disputes/clashes shall be published after proper verification of facts and presented with due caution and restraint in a manner which is conducive to the creation of an atmosphere congenial to communal harmony, amity and peace. Sensational, provocative and alarming headlines are to be avoided. Acts of communal violence or vandalism shall be reported in a manner as may not undermine the people's confidence in the law and order machinery of the State. Giving community-wise figures of the victims of communal riot, or writing about the incident in a style which is likely to inflame passions, aggravate the tension, or accentuate the strained relations between the communities/religious groups concerned, or which has a potential to exacerbate the trouble, shall be avoided.

(ii) Journalists and columnists owe a very special responsibility to their country in promoting communal peace and amity. Their writings are not a mere reflection of their own feelings but help to large extent in moulding the feelings and sentiments of the society at large. It is, therefore, of utmost importance that they use their pen with circumspection and restrain.

(iii) The role of media in such situations (Gujarat Carnage/Crisis) is to be peacemakers and not abettors, to be troubleshooters and not troublemakers. Let the media play their noble role of promoting peace and harmony among the people in the present crisis in Gujarat. Any trend to disrupt the same either directly or indirectly would be an anti-national act. There is a greater moral responsibility on the media to do their best to build up the national solidarity and to cement the communal harmony at all levels remembering the noble role they had played during the pre-independence days.

(iv) The media, as a chronicle of tomorrow's history, owes an undeniable duty to the future to record events as simple untailored facts. The analysis of the events and opinion thereon are a different genre altogether. The treatment of the two also thus has necessarily to be different. In times of crisis, facts unadorned and simply put, with due care and restraint, cannot be reasonably objected to in a democracy. However, a heavy responsibility devolves on the author of opinion articles. The author has to ensure that not only are his or her analysis free from any personal preferences, prejudices or notions, but also they are based on verified, accurate and established facts and do not tend to foment disharmony or enmity between castes, communities and races.

21. Headings not to be sensational/provocative and must justify the matter printed under them:

In general and particularly in the context of communal disputes or clashes

(a) Provocative and sensational headlines are to be avoided;
(b) Headings must reflect and justify the matter printed under them;
(c) Headings containing allegations made in statements should either identify the body or the source making it or at least carry quotation marks.

22. Caste, religion or community references:

(i) In general, the caste identification of a person or a particular class should be avoided, particularly when in the context it conveys a sense or attributes a conduct or practice derogatory to that caste.
(ii) Newspapers are advised against the use of word 'Scheduled Caste' or 'Harijan' which has been objected to by some.
(iii) An accused or a victim shall not be described by his caste or community when the same does not have anything to do with the offence or the crime and plays no part either in the identification of any accused or proceeding, if there be any.
(iv) Newspaper should not publish any fictional literature distorting and portraying the religious characters in an adverse light and offending the religious susceptibilities of large sections of society who hold those characters in high esteem, invested with attributes of the virtuous and lofty. change made on 16/12/04.
(v) Commercial exploitation of the name of prophets, seers or deities is repugnant to journalistic ethics and good taste.
(vi) It is the duty of the newspaper to ensure that the tone, spirit and language of a write up is not objectionable, provocative, against the

unity and integrity of the country, spirit of the constitution seditious and inflammatory in nature or designed to promote communal disharmony. It should also not attempt to promote balkanisation of the country.

(vii) One of the jobs of the journalists is also to bring forth to the public notice the plight of the weaker sections of society. They are the watchdogs on behalf of the society of its weaker sections.

23 *Paramount national interest:* (i) Newspapers shall, as a matter of self-regulation, exercise due restraint and caution in presenting any news, comment or information which is likely to jeopardise, endanger or harm the paramount interests of the State and society, or the rights of individuals with respect to which reasonable restrictions may be imposed by law on the right to freedom of speech and expression under clause (2) of Article 19 of the Constitution of India.

(ii) Publication of wrong/incorrect map is a very serious offence. It adversely affects the territorial integrity of the country and warrants prompt and prominent retraction with regrets.

24 *Foreign Relations*: Media plays a very important role in moulding public opinion and developing better understanding between countries. Objective reporting so as not to jeopardise friendly bilateral relations is therefore desirable.

25. *Newspapers may expose misuse of diplomatic immunity:* The media shall make every possible effort to build bridges of co-operation, friendly relations and better understanding between India and foreign States. At the same time, it is the duty of a newspaper to expose any misuse or undue advantage of the diplomatic immunities.

26. *Investigative journalism, its norms and parameters*: Investigative reporting has three basic elements:

(a) It has to be the work of the reporter, not of others he is reporting;
(b) The subject should be of public importance for the reader to know;
(c) An attempt is being made to hide the truth from the people.

The first norm follows as a necessary corollary from

(a) That the investigative reporter should, as a rule, base his story on facts investigated, detected and verified by himself and not on hearsay or on derivative evidence collected by a third party, not checked up from direct, authentic sources by the reporter himself.

(b) There being a conflict between the factors which require openness and those which necessitate secrecy, the investigative journalist should strike and maintain in his report a proper balance between openness on the one hand and secrecy on the other, placing the public good above everything.

(c) The investigative journalist should resist the temptation of quickies or quick gains conjured up from half-baked incomplete, doubtful facts, not fully checked up and verified from authentic sources by the reporter himself.

(d) Imaginary facts, or ferreting out or conjecturing the non-existent should be scrupulously avoided. Facts, facts and yet more facts are vital and they should be checked and cross-checked whenever possible until the moment the paper goes to Press.

(e) The newspaper must adopt strict standards of fairness and accuracy of facts. Findings should be presented in an objective manner, without exaggerating or distorting, that would stand up in a court of law, if necessary.

(f) The reporter must not approach the matter or the issue under investigation, in a manner as though he were the prosecutor or counsel for the prosecution. The reporter's approach should be fair, accurate and balanced. All facts properly checked up, both for and against the core issues, should be distinctly and separately stated, free from any one-sided inferences or unfair comments. The tone and tenor of the report and its language should be sober, decent and dignified, and not needlessly offensive, barbed, derisive or castigatory, particularly while commenting on the version of the person whose alleged activity or misconduct is being investigated. Nor should the investigative reporter conduct the proceedings and pronounce his verdict of guilt or innocence against the person whose alleged criminal acts and conduct were investigated, in a manner as if he were a court trying the accused.

(g) In all proceedings including the investigation, presentation and publication of the report, the investigative journalist newspaper should be guided by the paramount principle of criminal jurisprudence, that a person is innocent unless the offence alleged against him is proved beyond doubt by independent, reliable evidence.

(h) The private life, even of a public figure, is his own. Exposition or invasion of his personal privacy or private life is not permissible unless there is clear evidence that the wrong doings in question have a reasonable nexus with the misuse of his public position or power and has an adverse impact on public interest.

(i) Though the legal provisions of Criminal Procedure do not in terms, apply to investigating proceedings by a journalist, the fundamental principles underlying them can be adopted as a guide on grounds of equity, ethics and good conscience.

27. *Confidence to be respected*: If information is received from a confidential source, the confidence should be respected. The journalist cannot be compelled by the Press Council to disclose such source; but it shall not be regarded as a breach of journalistic ethics if the source is voluntarily disclosed in proceedings before the Council by the journalist who considers it necessary to repel effectively a charge against him/her. This rule requiring a newspaper not to publish matters disclosed to it in confidence, is not applicable where:

(a) consent of the source is subsequently obtained; or

(b) the editor clarifies by way of an appropriate footnote that since the publication of certain matters were in the public interest, the information in question was being published although it had been made 'off the record'.

28. *Newspapers to avoid crass commercialism*

(i) While newspapers are entitled to ensure, improve or strengthen their financial viability by all legitimate means, the Press shall not engage in crass commercialism or unseemly cut-throat commercial competition with their rivals in a manner repugnant to high professional standards and good taste.

(ii) Predatory price wars/trade competition among newspapers, laced with tones disparaging the products of each other, initiated and carried on in print, assume the colour of unfair 'trade' practice, repugnant to journalistic ethics. The question as when it assumes such an unethical character, is one of the fact depending on the circumstances of each case.

(iii) The practice of taking security deposit by an editor from the journalists at the time of their appointment is unethical.

29. *Fraudulent activities*: Defrauding the public by closing down a publication subsequent to collection of subscription is unethical on the part of management of the paper/periodical/magazine. If the closure is inevitable, the subscription amount due should be returned to the subscribers.

30. Professional misconduct: Blackmailing or extortion of money from people under threat of maligning them through the columns of newspaper amounts to gross violation of journalistic norms.

31. *Professional rivalry*: Newspaper columns should not be misused by rival newspapers to gratify their private spite against each other out of commercial rivalry.

32. *Plagiarism:* (i) Using or passing off the writings or ideas of another as one's own, without crediting the source, is an offence against ethics of journalism.

(ii) Violation of copyright also constitutes violation of journalistic norms.

33. *Unauthorised lifting of news*: (i) The practice of lifting news from other newspapers publishing them subsequently as their own, ill-comports the high standards of journalism. To remove its unethicality, the 'lifting' newspaper must duly acknowledge the source of the report.

(ii) The position of features articles is different from 'news': Feature articles shall not be lifted without permission/proper acknowledgement.

34. *Illegal reproduction*: The Press shall not reproduce in any form offending portions or excerpts from a proscribed book.

35. Non-return of unsolicited material

(i) A paper is not bound to return unsolicited material sent for consideration of publication. However, when the same is accompanied by stamped envelope, the paper should make all efforts to return it.

(ii) Whenever articles from the contributors are published free of remuneration, there must be an agreement not to pay and the newspaper should follow this practice as a rule.

36. *Advertisements*: (i) Commercial advertisements are information as much as social, economic or political information. What is more, advertisements shape attitude and ways of life at least as much, as other kinds of information and comment. Journalistic propriety demands that advertisements must be clearly distinguishable from news content carried in the newspaper.

(ii) *Newspaper should not publish Liquor and Tobacco Advertisements*: No advertisement shall be published, which promotes directly or indirectly production, sale or consumption of cigarettes, tobacco products, wine, alcohol, liquor and other intoxicants.

(iii) Newspaper shall not publish advertisements, which have a tendency to malign or hurt the religious sentiments of any community or section of society.

(iv) Advertisements which offend the provisions of the Drugs and Magical Remedies (Objectionable Advertisement) Act, 1954, or any other statute should be rejected.

(v) Newspapers should not publish an advertisement containing anything which is unlawful or illegal, or is contrary to public decency, good taste or to journalistic ethics or propriety.

(vi) Journalistic propriety demands that advertisements must be clearly distinguishable from editorial matter carried in the newspaper. Newspapers while publishing advertisements should specify the amount received by them. The rationale behind this is that advertisements should be charged at rates usually chargeable by a newspaper since payment of more than the normal rates would amount to a subsidy to the paper.

(vii) Publication of dummy or lifted advertisements that have neither been paid for, nor authorised by the advertisers, constitute breach of journalistic ethics specially when the paper raises a bill in respect of such advertisements.

(viii) Deliberate failure to publish an advertisement in all the copies of a newspaper offends against the standards of journalistic ethics and constitutes gross professional misconduct.

(ix) There should be total co-ordination and communication between the advertisement department and the editorial department of a newspaper in the matter of considering the legality propriety or otherwise of an advertisement received for publication.

(x) The editors should insist on their right to have the final say in the acceptance or rejection of advertisements, specially those which border on or cross the line between decency and obscenity.

(xi) Newspapers to carry caution notice with matrimonial advertisements carrying following text*:

> "Readers are advised to make appropriate thorough inquiries before acting upon any advertisement. This newspaper does not vouch or subscribe to claim and representation made by the advertiser regarding the particulars of status, age, income of the bride/ bridegroom".

(xii) An editor shall be responsible for all matters, including advertisements published in the newspaper. If responsibility is disclaimed, this shall be explicitly stated beforehand.

(xiii) Tele-friendship advertisements carried by newspapers across the country inviting general public to dial the given number for 'entertaining' talk and offering suggestive tele-talk tend to pollute adolescent minds and promote immoral cultural ethos. The Press should refuse to accept such advertisements.

(xiv) Classified advertisements of health and physical fitness services using undignified languages, indicative of covert soliciting, are violative of law as well as ethics. The newspaper should adopt a mechanism for vetting such an advertisement to ensure that the soliciting advertisements are not carried.

(xv) Advertisements of contraceptive and supply of brand item attaching to the advertisement is not very ethical, given the social milieu and the traditional values held dear in our country. A newspaper has a sacred duty to educate people about precautionary measures to avoid AIDS and exhibit greater far sight in accepting advertisement even though issued by social welfare organisation.

37. *Management-Editor Relationship*

(i) There is a well-recognised distinction between the editor and the journalists on the one hand and the Manager, the Executive or the Administrator on the other, whatever the nomenclature that they may carry in a particular newspaper establishment. The duties and responsibilities of the editor and the management differ and whatever the co-ordination may be required to efficiently manage the establishment to bring out the journal, the functions of the two are separate and have to be kept as such.

Once the owner lays down the policy of the newspaper for general guidance, neither he nor anybody on his behalf can interfere with the day to day functioning of the editor and the journalistic staff working under him.

It is well established that the freedom of the press is essentially the freedom of the people to be informed accurately and adequately on all issues, problems, events and developments. In discharge of the editorial functions the editor is supreme and superior even to the owner.

The independence of the newspaper is essentially the independence of the editor from all internal and external restrictions. Unless the editor enjoys this freedom he will be unable to discharge his primary duty which is to the people and without such freedom, he can be held responsible in law for all that appears in the newspaper.

In the running of the newspaper, the managerial, administrative or business side of the newspaper has to be kept independent of its editorial side and should not be allowed to encroach upon or interfere with the editorial section. This precaution is to be taken even when the owner and the editor is the same. The proprietor must not allow his business interests and considerations to either dominate or interfere with the newspapers obligation to the people.

That is why there is also an obligation on the management to select a person as the editor who is competent and bears integrity of character and independence of mind.

The successful working of any arrangement in the ultimate analysis would depend on mutual understanding, cooperation and goodwill between the management, the editor, editorial journalist staff and all those who are faithfully working in the production of a paper.

If the co-ordination between the different departments including the editorial is effected by the Brand Management without in any way interfering with the freedom of the editor to include or exclude news or views, the length or details as well as their language and the place where they are to be published, and the prominence with which they should appear, there may not be much grievance that such co-ordination is in violation of the freedom of the editor. However, if the choice of the editor with regard to selection of material in any manner is sought to be interfered with, it is undoubtedly an unwarranted encroachment on the said freedom.

(ii) The editor under no circumstances can be asked by the proprietor to serve his private interests. To require an editor to cater to the personal interests of the proprietor is not only to demean the office of the editor but also to encroach upon his status as a trustee of the society in respect of the contents of the newspaper. In any country which swears by the freedom and the independence of the press, an attempt by any proprietor of a newspaper to use his editor as his personal agent to promote his private interests and to compel him to act and to write, to serve them is both offensive and reprehensive. Any editor or for that matter any journalist who accepts or condescends to do such jobs not only degrades himself but also the profession of journalism and does not deserve the calling. He betrays the trust the society keeps in him for furnishing fair, objective and comprehensive news and views.

Part B deals with Guidelines on Specific Issues

These issues are:

b) Norms for observance by the Press in the wake of communal disturbances 1969
c) Coverage of Handouts of Militants/Terrorists-Guiding Principles 1991-1992
d) AIDS and the media
e) Financial Journalism-1996
f) Election Reporting-1996
g) Allotment of houses to journalists-1996
h) Guidelines on undue favours to -1998
i) Right to privacy-Public figures and the press-1998

Part C Deals with Laws Relating to the Press

a) Constitution of India
b) Press Laws/Acts
c) Relevant Provisions of Indian Penal Code, 1860
d) Relevant Provisions of Cr. P.C., 1973 (Act No. II of 1974)

Part D deals with Press Council's Powers, Practice and Procedures

Unit 6: Sting Operation and Ethics

31

Sting Operation

Introduction

Sting Operation is a deceptive operation meant to catch a person committing a crime. It is often used by law enforcement agencies in western countries to expose crimes like buying or selling contraband, soliciting prostitutes or even trapping paedophiles by trying to lure children over the internet.

The word, 'sting' derives its origin from American usage to mean a police undercover operation designed to ensnare criminals. It is a synonym for the expression '*set a trap to catch a crook*'. In terms that are more refined, it can also be called as '*investigative journalism*' or '*undercover journalism*'.

Sting operation is an information gathering exercise. The purpose is to expose something that the culprit tries to conceal or suppress. Through the sting operations the journalists look out for facts that are not easy to obtain by simple requests or searches.

The concept is not a new one. In the 1880s, *New York World* reporter Elizabeth Cochran, under the byline Nellie Bly faked that she was insane to get access to a New York asylum.

In America and elsewhere, the term is generally used to describe the action of a law enforcement agency in which officials plot a deceptive operation to trap a criminal. The agents act like a partner in crime or a possible victim and lure the offender into the trap. It's common for agents to deploy a 'bait car' to catch an auto thief or pose as clients to crack prostitution or drugs racket. Recently, the American police has executed many stings to lure child molesters in chat rooms. The 2004-07 reality TV series "To Catch a Predator" was a sting, using spy cameras to identify potential sexual predators.

However, in India, Sting Operations have become synonymous with journalists, usually television journalists, who use miniaturised audio and video technology, especially pin hole camera technology to clandestinely make a video or audio recording of a conversation or actions of individuals. It caught the country's imagination when in 1999, a news website, *Tehelka*, blew open the lid on match fixing in cricket. *Tehelka* followed this with an even bigger Sting Operation in 2000 on corruption in defence deals on the country.

Laws Governing Sting Operation

In India, there are no specific laws regulating the use of covert surveillance equipment by private individuals. However, the government has referred to Rule 6 of the Cable Television Network Rules, 1994, to warn the channels against showing objectionable visuals from Sting Operations. Rule 6 prohibits carrying of any programme in the cable service which offends good taste or decency; contains anything obscene, defamatory, false and suggestive innuendos and half truths and is not suitable for unrestricted public exhibition. The initial *Tehelka* Sting Operations raised questions about special privileges accorded to the media and whether it meant the media could invoke 'public interest', 'public person' and 'due diligence' as defence in conducting Sting Operations.

The Supreme Court has stated as far back as 1975 that privacy-dignity claims deserve to be examined with care and ought to be denied only when an important countervailing interest is shown to be superior. The court has also stated that both the public and the media interest would be adequately reconciled if the media acted bona fide and reasonably diligently in its exposure of public officials. Among the cases slapped against *Tehelka* for the expose were cases of defamation.

Admissibility of the Tapes of Sting Operation admissible as Evidence in a Court of Law

Revelations of a Sting Operation are admissible in law if it is proved that it is untampered and authentic. India does not follow the American legal system that does not allow the use of any evidence obtained using illegal means. The Supreme Court has constantly held that candidly collected evidence is admissible in law. The court was of the view that it would be wrong to deny the law of evidence and the advantages of the advances made in technology and devices. An apex court bench had pronounced that just the fact that tape recorded conversations could be tampered with was no reason to reject it as evidence as there was possibly no piece of evidence that could not be tampered with.

The court felt a recorded conversation, though procured without the knowledge of the accused, could be used as long as it is not elicited by duress, coercion or by force. Charges have been framed against various defence ministry officials on the basis of the *Tehelka* sting demonstrating that revelations from sting operations are admissible in India courts. And in the *Tehelka* cash-for-question expose, the accused MPs have been expelled from the Parliament on the basis of the evidence procured by the Sting Operation.

Laws in Other Countries regarding Sting Operations

In UK, the courts do not feel that evidence should be refused on the basis of its method of collection. The decision to exclude or include evidence on the basis of its method of collection is made taking into consideration the seriousness of the crime.

In the US, only law enforcement officials are allowed to use hidden recording equipments under certain circumstances and under carefully controlled conditions. No private individual, not even journalists are allowed to use such equipments.

The US courts hold that the state cannot prosecute a person for a crime after instigating the person to commit it i.e. entrapment. Yet, this defence of entrapment can be countered by proving that the accused was pre-disposed to committing the act. Despite the legal safeguards in the US, there have been growing complaints of the misuse of such covert equipment not only by private individuals but also by the law enforcement agencies.

Undercover Journalism

The form of journalism in which a reporter infiltrates a group to get stories is perhaps as old as the profession. Perhaps the most notable example from the early days of such journalism was the 1887 asylum expose done by Nellie Bly, an American journalist, working for Joseph Pulitzer's the New York World. Her reports depicted the poor condition of the patients. The reporting resulted in a probe and subsequent increase in the budget of the Department of Public Charities and Corrections by $850,000. In the early days, reports were based on a journalist's accounts.

To sting or not to sting?

According to the authors Kovach and Rosentiel, journalists should use a three-step test while conducting sting operations:

1. The information should be sufficiently vital to the public interest to justify the deception.
2. Journalists should not engage in the masquerade unless there is no other way to get the story.
3. Journalists should explain their audience as to why the story justifies deception and why this was the only way to get the facts.

The Significance of Sting Operations

Investigative journalists today seem to have taken media to a whole new level. Indeed, sting operations have become the most favoured tool for journalists, the recent spate of such operations, especially the 'string of sting operations' by Tehelka bear witness to this fact.

At the onset, let me distinguish between investigative journalism and sting operations. A sting operation is an operation designed to catch a person committing a crime by means of deception or exposing a wrong deed by a hidden camera. Sting operations are just one of the tools of investigative journalism.

Dubbed the fourth estate or the fourth pillar of democracy, media has taken upon itself the right to carry out operations that are carefully scripted to apprehend defaulters as they take the bait offered. In an era of sensational reporting, news channels have a field day covering the expose in the name of working in the interest of the public. The public too, deprived of transparency about the working of public servants in office, save the lone RTI act, are ever willing to absorb the news they are fed.

Most sting operations are carried out against public servants in the system. Media Houses claim that they are in such cases, acting out of interest for Truth and Justice. They argue that in cases where the whole society is at stake, like corruption, cash for votes, et cetera, they are justified in carrying out deliberate operations, as this is probably the only way the defaulters can be caught red handed. That too in a situation where there is conscious concealment of information, there seems to be no better way than this. In fact, in the police department this is a time tested method to nab criminals.

People argue that it keeps people on their toes, makes officials answerable. So you might say that the operation against Uma Khurana was unethical but the one showing 14 MP's taking bribe is justified.

To a great extent, sting operations have contributed to the change in the media-government relations. When the state tries to gag the media freedom it shows the success of the media. Hidden camera investigations have kept the politicians on their feet. This was clear when the present government tried to regulate sting operations immediately after the cash-for-questions scandal.

Thus, sting operations have an important role to play in India as the country is infested with corruption, dishonesty and fraudulent activities in all sectors-both public and private. But, provided the Media outlets do with 'public interest' as the sole motive and not their own 'private interest' to raise TRPs.

The Hazards of Sting Operations

Sting operations are a matter of contention because there are myriad questions of ethics, which are very subjective. Traditionally, the role of the media has been that of a 'watchdog'. With the coming of the TV, that role has begun to change-infotainment is a necessity. The media saw sting operations as a news strategy that would fulfill their role of a 'watchdog' at the same time provide a sense of entertainment. Sting operations make people sit up and watch.

The problem is that, somewhere the distinction between exposing a wrong-doing and sensationalizing it is lost. Stings have been a part of UK's tabloid culture for a long time now. But in India, it is difficult to distinguish between serious and tabloid journalism, thus the situation is dangerous.

Another common contention is that sting operations are an invasion of an individual's privacy. The problem is compounded by the lack of a commonly accepted definition of privacy. Right to privacy in India is derived both from the common law and the constitutional law (Article 21). But when we discuss Right to Freedom of Speech and Expression of the media in the same length as the privacy of an individual, we reach a deadlock. In that, there cannot be a rule to place one above the other at all times.

Therefore, the next question will be, if we accept that the sting operations uphold the freedom of speech, is it for our common good? Who decides what is common good or 'public interest'? The media have time and again proved convincingly that they are capable of sensationalizing issues in the name of 'public interest'.

On the other hand, our democracy has come to such a pass, that people take its evils as a given, and you need the media to use newer, innovative methods to induce the public into action.

For instance, corruption in the Army/Defense Ministry was public knowledge but the *Tehelka* investigation made people react to it because it was a visual document.

There is always a danger of the public taking these sting operations for granted, if they are too many in number. There are weekly TV shows full of stories obtained from hidden camera investigations like *parda fash* or *sansani*. These are, beyond doubt, sensational, and are a gimmick to draw more eyeballs.

Sting journalism in today's time is considered to be nothing more than 'entrapment journalism'. The media induce people to commit a crime and then cry foul. One school of thought believes that this is unethical because it could be assumed that the crime would not have been committed if there had been no 'deception' or 'entrapment'. But this argument is on shaky grounds because of two reasons. First: that the crime was committed is enough to justify that the person is guilty (assuming that the sting was authentic). Second: it is only an assumption that the crime would not be committed had there not been an entrapment. However, an expose would be on sounder ethical grounds than 'entrapment'. Also, those who mount an entrapment story themselves commit offences of impersonation, criminal trespass under false pretenses *et al*.

Sting operations break two classic journalistic traditions/practices. One: the distinction between 'off-the-record' and 'on-the-record' briefing is blurred. This typically happens in the case of an expose. A journalist's responsibility towards her source is questioned here (again 'public interest' becomes the parameter to judge whether the story must be done or not). Second: with the coming of sting operations, not all 'breaking news' is topical- they are constructed and created. How many times have we seen 'breaking news' which are hidden camera exposes by the channels? All this makes us wonder if stings are merely sensational, done in the interests of the commercial media. Due to the technological advancement authenticity of the hidden camera exposes are questioned. You don't need a technologically savvy person to concoct tapes.

In most cases, proving the authenticity of the tapes takes up a lot of valuable time and the public would have lost interest in the case by the time the report comes out.

The easy availability of technology has brought about the phenomenon of 'citizen journalism'. Exposes by individuals could be another gray area. The photograph of Shahid and Kareena taken from a camera phone by a by stander was a clear case of invasion of privacy.

Especially in the area of sting journalism if the lines between a journalist and a common man is blurred, it could be dangerous. However, the channels have to take utmost care while accepting tapes from citizens and check its authenticity. To a great extent, sting operations have contributed to the change in the media-government relations. When the state tries to gag the media freedom it shows the success of the media. Hidden camera investigations have kept the politicians on their feet. This was clear when the present government tried to regulate sting operations immediately after the cash-for-questions scandal.

While politicians have been the targets of the stings very often, corporate firms, big MNCs have rarely/never come under the scanner.

This tells us something about the media. They cannot take on the corporates, who form the major source of their revenue. It wouldn't be wrong to say that sting operations have the potential to affect a social change. But today's journalism is fast paced. Follow-ups are not vigourous. Thus perhaps, stings end up being isolated events and have a limited impact.

Having gone over the pros and cons of sting operations, I have a few conclusions to draw. If we have to choose between the people in power and the media then, like Thomas Jefferson did, I would choose the media because Indian media is very diverse and can accommodate many viewpoints. However, the day is not far when the media is in the danger of losing this trust.

Despite all the shortcomings sting operations are a powerful tool in the hands of the media, they are justified as long as they are used responsibly.

Journalist's Views on the Ethics of Sting Operations

Times of India on September 1, 2007 published an article: 'Sting ops part of journalism'.

In the backdrop of criticism against the television sting expose on a Delhi school teacher, who was allegedly pushing her students into prostitution, broadcasters have defended the sting operation describing it as an extension of investigative journalism and an expose of a terrible crime. The broadcasters rejected the suggestion, as made by some, that the I&B ministry's proposed content code for broadcasters would have prevented mob violence.

The aforementioned article quoted a few media persons whose statements are as follows:

G. Krishnan, Executive Director and CEO, Aaj Tak: "TV channels have a right to conduct sting operations, just as newspapers do investigative reporting. It will be incorrect for the government to be given the authority to impose restrictions."

On the mob reaction, Krishnan said, "People have the right to express their views. Unfortunately people reacted very emotionally to the sting, they should have gone to the police or the courts. But a few days back when a girl went to report her stolen mobile to the police she was raped. We don't know how many such cases are taking place. The media is only putting it in front of the people."

Sudhir Choudhary, Live India: "Our sting on human trafficking was in public interest. It was not TRP oriented or we could have carried sleaze, a bedroom story about politicians, if we wanted to garner higher TRPs. And as a news channel we get 20 sting operations. We reject most of them. We only accept those that are in public interest."

He added that the channel had taken the precaution of informing the police about the sting before it was aired. "It is the police's job to maintain law and order. They did not take us seriously and sent only 4-5 constables. In fact, later when a large crowd had collected, the police asked us to stop live broadcast of the mob fury. We immediately removed our reporter and OB van."

Choudhary added that the channel had by evening submitted all the tapes to the police and the education department. On bringing about a content code, Choudhary said, "There is no need for a government controlled content code. I feel that all channel heads are capable of self-regulation. There will be no meaning of a free media in this country, if there is a code."

Sunil Lulla, CEO, Times Now: "I feel each channel has its own guidelines and mode of sensibility. To say that an umbrella code should be established is declaring a police state. Channels don't air sting operations to instigate violence. To link it to a reaction in this extreme case would be wrong."

Amitabh Thakur, DIG Editor: "If editors can take a call on other stories, why not sting operations? Not just a sting but any story should be done with journalistic intentions. The reaction to any story is not the media's responsibility."

Rajdeep Sardesai, CNN-IBN Editor-in-Chief: "Any sting operation must squarely be in public interest and not entrapment. I don't know enough about this case to comment on whether it was in public interest or not. But having said that, it is wrong to say that the mob fury could have been incited only by media coverage. There could be numerous factors for what happened on that day and media coverage was one of them. However, I do feel that there is need for various filters to be gone through before a sting is aired."

We believe that sting operations are a valid form of investigative journalism. The touchstone for judging the validity of any expose – stings included – is whether or not it's in public interest; they can just be judged by the kind of reaction an expose may provoke. To cite the latter and push for the content code is to push for censorship and government control over media on a flimsy pretext. Would you after all not want to expose a teacher who is allegedly driving her students into prostitution?

Poonam Saxena, Editor Brunch, *Hindustan Times:* In the article, 'Breaking the news into a sleazy, sad story', in *Hindustan Times* on 1.09.2007, she quoted, "Sting operations have become the staple of hindi news genre. Nobody in his right frame of mind will deny that a school teacher who blackmails her students into becoming call girls deserves to be exposed. But why is that stings tend to focus on individual schoolteachers and stories with sexual component? In a country where there is so much injustice, why do so few channels bother to use their hidden cameras to reveal police corruption, governmental neglect or the oppression of the little guy? The stings that have made an impact – Aniruddha Bahl's story about MPs who accepted money to ask parliamentary questions or Poonam Aggarwal's suggestion that the prosecution and defence were colluding in the BMW case – are the ones that dealt with serious issues. Sadly, they are becoming rarer and rarer. Instead, the channels concentrate on salacious stories and much of what they do is pure and simple entrapment. It's become almost a mantra within the media to say that the hindi news channels need some content regulation, ideally self censorship rather than governmental intervention. But I sometimes wonder if we're being unfair in singling out the hindi channels. All of television seems to operate in a different ethical universe to print… So, yes, let's have a debate on ethics in television. And let's have some self regulation. But let's end the hypocrisy of acting as though the hindi chanels are patiahs. And let's accept that for all our self righteousness, even the English language media have serious ethical issues that need to be debated."

Rajdeep Sardesai, Editor-in-chief, CNN-IBN and IBN 7: In the article, "Media's mediators", in *Hindustan Times* on 14.09.2007, he quoted, "A few weeks ago, I received an SMS: "Dear sir, I am from Patna. I have more than 40 stings with me. Meet me once, you will not be disappointed. Trust me, together we will create a tehelka (pun possibly intended)!" I chose not to respond in the firm belief that this was one tehelka I did not want to part of. After all, 40 sting operations at one go sounded a bit unreal. I have little doubt though that someone, somewhere would have responded to the man from Patna. In this open season for outsourcing sting journalism, there must be a buyer who found the offer attractive. As perhaps did the editorial team of the news channel that aired the now infamous Uma Khurana sting, where a schoolteacher was alleged to be a willing accomplice to a prostitution racket till it was discovered that the schoolgirl who was being used as bait wasn't a student after all.

To practitioners in the television news whirl, the Khurana episode should come as no surprise. It was, in a sense, an incident waiting to happen. Which is why some of the self-righteous hand-wringing that has followed the arrest of the television reporter who did the sting is a bit strange. Suddenly, the cheerleaders of the hidden cam expose are turning on their favourite target: television news. As if one sting operation with its shades of grey should be reason enough to tar the entire profession with the brush of unprofessionalism, and worse, criminality.

Let's be honest. The sting has become a legitimate weapon in a journalist's armoury, the hidden camera and its sophisticated variants are now part of the media landscape. Every channel, large or small, has used the hidden camera, often to devastating effect. Let's also be clear: every sting involves an element of deception Then, whether you are posing as a defence dealer or an NGO, (or, as in the Khurana case, a schoolgirl), the sting necessarily involves luring someone through false pretence: as a result, the lines between an expose and entrapment can often be very thin.

In the United States, the law and professional news organizations have stepped in to define the limits of the hidden camera. Take for example CNN's policy guidelines in this regard. The policy clearly states, "the information or evidence to be gathered by a hidden camera should significantly contribute to a story that is of substantial value to society or of vital public interest." Secondly, the expectation of illegal behaviour or wrongdoing should be strong (i.e. no fishing expedition). Thirdly, before using a hidden camera a journalist must first try and exhaust alternatives for obtaining the interview or information. Fourthly, all hidden camera shoots must have the prior approval of the senior news management. In some instances, permission of the federal authorities may also be required before the shoot. Moreover, simply because it is "good television" is not a good reason to use the hidden camera. Bottom line: a hidden camera can be an important tool for solid, investigative journalism, but must be subject to well laid out rules and procedures.

India is different. We have no law that governs sting operations nor have most news organizations chosen to establish a code of conduct in such cases. At the same time, we are a notoriously opaque society, with an extended history of corruption and non-accountability. In such a system, a blanket ban on sting operations, as was hinted at by a Supreme Court judge, is no solution. In the Indian system, the hidden camera can become a valuable instrument of empowerment, a technological tool to expose those who misuse and abuse their authority. Then, whether it be Members of Parliament who are ready to ask questions in parliament for a price, ministers willing to courier drugs, doctors who will amputate the limbs of beggars or lawyers who will collude with witnesses, a sting operation can be staunchly defended for being in the public interest space.

The question is, who will decide what is in the "public interest": the government (as it wishes to do in the Broadcast Bill), the viewers (who continue to have a Jekyll and Hyde approach to the blurred images), the courts (who see themselves as custodians of morality) or the editors (who are well paid to ensure standards)? In the final analysis, notions of public interest must necessarily be subjective, exercised on a daily basis in a 24 x 7 news wheel by those who are responsible for channel content.

Unfortunately, the real flaw in the system lies not in the idea of a sting, but in the process of editorial filtration that must accompany the selection of content. It's that process which is under severe strain in this era of quick-fix, and almost reckless journalism, where almost every hour seems to demand a new breaking news headline, where the battle for eyeballs has become increasingly frenzied, where a sense of editorial worth is seemingly determined by the channel ratings. The resultant pressures have meant that otherwise sensible editorial minds end up doing the most irrational journalism: sensationalizing and titillating instead of informing and enlightening. At one of those endless debates on media ethics, the editor of a leading news channel made the stunning submission that for him, "conscience did not matter, only numbers did!" (by the way, there is no established connection between a sting and television rating points).

When the ethical foundation of journalism has been dismantled so starkly by editorial heads, is it any wonder those who are just entering the profession are gripped by a sense of moral vacuousness? In that sense, the young reporter who has been arrested in the Uma Khurana is as much a "victim" of the new rules of the journalistic game as was the lady who was "stung". How does a young reporter with stars in his eyes make a mark in an increasingly cluttered news market? By simply out-sensationalising his peers even as his seniors mistakenly applaud "cowboy" journalism for serious investigation. Perhaps, the latest controversy provides us news practitioners with a final opportunity to evolve a much-needed industry code of conduct before the government steps in. Self-regulation is only part of the answer: how would self-regulation ensure a uniform adherence to standards in an industry where everyone, from political fixers to real estate sharks, believe they can bring out a news channel? Unless there is an industry-prescribed broadcasting code of conduct, with strict penal provisions for non-observance, news journalism is in danger of hurtling down a slippery slope of normalessness, with a resultant loss of credibility.

Lets also not make the sting fallout a bitter television versus print debate. This must be a debate about media ethics, which involves the entire news media. There are no easy solutions either, for ethical choices are often shaped by commercial pressures. But it is no longer enough to blame smart-suited marketing men alone for compromising editorial integrity. In the end, the editorial leadership of newspapers and channels need to take a hard look at themselves: have we succumbed to temptation too easily: the extravagant lifestyle, the fame game, the cosy, incestuous relationships, the low attention to detail? Journalism is still, at its very core, a noble profession, reporting fearlessly, engaging with the spirit of ideas, challenging those in power, rigorously questioning prevailing wisdom, celebrating human achievement, and offering a mirror to a wide world. If journalism is being debased, it is we who have made this a career choice who must take the responsibility. Rather than live in denial, this must be seen as a collective failure that calls for urgent remedial action. Else, who knows, the next sting could well be on us editors!"

Court Judgments on Sting Operations

Certain important judicial responses in this aspect may further be studied so as to understand the concept better.

In *Court On Its Own Motion v. State*, [146(2008) DLT429], certain guidelines were given by the Delhi High Court as regards sting operations after there was false reporting of a school teacher, Uma Khurana's involvement in a prostitution racket. These include the following-

1. The Court argued against the entrapment of a person even if it was to further the 'public interest.' The right to privacy of a person is to be respected unless there is a larger interest involved.
2. A channel proposing to telecast a sting operation had to obtain a certificate from the person who recorded or produced it saying that it was genuine to the best of his or her knowledge.
3. The channel has to obtain permission from a committee appointed by the Ministry of Information and Broadcasting to telecast the sting operation.
4. While the transcript of the recordings could be edited, the films and tapes cannot be edited. Both edited and unedited tapes have to be produced before the Committee.
5. The chief editor of the channel is responsible for self-regulation and he has to ensure that all statutory requirements have been adhered to.
6. Reports or current events cannot deliberately be presented as true and any unverified or inaccurate facts must be avoided, so as to prevent trial by media so that the public does not get misled.

7. Deliberately overplaying certain parts while underplaying others is also not to be allowed.
8. Reports should not be such as to create alarm or panic or amount to incitement to commit any crime.
9. Media to observe general standards of decency, having regard of the sentiments of viewers, particularly that of children.

Another important issue at the Delhi High Court as regards such operation was the *Cash-for-queries scam* as has been seen earlier. The Delhi High Court in September 2010 upheld the legality of the sting operation conducted by journalists Aniruddha Bahal and Suhasini Raj in 2005 to expose corruption in the Union Parliament. The Delhi Police had previously charged the journalists under the Prevention of Corruption Act for seeking to bribe the MP s. The prime issue which arose in this case was whether any citizen of this country can carry out such an operation and offer bribe to a public officer to expose corrupt practices. The single Delhi High Court judge opined that such a right flowed from the fundamental duty to cherish the noble ideals which inspired the freedom struggle as under Article 51A(b), and creating a corruption-free and independent India is one such ideal. It was also stated that this fundamental duty is linked with every other duty enshrined in Article 51A and more importantly, it is necessary to protect the sovereignty, integrity and unity of the country. Thus, what needs to be seen is that the judge equated the rights of these journalists to that of ordinary citizens, thereby entitling the protection of law to every citizen in such case. As regards offering bribes by the journalists is concerned, the learned judge was of the opinion that in the instant case, the intention of the journalists must be seen, which was clearly to expose corruption amongst the top brass of the government. Further, the journalists deposed truthfully before the Parliamentary committees investigating the matter and the same must be considered.

The journalists have now filed a caveat in the Supreme Court, in case the Delhi Police decides to file an appeal.

A case dealing with sting operations is the judgment given by the Supreme Court in *Raja Ram Pal v The Hon'ble Speaker, Lok Sabha & Others,* ((2007) 3SCC184) concerning the Cash-for-queries scandal and the MPLAD scandal. In this case, certain members of Parliament had challenged their expulsion by way of writ petitions before the apex court. The expelled members contended that the journalists who had carried out the 'sting operation' had admitted to have received monetary and other benefits from the same. It was thus argued on behalf of the tainted MPs that these journalists were driven by motives of self and profit. However, the court held that irrespective of the fact as to whether or not there was any motive to extract money from such operations, the expulsion of the members is not invalid due to the conduct which they had exhibited.

However, it is not just the executive or the legislature which has come under the Media's eye. The Supreme Court in its judgment in *Vijay Shekhar v. Union of India*, ((2004) 4 SCC 666) discussed about corruption in the judiciary and upheld that warrants obtained against certain eminent persons (including former President, Dr. Abdul Kalam and former Chief Justice of India, Mr. Y.K. Sabharwal) in pursuance of a sting operation to expose corruption in the subordinate courts of Gujarat were illegal. It was argued that these warrants had been fraudulently obtained. In fact, the then Chief Justice of India, Mr. K.G. Balakrishnan asked the journalist who had conducted the operation to tender an unconditional apology. A question would thus arise herein as to whether the judiciary was in fact trying to protect its own members while delivering such a judgment. Further, taking into consideration the principle of independence of the judiciary, was the Chief Justice entitled to hear a case in which he was probably interested himself?

Another case was the *Judeo case* which dealt with a sting operation which showed former environment minister Dilip Singh Judeo receiving a bribe from an Australian firm for mining rights in Chhatisgarh. This case came before the Supreme Court after Justice Markenday Katju of the Delhi High Court opined that such sting operations are essential to bring issues such as corruption to light. It was argued on behalf of the journalists that the media act as 'whistleblowers' in public life and thus cannot be prosecuted. However, the CBI on the other hand contended that even journalists involved in such sting operations may be prosecuted where there is active inducement to commit a crime by such persons or where there are other vested interests involved and not just public interest. The premier investigating agency of the country argued that law enforcement is solely within the ambit of the powers of the government. Others can merely assist the government, but they cannot take the law into their own hands. The CBI was of the opinion that any person carrying out such operations may be prosecuted under the Prevention of Corruption Act. The journalists in the instant case, they said, should have informed law enforcement agencies either prior to or immediately after carrying out the operation. Thus, it was reiterated that though the media acts as a guardian of the fundamental rights of citizens, it must do so responsibly.

Judiciary Validates Sting Operations

Sting-Operations Legally Valid: High Court: 25 Jan, 2011

Upholding the legality of sting-operations, the Delhi High Court in a recently reported decision [*Aniruddha Bahal v. State, (2010) 172 DLT 269*] has declared that "it is built-in duties that every citizen must strive for a corruption free society and must expose the corruption whenever it comes to his or her knowledge and try to remove corruption at all levels more so at higher levels of management of the State".

Justice Shiv Narayan Dhingra of the Delhi High Court, quashing the criminal charges for having "conducted a sting operation to expose the practice prevalent amongst some of the Members of Parliament of taking money for asking question in the Parliament", opined as under;

The question that arises in these petitions is whether a citizen of this country has a right to conduct such sting operation to expose the corruption by using agent provocateurs and to bring to the knowledge of common man, corruption at high strata of society.

The Constitution [Part-IVA] lays down certain fundamental duties for the citizens of this country and Article 51A(b) provides that it is the duty of every citizen of India to cherish and follow the noble ideals which inspired our national struggle for freedom. I consider that one of the noble ideals of our national struggle for freedom was to have an independent and corruption free India. The other duties assigned to the citizen by the Constitution is to uphold and protect the sovereignty, unity and integrity of India and I consider that sovereignty, unity and integrity of this country cannot be protected and safeguarded if the corruption is not removed from this country. Another duty of every citizen is to defend the country and render national service when called upon to do so. I consider that a country cannot be defended only by taking a gun and going to border at the time of war. *The country is to be defended day in and day out by being vigil and alert to the needs and requirements of the country and to bring forth the corruption at higher level.* The duty under Article 51A(h) is to develop a spirit of inquiry and reforms. The duty of a citizen under Article 51A(j) is to strive towards excellence in all spheres so that the national constantly rises to higher level of endeavour and achievements *I consider that it is built-in duties that every citizen must strive for a corruption free society and must expose the corruption whenever it comes to his or her knowledge and try to remove corruption at all levels more so at higher levels of management of the State.*

This Court can take judicial notice of the fact that of widespread corruption on a large scale which was unheard of before was now a common place. In 1988 (2) SCC 602 (Antulay's case), Justice Sabyasachi Mukharji observed as under:

> "Values in public life and perspective of these values in public life, have undergone serious changes and erosion during the last few decades. What was unheard of before is common place today. A new value orientation is being undergone in our life and in our culture. We are at the threshold of the cross-roads of values. It is, for the sovereign people of the country to settle those conflicts yet the Courts have vital roles to play in such matters."

These observations were made in 1988. Situation today is much worse.

I consider that it is a fundamental right of citizens of this country to have a clean incorruptible judiciary, legislature, executive and other organs and in order to achieve this fundamental right, every citizen has a corresponding duty to expose corruption wherever he finds it, whenever he finds it and to expose it if possible with proof so that even if the State machinery does not act and does not take action against the corrupt people when time comes people are able to take action either by rejecting them as their representatives or by compelling the State by public awareness to take action against them.

10. This Court had considered as to whether a person making complaint regarding corruption can be considered as an accomplice or not in *State v P.K. Jain and another 2007 Crl. L. J 4137* and observed as under:

10. I consider that observations of learned A.S.J brandishing the complainant in a trap case as accomplice amounts to discrediting the criminal justice system itself and portrays that the criminal justice system cannot respect the witnesses. This country is facing unprecedented rise in corruption. Situation has come to a stage that MCD officials, due to the corrupt practices, have turned the whole city into a slum by allowing all types of unauthorized construction, encroachment, squatting over public land. Engineers of local body who were supposed to check the unauthorized construction and encroachment of the public land, encroachment of roads, encroachment of pavements, turn a blind eye to all this, since their pockets are warmed and palms are greased. Similarly the observation of the trial Court that complainant and his son are interested witnesses and not trust worthy, is unfortunate. In case of a legitimate trap, the persons and police officials taking part in trap, in no sense can be said to be accomplice or un-credit worthy witnesses so that their evidence would require, under law to be corroborated by independent witness. The rule of corroboration is not a rule of law. It is only a rule of prudence and the sole purpose of this rule is to see that innocent persons are not unnecessarily made victim. The rule cannot be allowed to be a shield for corrupt. Moreover, the corroboration need not be by direct oral evidence and can be gathered from circumstantial evidence. The sole evidence of a complainant is sufficient to convict a person, if it is reliable, acceptable and trust worthy. There was a stage under our criminal justice system when the victim of rape was also considered as an accomplice. However, the law rectified itself over the time and gradually it was realized that it was unjust to consider and brand, a victim as an accomplice and seek corroboration of her testimony. Ultimately, Supreme Court laid down that sole testimony of a victim of rape, if trustworthy, was sufficient to convict the accused. In case of bribe giving and taking, normally people do not report the instances of bribe because it suits them to give bribe as they get their illegal works done. Only few persons come forward who either do not believe in giving bribe or who are on the right track or who are fed up by giving bribe. It requires great courage to

report a matter to the Anti Corruption Branch in order to get a bribe taker caught red handed. In our judicial system complainant sometime faces more harassment than accused by repeatedly calling to police stations and then to court and when he stands in the witness box all kinds of allegations are made against him and the most unfortunate is that he is termed as an accomplice or an interested witness not worthy of trust. I fail to understand why a witness should not be interested in seeing that the criminal should be punished and the crime of corruption must be curbed. If the witness is interested in seeing that there should be corruption free society, why Court should disbelieve and discourage him. The witness who reported the demand of bribe so as to trap the culprits cannot be considered as an accomplice or non-trust worthy or interested witness. There is no reason for the court insisting upon an independent corroboration of the complainant's evidence in regard to the demanding of bribe before the trap was laid. When a given complainant first visits a public servant for doing or not doing some task for him, he does not go to him as a trap witness. He goes there in a natural way for a given task. To require him to take a witness with him at that stage would amount to attributing to the complainant a thought and foreknowledge of the fact that the accused would demand bribe. (*Rajinder Kumar Sood Vs. State of Punjab, 1982 Cr. LJ 1338* (PandH). The necessity for court to search for independent witness in case of charges for corruption cannot be insisted upon. Such crimes are committed in secrecy and normally bribe are not taken openly (although there are bold public servants who do even that). In case of trap where accused has not been lured and goaded in some form to accept bribe but the accused himself has created a situation so that he gets bribe money or the accused indulges in the harassment of the complainant to compel the complainant to give bribe and the complainant reports the matter, the absence of independent witnesses to support the version of the complainant cannot be a ground to acquit the accused".

Disadvantages of the Validity of Sting Operations

R Jagannathan on the website *www.firstpost.com* clearly stated the negative aspects that can arise after the Supreme Court validated the sting operations. The headline of the article dated Oct 19, 2011 states, "*SC Opens a can of worms by sanctifying sting operations*".

The Supreme Court's *dismissal* of the Delhi police's appeal to prosecute two journalists for conducting a sting operation against members of Parliament in 2005 in the cash-for-questions scam has wide ramifications.

In its judgment, a bench headed by Justice Aftab Alam quashed the special leave petition filed by the police against an earlier Delhi High Court verdict junking their charge-sheet against journalists Aniruddha Bahal and Suhasini

Raj of Cobrapost.com. *The Times of India* reports that the two journalists had conducted a sting operation called "Operation Duryodhan" which was aired in December 2005. Following this and a parliamentary enquiry, 11 MPs were expelled for taking cash to ask questions in parliament.

The police claimed sting operations needed their sanction, since any person who was aware of the possibility of an offence had to inform the police about it.

The apex court would have none of it, but the judgment opens a entire can of worms.

First, the judgement essentially sanctifies sting operations. This means that, ultimately, the BJP MPs (and ex-MPs) who are now in jail in the cash-for-votes scam for allegedly "entrapping" bribe givers before the July 2008 confidence vote (which the UPA won), can claim the same legitimacy for their operation. Does the court want a stings-without-strings situation?

Second, the Supreme Court also seemed to justify the position that the police need not be informed in advance about sting operations. The court ruled out this possibility on the ground that "the respective MPs would have been given information by the police beforehand and would have been cautioned about the entire operation." This is an extraordinary admission and amounts to saying that the police can be assumed to be in league with politicians and MPs.

If this argument is valid, the whole claim of the police – that the BJP ex-MPs should have gone to the police if they had information about attempts to buy votes in 2008 – falls flat. Sudheendra Kulkarni, former aide of LK Advani, and three MPs and ex-MPs who have been arrested in the cash-for-votes scam, claim they were whistle-blowers. They are likely to use this judgment to extricate themselves from their predicament.

Third, if journalists and political parties take this verdict to mean that they can pry and probe whatever they think is a crime, the potential for misuse of the information is enormous. Consider the possibility that someone who has filmed or taped such evidence could use the information to influence the person targeted. What is to stop crooked journalists or politicians from using stings to coerce and blackmail targets? This is what foreign spy agencies do. Should it now be a free-for-all?

Quite clearly, the Supreme Court – while correctly upholding the validity of bonafide sting operations – has opened a pandora's box of troubles. In view of this, journalists and whistle-blowers need to evolve a code of conduct to ensure that stings do go out of hand.

While it makes sense not to tell the police – as the Supreme Court itself seems to suggest – journalistic stings do need some kind of prior sanction from self-regulatory organisations before they are conducted.

Perhaps sting operations should have some kind of pre-sanction from the chief of the Press Council or some statutory body whose *bona fides* are not suspect. In fact, this is necessary for their own protection.

Let's take a situation where a journalist actually gets caught while conducting a sting. Who will be able to vouch for the authenticity of the sting? It could be the editor, but editors of small-time journals and dubious media organisations may be as culpable as the journalists themselves. It is, after all, a well-known fact that in many regional newspapers and channels, journalists and management are sometimes in cahoots to extort money from advertisers or others by using negative news as a threat.

Moreover, stings can be conducted for the wrong reasons. What is to stop unscrupulous people from using stings to film private material – secret liaisons and family matters? This would be a gross invasion of privacy.

Stings are a double-edged sword for journalists – and the better they are regulated, the more their credibility. Stings cannot become the norm in good journalism. They ought to be the exception rather than the rule.

32

Code of Ethics on Sting Operations

1. Press Council of India – Norms of Journalistic Conduct

Clause 26-Investigative journalism, its norms and parameters: Investigative reporting has three basic elements.

(a) It has to be the work of the reporter, not of others he is reporting;
(b) The subject should be of public importance for the reader to know;
(c) An attempt is being made to hide the truth from the people.

The first norm follows as a necessary corollary from

(a) That the investigative reporter should, as a rule, base his story on facts investigated, detected and verified by himself and not on hearsay or on derivative evidence collected by a third party, not checked up from direct, authentic sources by the reporter himself.
(b) There being a conflict between the factors which require openness and those which necessitate secrecy, the investigative journalist should strike and maintain in his report a proper balance between openness on the one hand and secrecy on the other, placing the public good above everything.
(c) The investigative journalist should resist the temptation of quickies or quick gains conjured up from half-baked incomplete, doubtful facts, not fully checked up and verified from authentic sources by the reporter himself.
(d) Imaginary facts, or ferreting out or conjecturing the non-existent should be scrupulously avoided. Facts facts and yet more facts are vital and they should be checked and cross-checked whenever possible until the moment the paper goes to Press.
(e) The newspaper must adopt strict standards of fairness and accuracy of facts. Findings should be presented in an objective manner, without

exaggerating or distorting, that would stand up in a court of law, if necessary.

(f) The reporter must not approach the matter or the issue under investigation, in a manner as though he were the prosecutor or counsel for the prosecution. The reporter's approach should be fair, accurate and balanced. All facts properly checked up, both for and against the core issues, should be distinctly and separately stated, free from any one-sided inferences or unfair comments. The tone and tenor of the report and its language should be sober, decent and dignified, and not needlessly offensive, barbed, derisive or castigatory, particularly while commenting on the version of the person whose alleged activity or misconduct is being investigated. Nor should the investigative reporter conduct the proceedings and pronounce his verdict of guilt or innocence against the person whose alleged criminal acts and conduct were investigated, in a manner as if he were a court trying the accused.

(g) In all proceedings including the investigation, presentation and publication of the report, the investigative journalist newspaper should be guided by the paramount principle of criminal jurisprudence, that a person is innocent unless the offence alleged against him is proved beyond doubt by independent, reliable evidence.

(h) The private life, even of a public figure, is his own. Exposition or invasion of his personal privacy or private life is not permissible unless there is clear evidence that the wrong doings in question have a reasonable nexus with the misuse of his public position or power and has an adverse impact on public interest.

(i) Though the legal provisions of Criminal Procedure do not in terms, apply to investigating proceedings by a journalist, the fundamental principles underlying them can be adopted as a guide on grounds of equity, ethics and good conscience.

2. News Broadcaster's Association-Code of Ethics and Broadcasting Standards:

Clause 9-Sting operations: As a guiding principle, sting and under cover operations should be a last resort of news channels in an attempt to give the viewer comprehensive coverage of any news story. News channels will not allow sex and sleaze as a means to carry out sting operations, the use of narcotics and psychotropic substances or any act of violence, intimidation, or discrimination as a justifiable means in the recording of any sting operation. Sting operations, will also abide by the principles of self regulation mentioned above, and news channels will ensure that they will be guided, as mentioned above, by an identifiable larger public interest. News channels will as a ground rule, ensure that sting operations are carried out only as a tool for getting conclusive evidence of wrong doing or criminality, and that there is no deliberate alteration of visuals, or editing, or interposing done with the raw footage in a way that it also alters or misrepresents the truth or presents only a portion of the truth.

3. Code of Practice for Journalists Adopted by Editors' Guild of India, August 20, 2002:

Clause 9 of Staff's domain: Information should not be obtained through the use of clandestine listening (and photographing) devices or by intercepting private telephone conversations or through misrepresentation or subteertuge, except when justified only in public interest and only when information cannot be obtained by any other means.

4. Society of Professional Journalists Code of Ethics: Avoid undercover or other surreptitious methods of gathering information except when traditional open methods will not yield information vital to the public. Use of such methods should be explained as a part of the story.

5. Content code including "self-regulation guidelines for broadcasting sector": July 23rd, 2007- The Indian government came out with a content code including "self-regulation guidelines for broadcasting sector" which mandates news channels to follow certain "do's and don'ts" while carrying out sting operations to avoid "unwarranted" infringement of privacy.

According to the guidelines, which run into 34 pages, "channels must not use material relating to a person's personal or private affairs or which invades an individual's privacy unless there is an identifiable larger public interest reason for the material to be broadcast". It also asked channels to ensure "senior editorial control" for selecting material in issues relating to privacy and intrusion into public affairs. The guidelines also suggested the appointment of one or more content auditors by the channels as part of their internal regulatory mechanism.

The Information and Broadcasting Ministry unveiled the code after a meeting with broadcasters, ahead of plans by the government to bring the Broadcast Bill in the monsoon session of parliament beginning early next month. The content code and the guidelines have come in the backdrop of growing concerns over the depiction of sex and violence, and also the manner in which sting operations were being carried out by news channels, reports The Economic Times.

News Broadcasters Association

On February 12, 2012, an article came in the website, www.thehoot.org, on the role of NBA as a self regulatory body.

The News Broadcasters Association is a voluntary self-regulatory industry body and act as a channel of redress for the public. Since its inception in 2008, the body has acted in response to the complaints received against news contents. However, a review of the decisions that were taken till now shows that, only 9 cases were taken into consideration. In view of the 239 complaints that were handed over to the NBA by the BCCC, the cases/ complaints against the channels that were dealt with are too less.

The complaints to NBA pertained to those contents in news items where the viewers wanted discretion. Many complaints had to do with the insensitive coverage of news stories that had been covered in Hindi news channels such as Aaj Tak, Zee News, India TV, etc. In one complaint, Aaj Tak was found to have violated the Code of Ethics & Broadcasting Standards and Guidelines issued by the NBA in the programme, "Operation Jai Jawan". The channel was found to have sensationalised corruption in Ordinance Maintenance Company (OMC), Ambala, which procures supplies for the Army. The channel also did not authenticate the identity of the officers who were shown as being bribed in the visuals. Such pernicious and unauthenticated reporting should have been dealt with stringently but the NBA simply let off the channel with an admonition.

Sometimes news channels get away unscathed despite showing images that not only violate the content code of the guidelines, but also raises questions on the channel's credibility as a disseminator of news. India TV had to face the ire of the NBA's self regulatory authority after it aired "Operation Gang Rape" that showed visuals of an MMS of a gang rape. But it was let off with simply a warning for not following the guidelines of reporting a court proceeding and for interfering with the judicial investigation of the Gang Rape and the accused. Times Now was issued a censure on the unwarranted point of view of the court proceedings of Kanimozhi. TV9's telecast of the programme, "Gay Culture Rampant in Hyderabad", on TV9 News Channel, also drew a number of complaints. Though the broadcaster defended that the programme was aired to warn the public about the "crime" of blackmail being committed by certain persons who were enticing the people into the gay community, the NBA held that the broadcaster had violated Clauses 5 (Sex and Nudity), Clause 6 (Privacy), and Clause 9 (Sting Operations) of the Code of Ethics.

India TV on December 2008 aired an interview of a Pakistani analyst. The analyst had given the interview to Reuters. Not only were the interview translated and read out by a female anchor against a picture of the analyst but it also claimed that the analyst was a spy for the US government. In this case, the channel violated copyrights because the interview was given to Reuters and did not accredit the news agency, but also misrepresented facts to their audience. The erring channel had to apologise and was imposed a fine of Rs 1 lakh. But surprisingly the channel withdrew its membership from the NBA after the decision and again got re- elected by the NBA for 2011- 2012.

Sting Operations and Ethics—Some Opinions

Q.1. What are your views on Sting operation? Reasons if you may provide.

Answers:

Prabhu Chawla[1]: Sting operations are one of the most credible and scientific method of collecting information. In an age, when criminals and scamsters are devising unique ways of committing crimes, it is absolutely essential for media organisations to acquire fail proof technology for gathering information so that they can face any legal action.

Prashanta Kumar Goswami[2]: Sting Operation is a legitimate mode of exposing the existing evil in the larger public interest. However, the distinction between a legitimate sting operation and entrapment must always be kept in mind.

Pranab Pathak[3]: The phrase Sting operation is a new word in the field of journalism. We heard it for the first time during the Tehelka expose of the match fixing scam. When it comes to privacy and accountability, people demand the former for themselves and the latter for everyone else. Recently a Delhi High Court judgment discussed about sting operations in a matter where some MPs were offered money for asking questions in the Parliament. The High court declared that such sting operations meant for public good is justified. And I share the same opinion.

Shripal Shaktawat[4]: Sting operation is a wonderful tool that we have as a journalist to expose the wrongdoers in our society. When we exposed the *Kokh Me Qatal* series on tv screen, we realised that how the doctors were into sex determination of foetus and directly or indirectly involved in female foeticide. Our expose helped people to realise what is happening in their locality. The doctors are vigilant that anytime they could be exposed and so they try and avoid certain wrongs. So, Sting operation is a weapon that should be used judiciously and in public interest; and also to upheld the interest of the public.

Further in my opinion, hidden cameras should be used to find solutions to some public problems instead of using them for spying on closed rooms or beds of heroes and politicians. With this thought in our minds, we directed stings operations towards finding solutions to societal problems. For example first of all, we did a sting on how an old woman was daily cheated by her rich children and exposed to the public how such old people were harassed within the four walls of their houses. And it gives us utmost happiness that our stings could bring about changes in the Indian society with new laws on protection of the rights of old people and ban on screening of the sex of unborn babies.

Gautam Uzir[5]: In law enforcement, a sting operation is a deceptive operation designed to catch a person committing or trying to commit a crime. Such crime may be of various types like murder, misappropriation of money, spying or any other action which is detrimental to the society. In my view, there is no dearth of criminals in the present day world and in order to expose the crimes of such unscrupulous people, a sting operation becomes necessary which may be carried out either by a law enforcing agency or by a journalist. The oldest sting operation carried out by a journalist was "Nixon's Water Gate Scandal of America" and for which Nixon had to resign as the President of America. In India, one of the oldest sting operations is known as "Tehelka".

Dhruvanshu Jha[6]: If done with integrity it can reveal hidden truth. Sting operations can be useful, since, it reveals truth in public and same can have deterrent effect upon people to refrain from doing things which they cannot do legally.

Mithun Pillai[7]: Sting operations could be necessary. They should be used cautiously.

Kirti Kumar[8]: Sting operations should be carried out. These are very much helpful in bringing out the evil side of any organisation & government. Corruption can be decreased by doing string operations because it can develop a sense of fear among the corrupt officials.

Rajiv Dogra[9]: There are at times limitations to journalism when the source of information wants to project facts in a certain fashion which may not be the real picture. To dig out the actual facts, it's sometimes necessary to go undercover and ferret out the truth. Sting operation is one such way of highlighting the truth.

Ved Prakash[10]: Sting operations are good as well as bad. Good as long as they expose for the public good and bad if they are conducted to achieve selfish interest.

Anil Sagar[11]: Should be used selectively for exposing real corruption. Its use for political ends and to blackmail individuals should be strongly curbed.

Q.2. Should a sting operation be conducted on sub judice matter as it may influence the judge?

Answers:

Prabhu Chawla: Normally, media should be careful while conducting a sting operation which involves a case pending in a court of law. But if it involves public interest and it is absolutely necessary to collect evidence which help in promoting a public cause, I don't see any reason for resorting to such tactics. But it should be done without malice.

Prashanta Kumar Goswami: Sting Operation may be conducted under certain circumstances in a sub-justice matter to assist the cause of Justice, more particularly, if the authorities concerned are not performing the duties in accordance with law. However, the persons conducting the sting operation must be ready to appear before the concerned Court a witnesses.

Pranab Pathak: Infact on a sub judice matter no one should give any comment whether he is a politician, bureaucrat or journalist.

Shripal Shaktawat: Ofcourse yes, if that sting can provide some evidence that can take the case forward or give a new twist to the case. Like in the case of Jessica Lal murder case.

In this age of technological advancement if content of emails and SMSs have been recognized as evidences, then why not stings be recognized as the same? In fact, what could be a better evidence than this? Anyway, the government that was once in a mood of raising questions on the justification of using stings, has itself acknowledged the fact that there could be no better way to expose female foeticide and to put a stop to it. After our exposure Governments like Madhya Pradesh's Shivraj singh government and Rajasthan's Ashok Gehlot government are conducting stings on female foeticide. Moreover, government now funds the stings with Rs two lakhs if they are conducted on such lines. Now we also heard that the government of Vasundhara Raje is going to increase the amount. Earlier Government was criticising us for sting but now they are following us.

Gautam Uzir: When a legal matter is pending in a court of law, the court itself can normally monitor the progress of the case. As such, in case of requirement of any document (relating to the legal proceeding) from the government or a private agency, the court has enough power to direct the concerned agency (or government) to produce the same before it. Hence, under such a situation, a sting operation is not advisable or may not be required until and unless the government or private agencies are withholding or destroying such vital documents. However, to my knowledge, till date there has been no sting operation as such on a sub-judice matter.

Dhruvanshu Jha: In *sub judice* matter sting operations should not be conducted, since, the matter backed by material is before the Court, which is bound to decide matter judicially. Sting operations in *sub judice* matter can affect justice delivery system; however, a judge with good judicial training would not be affected by any such operation.

Mithun Pillai: No. It has every possibility of influencing the judge and bringing in a subjective view.

Kirti Kumar: Yes journalist can conduct sting operation on sub judice matter if they are sure that they have enough proof to change the course of justice. For eg in Jessica Lal murder case. Courts believe only on evidences and journalists, through their sting operations can provide the court with evidences.

Rajiv Dogra: No. As per the basic principle of journalism, the law of the land needs to be respected and abided by.

Ved Prakash: I think sting operations can be conducted on sub judice matter because there are many examples where judiciary has taken suo moto action based on the reports of sting operations.

Anil Sagar: No harm, as long as it reveals the truth. Even the purpose of judiciary is to unravel the truth and decide accordingly

Q.3. Should journalists take up the role of the police and other investigative agencies and conduct sting operations?

Answers:

Prabhu Chawla: Journalists are expected to perform investigative journalism. They have to go deep behind a story. They have to find the truth. that is what a police officer does. But a journalist does such investigations to get any one punished. he does it in public interest and leaves the prosecution to the law enforcement agencies.

Prashanta Kumar Goswami: The roles of the police and journalists are not identical. The role of the journalists so for as sting operations are concerned are supplementary in nature and can be resorted to in the larger public interest to advance the cause of Justice.

Pranab Pathak: There is no question of a journalist taking up the role of police. The way detective and investigative agencies help the police in investigating a crime and provide them with circumstantial evidences to unerringly prove the guilt of the accused, similarly, the journalists can conduct such investigation and help the police with their investigation.

Shripal Shaktawat: A journalist should do everything possible to expose the wrongdoers. They should not take the role of police officers but they should work in tandem with the police so that culprits are brought to books.

I remember a case of 1999 where a Tibetan girl was kidnapped and gang raped in Jaipur. She was kidnapped in a government jeep with blue lights and taken to a jungle which was around 130 kilometres and gang raped and, just like the recent Damini case in Delhi, was thrown naked on the railway track. With the help of a railway employee she first reached Jaipur. Through my own investigation I had collected a lot of evidence and information which could have been exposed through newspapers and television reports. But I wanted to cast away the role of a journalist and instead chose to be a good citizen. Instead of making it into headlines we informed the SP-Jaipur North Mr Sourabh Srivastava who immediately arrested the culprits. I personally believe that apart from our professional callings and responsibilities we have to be a good citizen first and accordingly do our duties.

I remember another sensational news of Rajasthan when a Dalit lady named Bhanwari Devi who was also a folk artiste and auxiliary nurse in a government hospital was kidnapped and murdered. It was alleged that Bhanwari Devi was blackmailing the minister of stature, Maderna and Congress legislator Malkhan Singh based upon a CD in which Maderna and others were seen in a compromising position with Devi. The CBI had started investigating and grilling both Maderna and Malkhan Singh. But CBI failed to procure the explicit CD that was being referred to for backmailing the two politicians. The CBI was trying hard to get hold of the CD. When I got hold of the CD through my sources I did not break the news out in the public but chose to be a responsible citizen and handed a copy of the CD to CBI and Jodhpur Court without whose strictness CBI would not have carried on with their investigation. The result being that the politicians and their associates in crime were booked and CBI was in a position to prove their motive of murder. All we did was play the role of a good citizen but sadly the next day some news channels claimed that the CD was in their possession but neither they informed the CBI nor behaved in a responsible way.

Gautam Uzir: Journalists are allowed to conduct sting operations only as journalists and not like the police or other investigation agencies. On 30th of August, 2007, a news channel called LIVE INDIA broadcasted a programme based on a sting operation in which one lady teacher of a school run by Delhi Government was shown to force a female student of her school into prostitution. After the programme being aired on the channel, people entered the school campus and manhandled the said lady teacher. The lady teacher was first suspended and later dismissed from service. The police registered a case and started investigating into the matter. In December 2007, the Delhi High Court took suo-moto notice of the media reportage and in the course of pendency of the matter the Court was informed that the said female person who posed as a student was actually not a student but a journalist and such an episode was projected just for self-exposure. In the meantime, the Ministry of Information and Broadcasting, New Delhi, prepared certain guidelines for the broadcasting agencies.

Dhruvanshu Jha: No doubt, in todays perspective media is the fourth pillar of democracy; however, it has its limitations and parameters based upon ethics. Media may make a bare probe into an issue, but to say that media takes up role of police and other investigating agencies would be unfair and dangerous to process well prescribed in the laws of the land.

Mithun Pillai: Yes. Journalists are supposed to help police by their investigation.

Kirti Kumar: I do not think that a journalist is carrying on the job of Police or an investigating agency. It looks a bit similar to an investigating agency though it is very difficult to draw a line of demarcation between two jobs.

Rajiv Dogra: The job of a journalist is to reach to the bottom and bring the truth to the fore. Sting operation is one tool that can be employed to get closer to the fact. However, it should not be conducted in a manner that it hinders the working of any other government agency, including the police.

Ved Prakash: I don't think that journalists take up the role of police when they conduct sting operations. They can supplement and complement each other. Moreover sting operations exposes as it is.

Anil Sagar: Journalists have an inherent role of investigation to play. But they should not try and be judgemental on issues or bully people by adopting a police style of functioning.

Q. 4. If a journalist resorts to illegal and unethical activities to expose a matter of public interest, should he be provided with immunity?

Answers:

Pranab Pathak: There is a difference between unethical and illegal activities. Sometimes the journalist has to resort to certain unethical activities to expose a matter of public interest like that of offering bribes etc but the intention should be for public good. Therefore it is justified. But so far as illegal activities are concerned, no one should resort to it.

Gautam Uzir: No, the journalist should not be provided with immunity.

Dhruvanshu Jha: No, journalists should refrain from resorting to illegal means in quest for fact unknown. Police and other investigating agencies are authorised for the same.

Mithun Pillai: Yes. It should be understood that they are using those unethical means to expose some wrong doings. But they should inform their activities to police.

Kirti Kumar: If a journalist uses unethical methods while carrying on sting operation, he cannot be left Scot free.

Rajiv Dogra: No one is above the law, including journalists. One must abide by the law of the land and refrain from doing anything illegal or unethical, which would bring a bad name to the profession.

Ved Prakash: Yes they can if their motive is public good

Anil Sagar: No, he should be punished most severely to set an example for others as well.

Q.5. In relation to Right to privacy and public interest, what according to you should be given more weightage?

Answers:

Pranab Pathak: Basically, whenever Right to privacy and Public interest crops up, more emphasis should be given to public interest. But journalists should also respect the privacy of an individual. The Supreme Court of India in a judgement on *R. Rajgopal Vs Tamil Nadu and others* stated that there should be a proper balance between right to privacy and public interest.

Gautam Uzir: Both privacy and public interest are a right to any prudent individual. As such, association of greater weightage to either of these depends on the situation and the necessity.

Dhruvanshu Jha: Both are independent, important and valuable rights. However, Right to privacy does not give immunity from illegal acts and in such case, such right should be denied in larger public interest likewise, in the name of so called public interest, privacy of individual should not be compromised on mere suspicion. Right to privacy and public interest ought to be balanced reasonably in a given situation.

Mithun Pillai: Of course, Public Interest.

Kirti Kumar: Public interest should be given priority over privacy, just as when there is a conflict between security of the state & individual freedom security of the state has a greater weightage.

Rajiv Dogra: A matter concerning public interest at large certainly weighs more than the right to privacy.

Ved Prakash: Obviously public interest

Anil Sagar: Right to privacy is cannot be total and neither can all acts be justified in the name of public interest. However, generally speaking there is no harm in revealing what is good for a large number of people. But it should be remembered that an individual's private life is normally not of much public interest, while it may pander to the prurient desires of the masses.

Q. 6. Do you think means and modalities used in a sting operation is irrelevant where public interest is served in some way?

Answers:

Prabhu Chawla: I am in favour of using any means as long as it is meant for unearthing a truth in public interest and not to blackmail any individual or an authority.

Prashanta Kumar Goswami: Means and modalities used in a sting operation an are not totally irrelevant. Unethical or dishonest means can hardly result in proper results. The difference between legitimate sting operation and entrapment must always be kept in mind.

Pranab Pathak: No the means and modalities used during a sting operation can never be irrelevant. One should no the difference between unethical and illegal activities. And even if they are using unethical ways, that should always be the last resort, the motive solely being just public interest and good.

Shripal Shaktawat: No, I am not finicky about the usages of means and modalities. To expose mud, you have to step into it and in the process dirty yourself. But if your overall intention is clear and in the benefit of larger public interest and good, then I personally do not any problems with the means and modalities used in the exposes. In the *Kokh me Qatal* series we also used pregnant ladies but they were in fact more eager to help us.

I just remembered another incident relating to one such Presidential election where Bhairo Singh Shekhawat was a candidate for the post. I came to know through some sources that the next day, which was a Saturday, he would visit a *Tantric*-like person in Pali, Rajasthan to worship Lord Shani with cremation ashes. This was to please the deity and win the elections. At that time I had to lie to the Collector that Shekhawat himself had asked me to collect a pass for entering the temple. We conducted the sting under the veil of security provisions and exposed that politicians like Shekhawat resort to superstitious means to win Presidential elections. Had I not lied to get the passes and conduct the sting, it would not have been possible for us to bring this truth into people's notice.

Gautam Uzir: Means and modalities comprising a sting operation are put to action when there is no other way to catch a criminal or expose a scam. But under normal circumstances where public interest could be served in some way, the need for a sting operation (or the means and modalities of a sting operation) becomes less significant/irrelevant.

Dhruvanshu Jha: No, they are relevant not only morally but ethically as well. One cannot resort to illegal modes and methods to find an answer. Procedure calls for utmost care and caution, since, valuable rights are involved.

Mithun Pillai: No. Means used to expose something should be of prime concern. One should always use the right means, and only in extreme cases resort to something unusual but the motive of such exposes should only be public interest.

Kirti Kumar: It is true that public interest should be given priority but it should not be at the cost right & ethical modalities. However sting operations should function in decorum and should not play with one's personal life. Hence, sting operations must preserve human values. Sting operation is a very critical act which hampers someone's privacy. So for using such thing one should have evidences to do so.

Rajiv Dogra: It's essential that the conduct is carried out in the ambit of law since no one is above the law, including journalists.

Ved Prakash: Yes, I believe the means and modalities used in a sting operation are irrelevant as long as they expose the wrong doer with public good in mind.

Anil Sagar: No, you can't be using violence, sex or allurements for achieving the objectives. For in themselves all these means and modalities also constitute a crime.

Q. 7. Apart from various Journalistic Code of conducts, do you think there should be some statutory laws laying down the rules and regulations of conducting a sting operation?

Answers:

Pranab Pathak: It is a pity that both the legislature and the judiciary is silent on the subject. Yes, there is an urgent need of laws to govern sting operations. They should provide the journalists exactly and to what extent they can use their right to freedom of speech and expression in the form of sting operations.

Gautam Uzir: Yes, there should be some statutory laws. Referring to the Live India case regarding Mrs Uma Khurana, the Ministry of Information and Broadcasting, New Delhi, prepared certain guidelines where the broadcasting agencies—

1. Cannot deliberately present as true any unverified or incorrect fact, so as to avoid trial by media.
2. Cannot present facts and views in a manner which is likely to mislead the public (about their veracity) by mixing fact and fiction in such a way that the public is unlikely to distinguish between the two.
3. Cannot present a distorted picture of reality by over-emphasising or underplaying certain aspects that may trivialise or sensationalise contempt.
4. Cannot make public any activity or material relating to an individual's personal or public affairs or which invades a person's privacy unless it involves or is identifiable with large issues of public interest.
5. Cannot create public panic or unnecessary alarm that is likely to encourage or incite the public to commit any crime or, otherwise, lead to any disorder or offensive towards public or religious feelings.

Dhruvanshu Jha: Yes, such regulation is required as same would give it legitimacy and would provide parameters within which such operation can be conducted without coming in conflict with right and privileges of individual or group of individuals.

Mithun Pillai: No.

Kirti Kumar: Since sting operation is required in public interest, it is important that besides journalistic code of conduct the government must make law covering every aspect of sting operation, so that people should not misuse it.

Rajiv Dogra: Apart from the basic code of conducts, I don't think there should be any additional laws. Anything addition would stifle the purpose of conducting a sting operation.

Ved Prakash: Yes, there should be some statutory laws to guard the privacy of the individual during sting operation if that does not include public good.

Anil Sagar: Self control and a righteous approach are the best rules and regulations.

Q. 8. Where sting operation covers incidents relating to child victims or juvenile delinquents, should some restrictions be placed on the journalist?

Answers:

Pranab Pathak: Whenever sting operations depict child victims of molestation, rape, torture etc or juvenile delinquents, it is very important for the journalists to govern their identity so that they too can lead a life of social dignity.

Gautam Uzir: Yes, under such a situation, the journalist should operate in a very careful way as over-exposure of such incidents may destroy the future of such child victims.

Dhruvanshu Jha: Yes, such restrictions are reasonable in larger interest of a child or a juvenile delinquent. The procedure should be such which does not even remotely affect delinquents psyche

Mithun Pillai: Yes. In cases where child victims are involved their identity should be protected. Even during the investigation they should not be harassed. Their emotions should also be taken care of.

Kirti Kumar: Of course some restrictions should be placed on journalists while carrying on these operations.

Rajiv Dogra: It's necessary that the identities of young delinquents are not revealed when the tapes are beamed on the national network. And to an extent, the TV channels are quite clear about this policy.

Ved Prakash: Definitely, there should be restrictions during the cases that deal with child victims and juveniles but a mere concealing of their identity is also good enough.

Anil Sagar: Yes, their identity should be protected as per the requirement of law. The idea should be that the sting operation should help in improving the lot of child victims or juvenile delinquents.

Q. 9. Should there be a mechanism to test the motive of the sting operation and that it is not used to take undue advantage like blackmailing etc?

Answers:

Pranab Pathak: No, it is practically not possible to test the motive of a sting operation unless and until it is projected in front of the public. It is true that there are many stunts of Entrapment by the channels to garner TRPs but, even then testing the motives is not possible unless all the Journalists who are into sting operations report to a central authority who keeps track of their investigation objectively.

Gautam Uzir: Yes, definitely there should be a mechanism so as to avoid blackmailing etc. If any journalist is proved guilty of resorting to such means (like blackmailing) then he becomes a criminal and the criminal law of the land is applicable upon him (like any ordinary criminal).

Dhruvanshu Jha: Yes, any sting operation with ulterior motive ought to be dealt with heavy hand.

Mithun Pillai: No. I don't think any such mechanism will work. An expose is an expose. Most of the sting operations are done secretly so, there is no way they can be tracked and tested.

Kirti Kumar: Certainly, sting operation should not be carried out with malefic intentions. The only objective has to be public interest. Therefore if we can evolve a mechanism which can judge the intentions of journalist involved in sting operation.

Rajiv Dogra: There should definitely be a mechanism to keep a tab on any kind of anti-social activity. But then the moot question remains that who would decide the mechanism.

Ved Prakash: I believe that the government should frame rules and regulations for conducting of the sting operations and that should take care of it.

Anil Sagar: A mere look at the objectives of any such sting operation is enough to reveal the intent behind it. As long as the intent is good, the sting operations are okay, if not they are not less than crimes in themselves.

Q. 10. Should there be an independent statutory body to regulate the transmissions/ publishing or withhold it, if necessary?

Answers:

Prabhu Chawla: I am in favour of a rigorous scrutiny of media content. But it cant and shouldn't be done by any government agency or an organisation which is backed by it. We need a body of professionals from within the media which should have few representatives from the judiciary.

Prashanta Kumar Goswami: Statuary Regulatory body in respect of transmission, publication etc is not in the public interest. This idea partakes the character of censorship which historically has been proved to be detrimental to public interest. Any one aggrieved by any such sting operation has legal remedies to vindicate his right. However, legal regime dealing with such cases should ensure speedy disposal of such cases. Public interest is better served by keeping the doors of free competition of ideas & news without restrictive set up.

Pranab Pathak: The Press Council Of India and the Prasar Bharti should take up the role of regulating the sting operations. But yes the journalists should know that they should not be cowed down by government pressure nor be swayed away by private junkies and freebies. If they are here to serve the public, they should go ahead and expose all who indulges in wrong doings. And the bringing in of independent statutory body can lead to censorship which is unwanted in this case.

Gautam Uzir: There are some expert bodies even constituted by the journalists themselves under the Ministry of Information and Broadcasting, Government of India. Since there are several guidelines provided by the Ministry itself, a separate law or body is not necessary as such. It only needs to be ensured that the broadcasting agencies prepare any story within the parameters of such guidelines and in case of any deviation from the guidelines severe punishment can be imposed.

Dhruvanshu Jha: Yes.

Mithun Pillai: No. We have witnessed that organisations breed corruption. Let sting operations be guided by the motive of competition between channels to give its viewers the best. Though all channels would say that the motive of their sting is public interest but the underlying fact remains that they compete with each other. There should be no regulations here as there are chances of it becoming manipulated.

Kirti Kumar: No there is no need for any such statutory body as it will lead to reigning the freedom of journalists with unnecessary censorship and rules and regulations.

Rajiv Dogra: The whole purpose of a sting operation would be lost if it comes under the scrutiny of a statutory body.

Ved Prakash: For print we have the Press Council of India and for broadcast we have the National Broadcasters Association. But though PCI is a statutory body it has no right to withhold anything meant for publishing and broadcasting. It can only regulate and reprimand.

Anil Sagar: There are ample laws in existence to govern various aspects of sting operations. If their motive is to take "undue advantage", then they constitute a crime. But if the objective is noble then there is no need to regulate them.

Conclusion

1. Sting Operation is a weapon in the hands of journalists; and if used judiciously can be of great help to the society and it will expose the wrong doers.
2. The underlying motive should always be public interest and public good.
3. The motive behind an expose should never be of raising TRPs or gain undue attention.
4. The driving force behind Stings should never be yellow journalism or sensationalism. Example- *the casting couch sting of Shakti Kapoor and Aman Verma.*
5. The journalists should never resort to Entrapment or false implication of any innocent person. Example- *the Uma Khurana sting operation.*
6. Sting operations should be done in tandem with editors and police.
7. The journalists should also follow up their story and see that the concerned authorities bring them to book.
8. There should be some strict punishment for those journalists who flaunt all ethics of journalism and use sting operations for personal good and private good rather than public good. Such exemplary punishment would deter other journalists from treading in the same path.
9. Journalists should not resort to paparazzi or intrude upon the private lives of others unless there is overriding cause of public interest.
10. Journalists conducting stings should be given support and protection by police and government. Journalists like *Jyotirmoy Dey of Mumbai* laid their lives for the cause of exposing criminals.
11. In the proposed draft code for television broadcasters, the government has suggested that sting operations be banned. While the idea of formulating a codebook for broadcasters with clearly spelt out do's and don'ts is good one but banning sting operation is not desirable.
12. Sting operation has been criticised for being nothing more than entrapment. The detractors may be correct in their view of stings as the base form of journalism, but in banning a particular method of investigation, the government only creates an impression that it has something to hide.

13. The popular belief I found after taking into consideration opinions from various sources is that – to hide their misdoings politicians try to pass legislations to curb the freedom of press.
14. The sting operations might blur the lines between what is ethical and what is not- but the end results often justify the methods.
15. Sting operation is essentially an information gathering exercise. It looks for facts that are not easy to obtain by simple requests and searches, or those that are actively being concealed, suppressed or distorted. Some subterfuge may be necessary in order to obtain information required to bringunlawful activities to light.
16. Lastly, the growth of electronic media over the past decade has drastically altered the rules of the game for journalists. The media should decide what form of investigative journalism is acceptable and what is not. The I&B Ministry has no place interceding and peremptorily deciding to simply ban an entire method of reporting.

Notes

1. Prabhu Chawla, Editorial Director, *The New Indian Express* Group.
2. Prashanta Kumar Goswami, Former Additional Solicitor General of India.
3. Pranab Pathak, Former Addl. Advocate General, Assam, Former Advocate General, Mizoram.
4. Shripal Shaktawat, Former Sting reporter, Sahara Samay, Currently Bureau Chief at India News.
5. Dhruvanshu Jha, Senior Advocate, Supreme Court.
6. Gautam Uzir, Senior Lawyer, Guwahati High Court.
7. Mithun Pillai, Head of Department, Mass Media, SIES College, Mumbai University.
8. Dr. Kirti Kumar, Retired as Senior Reader, Indraprastha College, Delhi University.
9. Rajiv Dogra, Content Manager, *Times of India*, Mumbai.
10. Ved Prakash, Former Newsreader, Doordarshan.
11. Anil Sagar, Senior Correspondent, Deshbandhu.

Bibliography

Advertising and Sales Management by Mukesh Trehan and Ranju Trehan.
Bright's *Mass Communication and Journalism*.
Constitution of India and Professional Ethics by G.B. Reddy, Reddy.
Contempt of Court and Freedom of Speech: Exploring Gender Biases by Bibha Tripathi.
Emerging, Constitution and Democracy by N.M. Ghatate.
Encyclopaedia of Journalism and Mass Communication (5 Vols.) by Om Gupta.
Freedom of Speech and Assembly and Public Order by S.K. Ghosh.
Freedom of the Press: Using the Law to Defend Journalists – Human Rights Law Network.
Handbook of Journalism and Mass Communication by Vir Bala Aggarwal, V.S. Gupta.
History of Indian Journalism by J. Natarajan.
Human Rights in India by Asish Kumar Das, Prasant Kumar Mohanty.
In Defence of Journalists by Nolan Shutler, Nick Chapman, Harsh Dobha.
Indian Government and Politics by Abbas Hoveyda.
Indian Press since 1955 by S.C. Bhatt.
Industrial scenario in India by Nishi Sinha.
Information Technology Law and Practice by Vakul Sharma.
Introduction to the Constitution of India by Durga Das Basu.
Introduction to the Constitution of India by Sharma, Sharma B.K.
Journalism and Mass Communication by Hena Naqvi.
Journalism in India by Rangaswami Parthasarthy.
"Laws on access to official documents" in T.N. Chaturvedi, (*op. cit.*).
Mass Communication in India (4th Edition) by Keval J. Kumar.
Mass Communication in India by Keval J. Kumar.
Mass Media and Related Laws in India by B. Manna.
Media and Ethics by S.K. Aggarwal.
Media Ethics: Key Principles for Responsible Practice: Patrick Lee Plaisance.
Media Law and Ethics: Neelamalar.
Media Law and Ethics: Roy L. Moore, Michael D. Murray.
Medial Laws and Ethics by M. Neelamalar.
MPA-013, 'Public Systems Management' published by IGNOU.
"Open government and administrative culture in India" *Indian Journal of Public Administration*, Vol. 36, No.3, July-September by Jaytilak Guha Roy.
Political Science textbook +2 Stage by Durga Kanta Sarmah.

Political Science textbook for H S. First Year by Dr. Kripesh Chandra Paul.
Political Science textbook for H S. Second Year by Dr. Kripesh Chandra Paul.
Pratiyogita Darpan (various editions).
Press Laws and Ethics of Journalism by P.K. Ravindranath.
Press Laws and Ethics: P.K. Ravindran
Public Interest Litigation by Sampat Jain; Deep and Deep Pub. 2003.
Public Interest Litigation in India by S.K. Agrawala.
Right to Information Act, 2005: Implementation and Challenges edited by R.K. Gupta, P.K. Saini, Rakesh Kumar Gupta.
Routledge Handbook of Indian Cinemas edited by K. Moti Gokulsing, Wimal Dissanayake.
"Secrecy in government in India" in T.N. Chaturvedi (Ed.), Secrecy in Government by Shriram Maheshwari.
Social Background of Indian Nationalism (6th-Edn) by A.R. Desai.
Style book of All India Radio, New Delhi.
Textbook on the Indian Penal Code by Krishna Deo Gaur.
The Code of Criminal Procedure, 1973 by American Law Institute.
The Journalist's Handbook by M.V. Kamath.
The Law of IPR edited by Shiv Sahai Singh.
Women Dimension on Television: Policy, Personnel, and Programme by Ila Joshi.

Websites

http://www.ictregulationtoolkit.org/en/toolkit/notes/PracticeNote/1222
http://cyberlaws.net/cyberindia/convergencearticle.htm
http://www.ascionline.org/index.php/ascicodes.html
http://www.ascionline.org/images/pdf/asci_code1new.pdf
http://www.ascionline.org/index.php/mission.html
http://www.preservearticles.com/2012011821089/essay-on-prasar-bharati-broadcasting-corporation-of-india.html
http://prasarbharati.gov.in/Corporate/Pb%20act/Pages/default.aspx
http://dict.mizoram.gov.in/uploads/attachments/cyber_crime/cinematographact1952.pdf
http://www.ddindia.gov.in/business/commercial%20and%20sales/Pages/CodeforCommercialAdvertisements_C.aspx
http://www.shareyouressays.com/121423/essay-on-information-technology-act-2000-399-words
http://www.shareyouressays.com/121630/salient-features-of-the-information-technology-act-2000-essay
http://eprocure.gov.in/cppp/sites/default/files/eproc/itact2000.pdf
http://www.indiankanoon.org/doc/1465272/
http://indiankanoon.org/doc/1251904/
http://www.indiankanoon.org/doc/74909/
http://www.lawzonline.com/bareacts/Indian-Constitution/Article361A-Constitution-of-India.html
http://www.legalserviceindia.com/articles/media.htm
http://indiatoday.intoday.in/story/two-recent-orders-fuel-debate-on-contentious-issue-of-contempt-of-court/1/283425.html
http://www.thehindu.com/opinion/columns/truth-fair-criticism-help-fight-contempt-charge/article602279.ece
http://www.indiatogether.org/2010/dec/law-contempt.htm

http://www.nwmindia.org/articles/checkmated-by-the-judiciary
http://articles.timesofindia.indiatimes.com/2012-04-09/india/31312267_1_fair-trial-vacuum-constitution-bench
http://ibnlive.in.com/news/right-to-fair-trial-cant-overshadow-freedom-of-speech-ram-jethmalani/249621-3.html
http://scholar.valpo.edu/cgi/viewcontent.cgi?article=1808&context=vulr
http://www.thehindu.com/opinion/Readers-Editor/freedom-of-the-press-and-fair-trial/article431603.ece
http://www.rtiindia.org/forum/82318-rti-happenings-government-review-official-secrets-act.html
http://archive.tehelka.com/story_main50.asp?filename=Ws151011Internal_ Security.asp
http://www.dnaindia.com/india/report-colonial-era-official-secrets-act-to-be-tweaked-to-get-in-tune-with-rti-1598940
http://newindianexpress.com/magazine/voices/article390689.ece
http://www.indianexpress.com/news/relevance-of-official-secrets-act-now-limited-rti-act-will-prevail-if-there-s-any-direct-conflict-says-cic/228511/
http://articles.timesofindia.indiatimes.com/2009-02-26/india/28003463_1_cbi-case-delhi-court-official-secrets-act
http://www.hindustantimes.com/India-news/Mumbai/Bail-for-scribe-booked-under-official-secrets-act/Article1-700472.aspx
http://bbs.tianya.cn/post-english-172212-1.shtml
http://infamouspirateoflaw.blogspot.in/2013/04/the-right-to-privacy-in-cyber-era.html
http://www.christuniversity.in/uploadimages/LAWYERED%20_%20August% 20issue.pdf
http://presscouncil.nic.in/norms-2010.pdf
http://articles.timesofindia.indiatimes.com/2011-06-04/india/29620422_1_privacy-law-ministry-confidentiality
http://www.indianexpress.com/news/after-radia-tapes-govt-works-on-a-privacy-law/726598/
http://rti.gov.in/webactrti.htm
http://rti.india.gov.in/exempted.php
www.pfc.org.in/workshop
http://business.gov.in/legal_aspects/laws_ipr.php
http://www.forbes.com/sites/sallypipes/2013/09/16/indias-war-on-intellectual-property-rights-may-bring-with-it-a-body-count/
http://www.rkdewan.com/
http://www.ijuindia.org/wjact.html
http://www.indiankanoon.org/doc/1157189/
http://www.thehindu.com/todays-paper/tp-national/section-124a-of-ipc-unconstitutional/article1533394.ece
http://www.frontline.in/static/html/fl2802/stories/20110128280200800.htm
http://www.lawyersclubindia.com/forum/Sedition-law-S-124A-IPC-Repeal-this-colonial-legacy-31647.asp#.UnyYIPlASSq
http://www.rediff.com/news/slide-show/slide-show-1-five-high-profile-sedition-cases-in-india/20120913.htm#1
http://indiankanoon.org/doc/345634/
http://m.indiatoday.in/story/babri-masjid-demolition-case-sc-directs-expeditious-hearing/1/236367.html
http://indiankanoon.org/doc/771276/
http://www.indiankanoon.org/doc/1704109/

http://apiap.org/opinions/legal/opinion-the-law-on-pornography-in-india-and-implication-on-cyber-cafe-operators
http://www.indiankanoon.org/docfragment/1623275/?formInput=moral%20%20doctypes%3A%20judgments
http://indiankanoon.org/doc/601866/
http://indiankanoon.org/doc/983956/
http://indiankanoon.org/doc/1164912/
http://www.indiankanoon.org/doc/930621/
http://indiankanoon.org/doc/967463/
http://indiankanoon.org/doc/1134316/
http://frontierindia.net/section-144-at-india-gate-during-anti-rape-protests-invoked-without-proper-procedures-delhi-high-court#axzz2k5ikrazg
http://articles.timesofindia.indiatimes.com/2011-08-17/varanasi/29895691_1_prohibitory-orders-crpc-loud-speakers
http://articles.economictimes.indiatimes.com/2013-01-06/news/36162202_1_prohibitory-orders-crpc-criminal-procedure-code/2
http://www.thehindu.com/news/cities/Delhi/police-asked-to-explain-rationale-behind-imposing-prohibitory-orders/article4566761.ece
http://indiatoday.intoday.in/story/ramdev-fallout-section-144-of-crpc-imposed-in-new-delhi/1/140497.html
http://articles.timesofindia.indiatimes.com/2013-10-15/goa/43065117_1_meat-complex-section-144-criminal-procedure-code
http://ecell.in/eureka13/resources/Intellectual%20%20Property%20Rights.pdf
http://www.kmplegal.com/docs/INTELLECTUAL%20PROPERTY.pdf
http://www.rahindia.in/ipl-design.shtml
http://www.ipapharma.org/pt/july2012/19-22.pdf
http://ipindia.nic.in/
http://www.uclan.ac.uk/research/environment/projects/assets/cpe_innova_deliverable1_3.pdf
http://copyright.gov.in/Documents/CopyrightRules1957.pdf
http://www.frontline.in/static/html/fl2824/stories/20111202282408800.htm
http://www.irrawaddy.org/burma/govt-donation-to-press-council-draw-criticism.html
http://thehoot.org/web/What-the-Press-Council-could-have-been/6449-1-1-7-true.html
http://www.dnaindia.com/india/report-shut-down-ineffective-press-council-of-india-ex-chief-justice-js-verma-1607479
http://www.indiatogether.org/2004/jul/med-illusions.htm
http://www.arunjaitley.com/en/my-opinion-inside.php?id=82&mode= Read&icatId=17
http://www.greaterkashmir.com/news/2013/Mar/16/press-council-to-get-more-teeth-govt-31.asp
http://www.firstpost.com/india/press-council-act-to-get-more-teeth-govt-663260.html
http://www.mediamagazine.in/content/threats-media-freedom-real-and-imagined
http://www.deccanherald.com/content/296654/media-council-need-hour.html
http://indiatoday.intoday.in/story/journalists-welcome-katju—media-council/1/159487.html
http://www.thehindubusinessline.com/news/katju-pitches-for-bringing-electronic-media-under-press-council/article3881381.ece
http://www.indianexpress.com/news/press-council-wants-say-in-electronic-media-is-in-talks-with-i-b-ministry/859755/2

http://articles.timesofindia.indiatimes.com/2012-08-29/india/33475263_1_social-media-press-council-media-council

http://zeenews.india.com/news/nation/wind-up-press-council-or-revamp-it-parliamentary-panel_846911.html

http://www.hindu.com/businessline/2001/05/18/stories/1418391l.htm

http://www.hindu.com/businessline/2001/04/13/stories/141354u1.htm

http://m.economictimes.com/news/news-by-industry/media/entertainment-/media/self-regulation-is-no-regulation-markandey-katju-press-council-of-india/articleshow/18049430.cms

http://books.google.co.in/books?id=S1odp66bx1IC&printsec=frontcover&dq=media+council+bill+2010+in+india&hl=en&sa=X&ei=qYuCUsGOG8qkrQearYHgBA&ved=0CDAQ6wEwAA#v=onepage&q&f=false

http://www.epw.in/commentary/press-council-expensive-irrelevance.html

http://www.ipc.in/ipccriticism.html

http://www.indiancabletv.net/catvact.htm

http://www.thehindu.com/news/national/now-local-tv-channels-may-come-under-regulatory-net/article4320424.ece

http://www.prd.kerala.gov.in/comitte_tvchannel.pdf

http://articles.timesofindia.indiatimes.com/2013-05-21/goa/39417770_1_cable-tv-network-rules-national-regional-satellite-channels

http://www.business-standard.com/article/companies/news-channels-oppose-amendments-to-cable-tv-act-109011401062_1.html

http://www.business-standard.com/article/economy-policy/trai-for-changes-in-cable-tv-act-106060701134_1.html

http://www.business-standard.com/article/economy-policy/trai-for-cable-players-foray-into-internet-tv-108010501060_1.html

http://pib.nic.in/newsite/erelease.aspx?relid=35496

http://indiacode.nic.in/fullact1.asp?tfnm=200302

http://www.indianexpress.com/news/caught-on-camera/561105/0

http://www.indiastudychannel.com/resources/138492-Tehelka-History-Tehelka-scandals-exposed.aspx

http://www.newsbullet.in/video/india/13177-star-news-carries-sting-on-medical-colleges

http://news.nwn.in/2012/01/28/india-tv-sting-operation-mla-election-officers-to-register-offence-against-the-candidates/

http://mediabharti34.blogspot.in/2006/05/kokh-mein-qatl-story-of-sting.html

http://zeenews.india.com/news/nation/money-liquor-crowd-at-election-rallies_754409.html

http://www.outlookindia.com/printarticle.aspx?230080

http://www.rediff.com/money/2005/mar/29sting.htm

http://www.thehoot.org/web/home/story.php?storyid=5750&pg=1&mod=1&sectionId=9&valid=true

http://www.youthkiawaaz.com/2010/06/sting-operations-how-ethical-are-they/

http://theviewspaper.net/to-sting-or-not-to-sting/

http://ayjw.org/articles.php?id=871112

http://ibnlive.in.com/news/fake-sting-uma-khurana-wants-her-job-back/48733-html

http://articles.timesofindia.indiatimes.com/2007-09-10/india/27969579_1_fake-sting-uma-khurana-sting-operation

http://www.rediff.com/news/2008/feb/19sting.htm

http://www.expressindia.com/latest-news/doctor-accuses-tv-journalist-of-fake-sting-op/224245/

http://video.in.msn.com/watch/video/fake-sting-operation-assulters/fdz4uaj2

http://articles.timesofindia.indiatimes.com/2007-12-14/india/27992076_1_inquiry-probe-tv

http://www.legalserviceindia.com/article/l166-Sting-Operation.html

http://en.wikipedia.org/wiki/Tehelka

http://www.lawisgreek.com/sting-operation-laws-in-india

http://www.indiatvnews.com/news/India/India_TV_Sting_Operation_MLA_Exposes_UP_

http://infochangeindia.org/Media/./Case-law-on-sting-operations.html

http://articles.timesofindia.indiatimes.com › Collections

http://forbesindia.com/article/special/5-sting-operations-wed-like-to./1

http://indiacurrentaffairs.org › Media

http://pib.nic.in/release/release.asp?relid=79936

Newspapers

Times of India

Indian express

Hindustan Times

The Economic Times

The Hindu

Index